P

Who

"A profound, gorgeous, devastating book, entwining its compassion and its contemplation of pain. Part memoir, part everything—reportage, criticism, history, meditation—this is a book about the many translations of grief, suffering, and hope. It is also about performance and truth, staged necessarily and most urgently by refugees seeking asylum, and seeking the belief of others. *Who Gets Believed?* is that rarest of creations, an original work about a condition in which we are all implicated."

—Jeff Sharlet, bestselling author of *The Family* and *This Brilliant Darkness*

"Instantly gripping . . . An ambitious and moving exploration of the borders we draw around credible victimhood, and will cement Nayeri's position as a master storyteller of the refugee experience." —*The Guardian*

"Ardent, harrowing . . . An elegant telling of truth to power." —*The Observer*

"Memoir, philosophy, and social history collide in this compelling examination . . . [A] powerful, clarifying book." —*Esquire*

"This engrossing book ultimately makes the case for empathy across a range of situations, and for thinking critically about who does and doesn't get believed, especially about their own stories." —*Shondaland*

"With every passing day, Nayeri's book is an increasingly profound and medicinal shock to the system; a defoliant for the chronic, malignant self-deception that has crept like kudzu across the blighted landscape of Western liberal democracy." —*Another Chicago Magazine*

"Always engaging and informative, the book is another milestone in the career of a thinker and writer whom we will undoubtedly be hearing from for many years to come." —*Los Angeles Review of Books*

"Perhaps it's this razor-sharp understanding of the reality that plausibility often hinges on performance that makes Nayeri the perfect guide on her book's exploration of truth and believability . . . It's a juggernaut of a work that forces readers to rethink on whom we bestow credibility, and why. It's an important book, and the best thing may be to shelve a copy in every section of the store." —*Washington Independent Review of Books*

"*Who Gets Believed?* is an important, courageous, brilliant book; an interrogation of 'disbelief culture' and the injustice that both fuels it and is fueled by it, a form-shifting memoir of an already remarkable life, and a moving, harrowing investigation of love, loss, and care."
—Robert Macfarlane, author of *Underland*

"I was hugely moved by this book . . . To bear witness, to tell my own story in my own words, is a basic human right. And yet as Dina Nayeri's powerful, often harrowing, but ultimately inspiring account of injustice and survival shows, millions are denied that right on an almost casual basis. *Who Gets Believed?* is essential reading, an extraordinary labor of love and hope that is destined to become indispensable in the continuing struggle for justice, a day when everyone has the basic right to speak the truth openly and to have their testimony heard."
—John Burnside, author of *A Lie About My Father*

"A compelling, generous, and distinctive inquiry into the nature of belief, credibility, and, above all, the deeply unjust and unequal societies in which we live. Reading it, I was reminded of Joan Didion's famous and oft misconstrued observation that 'we tell ourselves stories in order

to live.' *Who Gets Believed?* shows the workings of Nayeri's singular and noble mind."   —Chitra Ramaswamy, author of
Homelands: The History of a Friendship

"Dina Nayeri's mesmerizing, genre-bending book braids together narratives of asylum seekers, exonerated felons, and religious converts to ask: Who gets believed? In an era of fake news and tribalism, her question is urgent. In lyrical prose, Nayeri dives into court cases, draws from history and literature, and shares her own family's journey as refugees from Iran. The result is both heartbreaking and hopeful. Reading this book will up-end your preconceptions about who is worthy of belief, as writing it did for Nayeri herself."   —Amanda Frost, author of *You Are Not American: Citizenship Stripping from Dred Scott to the Dreamers*

WHO
GETS
BELIEVED?

WHO
GETS
BELIEVED?

When the Truth Isn't Enough

Dina Nayeri

Catapult
New York

First Catapult edition: 2023
First paperback edition: 2024

Hardcover ISBN: 978-1-64622-072-4
Paperback ISBN: 978-1-64622-216-2

Library of Congress Control Number: 2022943511

Cover design by Nicole Caputo
Cover image © iStock
Book design by Laura Berry

Catapult
New York, NY
books.catapult.co

Printed in the United States of America

10 9 8 7 6 5 4 3 2 1

For Sam who loves strange stories and
for Elena who always believes them.

And for Maman Moti, my enigmatic London grandmother,
for whom I was ready to believe anything.
Rest in peace, defiance, and power.

The best lack all conviction, while the worst
Are full of passionate intensity.

——W. B. YEATS, FROM
"THE SECOND COMING"

WHO
GETS
BELIEVED?

ately, when opportunity strikes, I search strangers' backs for scars. Or scratches, scabs. Backs are raw, untreated landscape, a wild surface whatever your circumstance. Sometimes deeper marks suggest a story. My partner Sam has a surgical scar from his slipped disc. I'm the one who most frequently glimpses it, who is most often reminded of that day. To him it's invisible. Likewise, I have a shadowy stretch over each clavicle where, after a lifetime of sunburns and scratching, it's damn near impossible to break skin. Sam calls it "the hide."

Marred flesh is evidence. Every faded old mark explains a flinch, a tic, a nightmare. We can't curate these humbling old wounds. Or we don't. More often, others do it for us. As a child, I found it unremarkable to hear of a public lashing; the bodies of citizens, it seemed, were the natural jurisdiction of the state. It was both Koranic and Biblical, and we lived, after all, in the Islamic Republic in wartime. There were worse things than a shredded back.

Then I became a refugee. Years passed. I grew into a watchful, cynical adult. I asked why my body wasn't my own, why I kept bowing to authorities and creating new gods. I cast them off, becoming a kind of social apostate. Today, when I speak about refugees laying their stories at our gates, American mothers in bright scarves call me an idealist. I laugh. In what dark universe would I qualify as an idealist? I reject authoritarians and the privileges of birth. I'm deathly afraid of the bureaucrat's icy gaze. I don't believe words, not yours, often not even my own. I believe in expertise, and in what I observe—what experience allows me to observe. I'm rarely consistent, but rarely dogmatic; I can fathom how much I don't know. I believe stories that are etched on skin. Could I slip by my own past gatekeepers again? I have dark nights, a foggy lens, a bad heart. I want to survive. I love my kid more than other kids. Other people's pain short-circuits my imagination. I crave to run from it. I *did* run from it, last time it loomed near.

I am an unbeliever. But I see that now.

THE RULE OF
THE WORLD

A Miseducation

Speaking

1.

Now and then, the heavy door swung open and a man was shoved inside—or dragged out, never to return. But they always numbered around ten in the room, all Tamil, like K. The prisoners in the Pambaimadu army detention camp slept on the concrete floor, no bedding or cloth. The room stank of the sweat, urine, and bodily filth of many men crammed together. If they were lucky enough to be taken to the toilet, all the men washed in one vat. If they were allowed to bathe, they used that same water. For the last few men, there was hardly any point. When the soldiers brought K food, they kicked it away, laughing. "Even dogs are treated better than you," they said. It didn't matter because K's throat was too swollen for him to eat. Often, they urinated on the food before they left. Often, K was taken to another room for beatings with gun butts and wooden poles, until he could no longer bend his right knee.

It seemed strange, he thought, since he and the other young men traveling with him had surrendered to the army on May 10, 2009. They had carried white flags and declared themselves civilians. But K was asked to stand in another group, those suspected of being Tamil

Tigers, a Tamil guerrilla force fighting for an independent state. His group was taken to a brutal army camp, instead of a civilian one.

At first the torture was routine, a few hours every few days along with other prisoners. They were beaten, then photographed and coerced into signing confessions that they had helped the LTTE (the liberation group, the Tamil Tigers). K signed his confession on his fifth day in the camp. After signing, K thought his interrogations would ease. But soon, he was spotted by members of other political parties and paramilitary groups, EPDP and PLOTE, who identified him as having helped the Tamil Tigers to hide gold.

One August day, K was taken into the interrogation room with ten men who demanded to know where the Tamil Tigers hid their gold. As he knelt, panting, trying to convince them that he knew nothing, he felt a heat near his shoulder. He turned to see a soldier with a metal rod approaching. The end of the rod glowed red; even through a terrified gray haze, it was easy to make out the glow in the room. Before K could think, the rod sank into his right arm, an intense heat shot through his body, and he passed out to the sound of his own distant screams. He woke to more questions about the Tamil Tiger gold, and to the sensation of new wounds: now his back, too, was badly burned, though he didn't remember it happening.

Then the gaggle of men held him down and poured gasoline over his face, his back, covering his fresh wounds. They threatened to set him alight unless he revealed the location of the gold. "I swear I don't know," he said, for the hundredth time. "I'm not LTTE. I'm a jeweler's assistant." As K choked on gasoline, an itch crept up his back and arms and distracted him from the foul taste, the smell. Then the itch became a searing, and the screams poured out of him again. He glanced at his arm—strange the details one remembers—and saw the dry skin of his long confinement now wet and slimy and peeling away.

The other men in the concrete room stared as K was dumped back inside. It was always like this, when someone was taken out to be tortured and then returned: a silent reception, a mix of happiness that the man had survived (that they could all survive) and fear of what had been done. Then, for some moments, the collective realization that this might be how they *all* would die—and that this sorrow was shared, just then, by every other man in the room.

K curled up on his left side, the only side that wasn't burned. He tucked his knees into his chest. In that strange angle, he prayed for sleep. But the pain was too sharp, and the gasoline fumes too noxious. Alone in his corner, he trembled, waiting for sobs to release his aching muscles. But he had no strength and no tears, and he nodded off with the craving unquenched.

"Tomorrow," a kind voice nearby whispered, "if they let us bathe, you can be first."

In the morning, an officer announced that they could bathe, and everyone agreed that K should go first. The man who slept closest helped K remove his shirt. "Gentle, gentle," a third man whispered, wincing as the corner of a wound appeared. "Keep still," said the helper as he worked K's good left arm out of that sleeve. With the shirt halfway up, K moaned. The fabric was sticking to the wettest parts of the wound, and when his friend pulled the shirt fully up, K groaned and clung to the wall. He turned to see patches of skin, blood, water, and bits of mottled flesh stuck to the shirt. "How does it look?" he asked the third man, who quickly looked away.

Just then the door swung open. They froze. K retreated to the wall. An officer entered and threw a fresh shirt at K's feet. "Wear that, after you clean yourself." Then he left.

"It's clean," said one of the men. "It's better you wear so the burns aren't exposed."

K splashed some water on his body and put on the shirt. It was agony. He would wear that shirt for many months, until it was stained with blood, in the shape of the iron rods.

For days, K suffered a fever and worried that his burns had become infected. Still, he had no way of looking at them. The beatings didn't stop. Now and then, he was dragged away again for questioning. He was kicked, his food overturned. He wasn't burned again, but because of the gasoline and the dirtiness of his surroundings, his wounds didn't heal for three months. Each morning K asked his cellmates to look at the wounds. "Are they better? Describe them." Over time, it became a routine, and the other prisoners obliged.

As the months passed, the wounds lost their sting, and he was able to roll onto his arms and back with only a dull ache, or an itch, to remind him. After a while, he began to feel better. Sometimes, in the toilets, he spoke to an EPDP member named Sasi, with whom he unloaded the army's deliveries. K began noticing prisoners vanishing, though they weren't dragged out by the guards. Rumors spread. One night in November 2010, lying on the floor of the concrete room, a cellmate whispered that the EPDP were helping people escape in exchange for money.

The next day, in the toilets, K dared to mention it to Sasi. Sasi glared for a moment. Then he whispered, "Give me your parents' number." K's father was the more skilled jeweler and he, too, had melted gold for the Tamil Tigers. Afraid for his family, K had not contacted them for many months. But what choice was there? Sasi was a friend, and K gave him the number.

One day in December, Sasi found K in the toilets. "I spoke to your family," he said. "I'll need money to get you out." Then he went off to finish unloading the food and water vessels. He didn't say more until February 3, when he told K to be ready the following day.

On February 4, Sasi was reloading the empty food and water vessels back onto a truck. When K arrived to help, Sasi told him to lie down flat in the back and quickly stacked the vessels on top of him. Then he disappeared and the truck groaned and lurched forward. *Is this happening* now? K thought. As the truck sped up, K tried to quiet his breathing. But his heart was pounding too unsteadily, so he held his breath.

When the truck stopped at the camp's exit, everything felt finished. K heard Sasi talking to the officer, then the officer's voice grew louder, and K felt his presence just outside the truck bed. He closed his eyes, pressed his lips together. His scars burned, fear triggering his body's memory. He turned his thoughts to his mother, his father and brothers, to calm his heartbeat. But in a moment, the officer was gone and the truck was moving again. And then a minute passed, then five minutes, and by the time the truck stopped again, ninety minutes had passed and the camp was far behind them.

"I'm free," thought K, as the truck sped up and his enemy receded. He breathed in, briefly rapturous, unable to fathom the ordeal just beginning, the mighty, pitiless foe up ahead.

———

At twelve, I used to hide in the public library stacks and read gruesome stories that I knew would frighten my dogmatic immigrant mother. Stories of cults, witch burnings, and Native American rituals—anything she might call "satanic." Her fear of all non-Protestant spirituality disappointed me. This was a woman who had stood up to the scariest people on earth: the mullahs of the Islamic Republic. She flaunted her Christian conversion, though they could easily have hanged her from a crane. Days before being dragged out of her office by the moral police, she was still telling Mullah Nasrudeen jokes without a tremor. And here she was, brave fugitive, afraid of an old library paperback because of some fireside incantations and a few battleground scalpings? The ancient Persians played polo with their enemies' heads. Now they use cranes to slow death by hanging. Iranians don't get queasy; we're innovators in the field of humiliating murder. I said things like this out loud, defiant, shocking. Really, it was a simple fascination. My mother had almost been executed, so I was obsessed with executions. Gruesome ones.

Something else bothered me too: not just her fear, but her dwindling imagination. My mother didn't see how similar the Oklahoma preachers of our new home were to the mullahs of our old: how alike in their opinion of women, how narrow their view of God.

In high school, strange stories enthralled me. I liked sin, messy moral tangles, disturbing sensory details. I fell deep into Golding's *Lord of the Flies,* with its feral boys, its irredeemable child. Jack was bad (maybe evil), and I wanted to know how he slipped beyond the pale. My ancestors were bad, I knew that much. My blood was bad. Despite my Christianity, I always felt so near the border of good, teetering on a precipice in slippery plastic church shoes. There was a reason I couldn't speak in tongues like the other Sunday School girls, why my skirt was always accidentally tucked into my tights while theirs were angelic and pristine. Jack's weird urges, his severed boar head impaled on a stick, these were vital clues. If I solved my own chronic errancy, I could crack a larger code and grow up performing the role of someone respected and believed. Then, one day—from inside the body of a successful American adult, with her Western passports and diplomas and bank accounts (I imagined myself, still eleven, sitting in a literal control room inside my own adult face)—I could gain access to an easier life.

I discovered Kafka's short story "In the Penal Colony" in an Oklahoma library when I was in middle school, months after a long-suffering English teacher had failed to make me appreciate *The Metamorphosis* (maybe because, as a refugee kid, transformation didn't seem so mysterious or strange a subject). But to a shell-shocked girl fresh from a war, crouched now in the dark and dusty stacks, Kafka's nightmarish penal colony, his bloody torture tale of the officer and the harrow, was effortlessly enticing.

"It's a peculiar apparatus," said the Officer to the Traveler . . .

That opening still gives me shivers.

A Traveler visits a penal colony in a foreign land, and is invited to watch an execution. An Officer, a true believer in the country's justice system, shows him a machine by which executions are carried out. The Condemned is strapped onto a bed of cotton wool, naked and facing down, and lump of felt is forced into his mouth. Money is tight, the Officer says, and the wad of felt is the same one all the previously Condemned have choked upon as they died. There is a Harrow shaped like the body of the Condemned, attached to an Inscriber. The Harrow lowers its many glass needles to inscribe "The Sentence" onto the flesh of the Condemned. The big needles inscribe; the small needles squirt water so the blood doesn't get in the way of a clear inscription. Each unique sentence is hidden from the Condemned, but entered into the Inscriber. Even if the Condemned were to catch a glimpse, the font is so elaborate that it blackens the entire page, and even the Traveler can't decipher it. "It's not calligraphy for schoolchildren," says the Officer. The many flourishes serve to cover the body. The Bed quivers; the needles begin their work. The cotton wool then rolls, simultaneously turning the body so that new parts can be inscribed, and cauterizing the recently inflicted wounds, so that in the next round, the inscription can go deeper. The used wool is tossed into a pit that also collects the blood and water. "It's not supposed to kill right away," the Officer explains. It takes about twelve hours to die, though the lump of felt is required only for six, after which point the Condemned seems to decipher "The Sentence," reading with his wounds what had been indecipherable to the eyes, and to accept it, succumb to it. He is quiet now, and the felt is removed. He can no longer physically scream.

At the sixth hour, the Officer likes to kneel down to look at the face of the Condemned. Hours later, the Condemned dies and the machine spits him out into the pit, where he is quickly buried.

Even now—seated comfortably inside the control room of that educated future self—I'm still obsessed with strange stories. Now I hide them from my daughter, Elena, as I once did from my mother. I'm still the misfit with a taste for the grotesque: here in my secluded French village, hushed by lockdown, I've been reading murder trials, squinting at eerie grayscale exhibits. Today it's a 1999 police interrogation transcript, the four-hour video playing simultaneously on my screen. I'm watching a real-life Harrow, every hair on my body standing at attention. I imagine my younger self, awkward, eccentric, socially inept, strapped by some unseen power to that chair, the machine.

In the last year, I've read thousands of pages of trial and police transcripts, interviews, appeals, expert testimonies. I've leafed through exhibit photos, charts. Most have come to me via defense lawyers or justice organizations like the Innocence Project and Freedom from Torture.

A surprising effect of watching interrogation videos is that, no matter how poor the film quality, no matter how many layers of pixels and smudge between you and that moment, you always slip into somebody's point of view: either the cop trying to get a confession, or the almost childlike innocent, trapped without a lawyer, unaware that the chitchat about television and childcare and shoddy carpentry is all designed to trip him up. I say *innocent*, because these cases come to me already finished—their wrongful conviction established, sometimes after decades. Watching the videos, then, I tend to imagine myself as the accused: I am always the awkward suspect in the chair, withering under the cop's wolfish grin, grasping for words. I speak. It's always a misfire. It ricochets and wounds me. Was there any chance I might have stumbled upon the right words, the ones that might have saved me?

Many of my family members are on the autism spectrum. A few years ago, my mother called to tell me that I am the family's biggest undiagnosed case—I'm paranoid, obsessive, I count everything on my fingers. I can't go to sleep until I perform my rituals. I'm afraid of money, and of most numbered things. I know every scab on Sam's body by heart, and I've come to terms with the fact that I'm not allowed to pick them, even in his sleep, that doing that is considered wicked and nonconsensual. I fixate on a different food item every three weeks on the dot—right now it's pita bread. Last month it was unspotted bananas. Before that, purple cabbage.

Certainly I'd crumble under any kind of police questioning, believing every lie in the toolkit. Sometimes, in social settings, I have to remind myself that others can't read my mind. I may or may not be on the autism spectrum. I'm no longer interested in a label, as I have my family and my coping mechanisms. Sam takes care of me. He tells me when I need to go outside or when I need to tend to "hermit Dina"—a version of me that college friends called "Econ Dina."

About a year ago, I called one of these college friends, Frances Kim Walters, then an attorney for the Mid-Atlantic Innocence Project. I had been reflecting on the many ways I'd doom myself in today's cynical justice systems, and Frances had spent years buried neck-deep in wrongful conviction cases: usually a person of color, too poor for a private lawyer, who had already spent decades in prison. "Oh Dina, you won't believe what passes for justice in America," she said.

Frances told me two stories:

Two men were accused of arson, of planning to murder their wives. Standing outside his burning house, with his family inside, the first didn't react strongly enough. The second drew suspicion because he overreacted, trying too hard to get back in. The first, a humble man with no higher degrees and an undiagnosed psychological disorder, was coaxed into a false confession. The second was college educated. Both men spent two decades in prison.

Michael Ledford, the stoical man, didn't run in. He was a volunteer firefighter, yet he stood outside, dumbstruck. He wasn't well liked in the community. He was abrasive, cold, quiet. He had a weird personality, a mess in social situations. Teachers said he might be on the autism spectrum, and later forensic psychiatrists confirmed this in his behavior. Sometimes he had a temper, sometimes a deep gloom. He was just "odd," people said, and very quiet. Later, his actions were hotly debated by lawyers and police: *Of course he didn't run in: he knew adding oxygen would spread the fire; why would he break open a window and doom more people?* Ledford's confession was grueling. At twenty-three, he had just lost his one-year-old son. His wife, horribly burned, was in critical condition. Despite an undiagnosed spectrum disorder and all that new trauma, he was interrogated, without a lawyer, for four solid hours.

The other, dramatic man (let's call him Dru) fell asleep with his children on the second floor as his wife slept below. He smelled smoke and climbed onto the roof with the kids. He lowered them down and sent the oldest to call the police. In front of the house, with his children safe and first responders rushing about, he screamed, "Oh my God, my wife!" To keep him from running in, firefighters bear-hugged him until he passed out. They eyed each other. Dru's struggle to get inside was a little "over the top," suspicious for an educated guy. Despite no further evidence against Dru, his wife's family (and the insurance company, who preferred arson) paid for experts.

Both men performed their grief badly. Sometimes, one's specific performance is just their singular nature. Why doesn't that uniqueness ever seem to work *for* the vulnerable, I asked, instead of always damning their case? Frances laughed, the tired chuckle of someone who's asked that question so often it's lost its meaning.

Frances couldn't tell me more about Dru—his struggle continues. But she asked Michael Ledford's lawyers to send me his file, including his tedious 1999 interrogation. Though the image is grainy and the audio fuzzy, and I can barely see his face under his baseball cap, right away I catch on to a certain cynical tone to the whole enterprise: the interrogators aren't after a truth that might surprise them. The question of what they *believe* is irrelevant here. They're trying to extract a particular set of words, a confession—that's their job. That's all they want; it's the way they measure success. Sometimes they pretend to be Michael's friend. Other times, they distance themselves from the investigation and express frustration that he won't let them *help him*. They understand, from early on, that Michael has an undiagnosed mental illness. Later, forensics psychologists flag this exchange as the first clear sign:

> Interrogator: Do you have any nicknames or aliases that you go by?
> Mike: *Well, the fire company called me Kamikaze one night. My wife calls me her big cuddly pooh-bear. Other than that I don't have any.*
> Okay.
> *Not too many people call me names. They usually call me Mike or Michael.*
> Okay. Do you prefer Michael?
> *I prefer Mike.*
> Mike?
> *Yeah. If the law says you have to call me Michael, that's fine.*

Michael has trouble adjusting to context. He overshares; then, per habit, he calls up the rules he's learned, like a crutch. This exchange alone shows his childlike belief in the law. But it doesn't sway the officers toward caution—instead, they double down on coercive questions. His autism isn't a pitfall on the way to the truth; it is the instrument with which they will wrench the words they need from their suspect. Later, with no authority to do so, they promise him treatment, the help he's yearned for his entire life. They say that confessing is part of "the rehabilitation."

Without explicit training, anyone on the autism spectrum would break under the Reid Technique, the terrifying interrogation method that is ubiquitous in America's police interview rooms. This is the method you see on *Law and Order: SVU*, the one we casually call the "third degree." Its limitations and safeguards have long been abandoned by many badly trained cops who've learned most of the tactics haphazardly on the job, through trickledown precinct culture.

The Reid Technique begins with an assumption of guilt. It was originally intended to be used only when the interrogator is absolutely certain of guilt. Even then, it was intended not to extract a confession that might condemn the suspect on its own (the technique is, after all, so torturous that even though the creators didn't believe it would cause an innocent person to confess, they seemed aware of that risk), but to uncover new, unknown details—intimate ones about the why and the how—that could *then be corroborated*. It was that supporting physical evidence that would convict the guilty—a body, a weapon, some real proof.

The technique works like this: as the interrogator, you go in, guns blazing, telling the suspect that his guilt is established, all evidence has been gathered, and that there is nothing he can say to disprove that fact (this is often a lie). "All I want to know today," says the interrogator, "is *why*." So he blocks every attempt to claim innocence—that kind of talk isn't tolerated. It's interrupted, waved away like a pestering insect. ("I'm going to be very frank with you, it's not a question anymore of who set the fire," the interrogator says to Michael.)

The suspect is in an either/or situation: confess, or be convicted of murder. There is no way anyone could see the mountain of evidence, just outside that door, and not convict him. Then, the interrogator offers an enticing "alternative question"—a more acceptable reason for committing the crime. A better story to cling to. The suspect is made to believe that if he chooses this alternative (more moral and conscionable) reason, and confesses to *that* instead of the heinous motive everyone now believes, the interrogator can help him. Michael's interrogator performs a kindhearted desperation to help: "The only option you leave me is to think, is to say one of two things: that you set back and planned this thing out, and planned it, and planned it out, and planned it out with the intention of either hurting your wife or your child, or it was just one of those things that happened . . . You set the fire, you leave, maybe come in and be the hero. That's fine and I, I can respect you for that." He then softens. "I understand why you did it."

Despite this unwinnable power dynamic, in the first hours, Michael is adamant:

> *I'm just telling you the truth. I did not set the fire . . . If I was going to set a fire as a joke . . . I'm not going to do it in the same building as I live in. If I was going to set a fire to put harm on someone, I certainly wouldn't have, I wouldn't have wanted to hurt my family.*

I don't think you did want to hurt your family. I think you wanted to save your family.

Why would I have started a fire in my own apartment?

That's a question you have to . . . you tell me.

I am telling you, I did not start the fire.

People do it because they do it. People do it because they do it, and, uh, that's only a question that you could answer. And only you can answer that. So you tell me.

I didn't start it.

Who did?

I don't know, but it wasn't me.

The Reid Technique is like Kafka's Harrow. It kills slowly, carving the sentence into its victim's flesh. Its final aim: acceptance of the outcome. The victim can finally read his sentence, realizes his life is over, and succumbs, even thanks the interrogator for the release. There is no untangling from the machine, and to the one operating it, it seems like justice. To continue the work, the interrogator must convince himself that the suspect is guilty. At the end, there's always a moment of kindness, of human connection, like the Officer kneeling down to peer into the face of the victim. The interrogator brings the suspect, raw from a confession, a Coke or a sandwich. The interrogator doesn't stop to marvel that, in effect, this technique is performed only on the poor, the uneducated, those who trust in the ruling systems. The most vulnerable don't realize (as the privileged always do) that they can stop the Harrow with four words: *I want a lawyer.*

Michael's interrogator performs a constant theatrical hand-wringing about the overwhelming evidence (a lie), the failed polygraph (inconclusive), and a suspect who refuses to be helped. Then, in a poignant exchange, Michael replies with religious conviction:

The only way I can say, sir, is do what you need to do, but I am going to claim my innocence until the day I die. I did not set the fire that took the life of my son and damned near took the life of my wife. There is no way in hell I'd have ever done that.

(Reading the transcript, I know what's coming next. Fangs receding, a show of empathy.)

I'd like to believe that. I really would. I would really like to believe that.
If I deliberately set that fire, may God strike me dead now. I did not set the fire.

(His interrogator changes tack smoothly, slipping from the helper's mask to that of the kind priest.)

Well, you know and understand he has the power to do that.
Right, says Michael.

(Michael's taken aback. Maybe he's interpreting it all literally again, as he's prone to do, afraid for his immortal soul. Maybe he hopes God will intervene. The interrogator says:)

He has the power to do it but for some reason he usually doesn't choose to do that.

———

The standard length of an interrogation is thirty minutes to two hours. Like the Harrow, the Reid Technique breaks you in exactly six. After six hours, an interrogation is considered undeniably coercive. Michael's video shows officers using those guidelines not to temper themselves, but as a kind of legal stopwatch. Though Michael's guilt is far from certain, they push him until he's exhausted. After hours of coercive tactics, Michael gives in. He writes out a confession, fueled by imagination and at odds with previous evidence. But he still can't think of a motive, so the investigators try to help him invent one. He loves his wife, he says, though he confides to the officers that his wife's family expected a lot of him. He tells them that he didn't know about any insurance policies until long after the fire. So, they ask, was it all that pent-up frustration? Was it a joke? Did he hope to save his wife and become a hero?

Did you burn the apartment thinking you could get out of the lease of the apartment?

Uh, the lease was already up.

You had planned to [move] into another apartment anyway, [inaudible] another house anyway, right? So you figured, well, I was starting to [inaudible] enough, and I'll, I'll be out . . .

(Another man): How about attention, or anything like that?

No.

They land on heroism. Per the alternative question suggested to him, Michael wasn't trying to kill; he threw a candle into a chair thinking he'd save his wife and live up to his in-laws' impossible standards. With the confession secured, the officers relax. They've done their job. They now chat with Michael about firesafe couch cushions, and television, and rehabilitation. When he follows up on the promise of being sent to a mental health facility, they say they'll go to bat for him, though (suddenly) they don't have the authority to promise anything. "I'm sticking my neck for you a little bit here," one interrogator says, relaxed now that he wants nothing more from Michael. Still, he has his social habits: hemming and hawing, suturing what was implied, roughly, to what is actually possible, "and I'm telling you, that I, I agree with, uh, with you that there is a problem here." Michael asks about out-of-state health benefits, and though he has just told the officers that he purposely set that fire, he speaks of visiting the hospital that night to see his dying wife. He has understood nothing of the bargain he's made.

The police report is quickly altered to reflect the shaky details (the candle) extracted from Michael. It now matches the confession. There is no further investigation to corroborate those details, as the Reid Technique requires. Instead, the *confession itself* is used to convict Michael, a clear misuse. At trial, the confession and the altered report (the shrug of experts) are the prosecutor's only proof of guilt. Having collected no physical evidence, they darken Michael's autistic behaviors (asking about his wife's life support) into something sinister. He is convicted and sentenced to fifty years.

Near the end of the video, the interrogator, in that flash of kindness when he asks Michael if he wants a soda, realizes that he hasn't been thanked.

"Mike, do you feel better?" he asks.

"Yeah," Michael mutters.

"Good," says the interrogator.

Another officer chimes in. "I saw relief on his face, before I did. Uh, uh, it's just like somebody took a burden off of him."

"I told him he would," says the first man. "Mike, just to satisfy my own curiosity, can you tell me why you, why you told him the whole truth."

Michael mutters, flatly, like a good student. "I was tired of lying to myself."

In America, an interrogator can claim to have evidence he doesn't have; he can offer phantom leniency, even present fake evidence—made-up charts and scans and lie detector tests. He can make the suspect believe that confessing is his best option, because somehow the world has turned upside down. Why would he not take this chance?

To someone for whom only the literal exists—for whom government authorities can't lie, their help always offered in good faith and backed by real power—fake evidence in the hands of a police investigator is unfathomable.

Proponents of the Reid Technique argue that an innocent person would never confess to a crime he didn't commit, even under such conditions. Yet people do just that, *all the time*. If you believe everything you're told, it is the only rational response. The technique is created on this very logic. In Iran, many political prisoners confess to lesser crimes because they understand that they're in the hands of an absurd captor, a Kafka villain who will harm their loved ones. If you're certain that your fate is prison, guilty or innocent, you will jump at a slightly better fate.

If the Reid Technique is being performed upon you, your only aim is to survive it without confessing. There is no better outcome. The rub is that you have no way of knowing this. It seems unfair, being forced to play for your life without hearing the rules of the game.

How could I have believed that all stories are heard the same way? That every story in the public record is entered by a neutral party with good faith, expertly crafted, details checked? How could I have assumed that the game is fair, and that every true story has an equal chance of being believed? The world has shown me, again and again, that we live by wildly different and ever shifting rules designed by the privileged for *their* children. I've always known this. The primary goal of my adult life, of my asylum-seeker adolescence, has been to convince the Americans in charge that I'm worthy, a high-quality candidate for their ostensible meritocracy; that I, born of doctors but unlucky in geopolitics, can be a decent spokesperson for it.

After we arrived in America, my younger brother, Khosrou, assimilated fast and was beloved by his classmates and community. Slapped with a new Western name, he was reborn "Daniel" and adapted, learned American football, backyard games, video games, the slang and the poetry. His accent changed with the same ease that, in the French village where we've been hibernating for the pandemic, Elena's is now Francifying. But by the time we became displaced, I had already spent three years in Islamic Republic girls' schools. Those three extra years had hardened me, making every small adjustment seem impossible. Or was it only that Daniel was younger? That I had learned Farsi script and the rules of the Iranian schoolyard? Was it that I had gone to class under a mural of a bloody fist? Or was it something more inborn? Once in early adulthood, my brother asked, "Are you sure all the crap you got in school was about being Iranian? Maybe it was just about being *you*." Maybe he was onto something.

There is more than one way of being an outsider, more than one type of misfit. Without my Western education, all I am is another prickly, highly literal oddball. A refugee from polite society who keeps stumbling over herself, who can't manage to assimilate to the "normal" culture. But I've been lucky. How do we invite the most vulnerable, those untrained in social performatives, to recount their traumas? How do they fare with those in charge: the caretakers and the enforcers and the protectors? To what lengths does society go to protect its comfortable insiders from the seemingly discrepant?

In 2019, I came across the astonishing case of KV (or K), an ordeal that began in 2009 and ended a decade later in the U.K. Supreme Court. Though KV's identity is protected, I met with him and learned the details of his case. Sitting in a London law office with me and his lawyer, he was fidgety and timid, searching for words. I knew that this nervous demeanor bore no similarity to the real man, the person he was back home in Sri Lanka: an ordinary jeweler with a family. Afterward, when I listened to his recorded voice, all I thought about was Kafka's Harrow. I heard its every creak and jostle, imagining it scratching at my own back. That image burrowed deep, becoming unshakable. Then the similarities became farcical. KV had endured so many bad-faith interrogations, his back now covered with deep, terrifying scars.

———

On February 24, 2011, a twenty-five-year-old Tamil national of Sri Lanka, the son of a jeweler with a harrowing story and scars to match, arrived in the U.K. He claimed asylum, explaining that he had been tortured by the Sri Lankan government on suspicion of being a Tamil Tiger. KV confessed that from 2003 to 2008, he and his father were coerced into valuing jewelry and melting gold for the Tamil Tigers. Government forces arrested him in May 2009. In a detention camp, they beat him with gun butts and wooden poles, branded him, and demanded the location of the valuables. Twenty days before arriving in the U.K., a friend helped him escape the army camp in the back of a truck. After a substantial payoff from his family, KV was handed off to a smuggler named Dean, who took him to his own house in Negombo to stay with his wife and children. KV's mangled back had hurt him for eighteen months. For much of that time, he had worn the same blood-stained shirt to cover his wounds. That night, Dean gave him fresh clothes and painkillers, then a passport with a new name. Escorted by a third man, KV traveled through France to the U.K., where he requested asylum.

During his interview with the Home Office, the U.K. department that handles immigration, KV showed photos of his scars: five long ones on his back and two shorter ones on his right arm, consistent with branding with a hot metal rod. In that small office, he repeated the whole story: that in August 2009, his captors burned his arm with a hot soldering iron. That he felt a heat on his arm, turned, and saw the glowing rod. That the burning intensified, he fell forward, and passed out. That his captors branded his back cleanly while he was unconscious and, when he woke, poured gasoline on his wounds to increase the pain. That the wounded tissue didn't scar for three months.

By 2011, when KV arrived in the U.K. and requested asylum, it was widely known that the Sri Lankan police and military used torture, especially in prisons. Their brutalities (burning and branding with soldering irons, suspension by thumbs) had been well documented and condemned by the UN. Just in case the Home Office decided to ignore this, KV's lawyers provided a full country report, detailing the political situation in Sri Lanka, its history, and the implications for those suspected of helping the Tamil Tigers.

KV had every expectation that he would be believed. His captors were notorious. He bore the scars. He was finally free. But in March 2011, the Home Office rejected KV's asylum claim: "You are a fit and healthy young male who it is considered suffered no problems in Sri Lanka." They wrote that KV's account showed inconsistencies, no evidence of danger in Sri Lanka, and that KV had offered no definitive medical evidence of torture. They cited—as if that were even close to the pivotal point—a section of the Sri Lanka COI (Country of Origin Information) describing a robust medical system that would offer KV treatment. So, they reasoned, KV could live a normal life, or at least normal "by the standards that generally prevail in your country of nationality." With that pompous send-off, the Home Office formally absolved itself of any humanitarian responsibility on KV's behalf. They urged him to go home.

Though home was all KV craved, return was impossible. His muscles recoiled at memories of the searing rod. And besides, the bribe his family had paid went to smugglers and freelancing insiders; it didn't appease the government. Going back would mean he'd be in an army camp within months, even days.

"We'll appeal, of course," whispered his lawyer. "There are still paths to asylum."

And so the rejection launched KV into a maddening eight-year battle to be believed. Though his lawyer had explained that kindness or sympathy should not be expected from Home Office communications ("This is how bureaucrats sound. It isn't personal."), KV was baffled. *How did they explain the scars?* He had been branded with a rod—in the known fashion of Sri Lankan authorities, in a known Sri Lankan army camp—clear as grade-school calligraphy. *Who is writing the rules of the world?*

Kafka was consumed by the law, its embedded lies. He imagined nightmarish bureaucratic and legal tangles with a cold, indifferent enemy. KV seemed to have walked right out of Kafka's notebook, and not just because of the scars or that eerily familiar alias. This K, too, had a powerful adversary, one who crushed the weak, believed the fortunate, and remade the truth to its purpose. The Home Office, it seemed, was claiming that KV had climbed into Kafka's machine and switched on the Harrow by choice.

Asylum activists often bring up Kafka when describing the interview process: years of gritted teeth, watching helpless as the landscape melts into absurdity, all the wrong words crawling out of your mouth on their own like vermin, though you struggle to hold them in.

I think of my own family's asylum interview—the moment, presumably, when I became obsessed with running through barred gates. I remember the room, the officer, the one or two questions she posed to me. It sounded like small talk, but two minutes into the conversation, the officer was checking on my mother's apostasy: had she taught her children the Bible? "What's your favorite Bible story? Do you know the story of Jonah? What about Job?"

I guess I didn't botch it. Much more depended on my mother's words, her gestures. Was she telling the right story, using the most believable words? Was she meek? Hardworking? Was she humble and grateful, a true scarf-ripping Christian convert? Or was she an opportunist who would steal a menial American job and wear hijab to the grocery store?

Did American children have to prove that they were Christian enough for all that wealth and opportunity and education? *Probably*, I thought, then. *Probably there are tests for everyone.*

"I think closed doors are the nightmare you know best," Sam tells me.

"Not closed doors," I say. "Irrational gatekeeping, bureaucracies, double binds."

For decades I've been chasing the great discrepancy, the lie I sense at the core of the world. I can't shake the conviction that it's there. You've seen it too: the words and gestures that help lucky children, trained from birth, to break down doors, to be trusted without proof, funded without merit. I glimpse its shadow over every sensational story, every overlooked one—the code that breaks the spell of skepticism and doubt. What makes calcified hearts believe?

I wonder this aloud one evening as Sam is sorting books nearby, watching me dig through court transcripts of wrongful conviction cases sent by the Innocence Project, asylum interviews sent by Freedom from Torture.

"You can't answer that without going inward," he says.

Half listening, I ask why. "You mean because I was a refugee?"

"No." He pauses. "Because *you're* the skeptic now. You're suspicious of everyone, you have to fact-check everyone," he says, "and yet you expect to be summarily believed."

I stare at my files, stung. *No, I believe the vulnerable.* Am I, with my leathery heart, the wrong audience?

Susan Sontag writes that while we crave to witness authentic pain (in photos, in movies), modern audiences are "schooled to be cynical about the possibility of sincerity. Some people will do anything to keep themselves from being moved." The raw, unaltered pain we claim to respect will only make us cringe. Convincing sophisticated audiences requires even more calculation: subtler stories, better craftsmanship, a more polished routine, the very deceptions we're trained to detect.

What is the anatomy of a believable performance, when the heart secretes an armor against others' pain? It's hard to be objective from inside this feeble human mind.

2.

My relationship with belief has changed now that I have some power over myself. Today, I keep examining how *I* believe—whom and what stories; what myths draw me in. But when I was a poor Iranian kid in Oklahoma, with my jet-black hair and massive nose, I gave that up as a decided thing (by my mother, my community). All I cared about was what Americans believed, what they made true with the awesome power of their opinion. I wanted to understand how to change it, to influence it: how do I sound neutral and credible, here and now, to *these* people? I wanted to disappear, like a chameleon into every background. I became obsessed with the people who glided by, blissfully invisible, native to the land. How did they do it?

Everywhere I went, I felt noticed, extra, like the accidental chickpea in a plate of raisin rice. People looked up. In school, I was mocked for my shabby clothes, my Iranian food, my piles of witchy books plus dictionary, my tics and whatever lay undiagnosed beneath. *Are those boy socks? Did you wear those yesterday? Geez, is that pink with red?* "I wish there was a handbook for being American," I told my mother.

I did know one rule of Western society: if you had money, you could be a little more yourself. And we were poor. Soon I became obsessed with getting into Harvard, the place where the handbooks were written, a place that could remake me into a stellar American. But how was I supposed to make time for such ambitions, when half my time was spent correcting tiny, instinctive nothings that no one else ever bothered to think about?

———

Noah was in my advanced geometry class. He was the first American boy who caught my eye. In my Isfahan preschool, I had been openly in love with Ali Mansouri, an older boy (he was in kindergarten) whom I dutifully followed around the playground, calling him always by his full name. "Ali Mansouri, want sour plums? Ali Mansouri, can I play now?" I didn't have many words, and three or four questions stood for my entire spectrum of girlhood emotions. He feigned annoyance for his friends un- til one day, when I stayed home sick, a woman appeared at our door, Ali Mansouri peeking out from behind her long chador, demanding to know that I hadn't moved away. After that, his playground objections were loud as ever, but he kept glancing back to see if I was still a few steps behind.

For years after we landed in Oklahoma, the everyday demands of English and poverty, and the general strangeness all around, distracted me. My heart was too gummed up until seventh grade when, amid my twelve-year old turmoil, I met a boy with dark hair and kind eyes.

Noah was the nicest kid in school. He never made fun of my accent or my clothes. He didn't mind being paired with me in math. "Lucky you're the best at it!" he'd say. He laughed at my jokes and accepted Rolos from my bare hand, unconcerned with Iranian germs—which, since my arrival, had been going around. I carried the little chocolate pucks in my pencil case all through seventh grade, though they were full of grainy caramel. I preferred Crunch bars, but in every grocery store aisle I begged my mother for Rolos, loudly whining that they were only fifty cents (class-shaming is the kryptonite of Persian mothers) and all I ever did was get A's.

Noah and I never talked for long. I worried about my English—not the language, exactly, as I had studied vocabulary and worked on my accent with a tape recorder. But almost every day, I tripped up on the shorthand, the slang, pop culture, jokes. Each time Noah said "Hi," I didn't worry about my bad jeans or my accent or even my words. I worried about the metaphors. Phat and grody and chill pill and gnarly. Slammin' was good but shady was bad ("Why, though?" I kept whispering to my only two friends). A bag of chips was good; cheesy was bad ("Cheese is so much tastier!"). And, my God, so many references from TV, which my mother had banned.

But Noah was easy—he didn't lean on slang. He spoke simply, slowly. He smiled a lot. He explained jokes from his favorite shows. The first time he took a Rolo, he said, "Mmm, good," in that gooey, closed-mouth way you do when your teeth are all gummed up. For half a second, I felt normal—as in on things, as much a part of this new childhood, as I had been when Ali Mansouri tried to choose the sourest plum from the hollow of my cupped hand.

I never told Noah that I liked him, not the way I had with Ali Mansouri, or with the right proxy words. Childhood love, too, has its special language, metaphors, layers of protective tissue children use to wrap their hearts. In Iran: *you're bahal.* In America: *You're dope. You rock.* Those words, though, didn't belong to me. My own words were always the wrong ones. But one morning, as the bell rang, I said them: "I start to miss you as soon as the bell rings."

Noah gave me a strange look. He gathered up his books, nodded goodbye, and then my only friend was gone. How did I get it so humiliatingly wrong?

———

Some years ago, I met a dramaturge who moonlights as an editor for college application essays. My first instinct was to be furious: if belonging is a performance with a script, a dramaturge is one hell of an asset, and I didn't have any such help along the way. But her clients are mostly foreign kids, those without access to American storytelling tools. Often her students say, "My life isn't that interesting," though they've survived war, poverty, insane grandmothers, village coups. They want to edit *out* the beautiful oddities of their voices, like the kind that pepper my mother's speech. "Does this sound like authentic English?" they ask, wanting to scrub out anything that could be mocked or misunderstood. The dramaturge keeps them from shearing their essays of personality and applies her theater expertise to their on-paper "characters," bringing every decision and consequence to life on the page. She keeps their voices broken in surprising places, their charming sentimentality intact. No one but my spicy Iranian mother has stepped in dog shit and said (about all of America), "Here is all over poops!" No one else has lost phone service and shouted into the receiver, "I got no wave!"

The dramaturge knows, too, that her students' rivals, the kids from prep schools and country clubs, have a good script. In my brief stint at the American School of London, my literature students wrote with the instinct that their stories mattered. They held forth about every experience, as if our attention were their birthright. And they got into the best universities. Many substituted vulnerability with drivel and still got through. But while for the foreign applicant the language of home has its place, you can't be entirely yourself: you're allowed a quick flourish, controlled, performed according to familiar Western mores, signaling dignity and grace. You should be interesting and new, but not unrecognizable, or of another realm. The gatekeepers are intimate with Western quirks and mistakes. A foreign teen's forgivable oddities may alarm them.

In his essay "On Truth and Lies in an Extra-Moral Sense," Friedrich Nietzsche writes: "To be truthful means to employ the usual metaphors. Thus, to express it morally, this is the duty to lie according to a fixed convention, to lie with the herd and in a manner binding upon everyone." What we consider truth is only a herd truth, the truth of a particular community or language, their accepted lie. It has to be, because words are invented, and metaphors fail to correspond to or capture the essence of anything. Essences are brief, elusive, altered by perception.

What is truth, then, to most people? What is casual honesty and trustworthiness? Only the use of "the usual metaphors," the familiar, comforting images we've already imbibed. Last year I watched Elena learn French. One by one, she replaced the sounds for every item, every action. All language, Nietzsche says, is code, "a mobile army of metaphors, metonyms, and anthropomorphisms," and everything we take as true and canonical in human relations is a worn-out metaphor we've long ago accepted, "coins which have lost their pictures and now matter only as metal, no longer as coins."

But even specific words aren't exact. A leaf, Nietzsche writes, represents many objects with like traits, though they vary widely. Who knows if the platonic leaf even exists? Where does "leaf-ness" end? Not with size, shape, color, or texture. Other things grow from a tree. When, as babies, do we learn the boundaries of "leaf?" Once, as a toddler, my daughter informed me that a thick blade of grass wasn't a leaf, that I had used the wrong word. How did she know? "Mummy, you lied!" We come to understand the accepted metaphors as children, yet those metaphors are constantly remade.

"You know who you should talk to?" a friend said. "If you want to know about passing for a leaf in places where *everyone's* looking out for the blade of grass? Undercover cops."

How do you know if the new guy hanging around is an undercover cop? I go lurking in a chat group where people ask this question a lot. Undercover officers stake their lives on being believed by vulnerable insiders trained to disbelieve newcomers. How do they do it? What's the trick? The chat is brimming with charmingly specific (almost folksy) wisdom and lived detail:

You can spot an undercover cop by the sole of his shoes—you can beat up your shoes, but a real drug dealer walks through a lot of broken glass and needles.

No, no, the real giveaway is their hands—you can grime up your hands, but you need cracked nails and calluses formed over years.

Oh please, it's their teeth—you can avoid the toothbrush for a few weeks, but years of neglect is hard to fake. And anyway, who'd do that to themselves for a gig?

There's their confident, almost arrogant stance, their searching eyes, the constant pings to a target's phone for tracking. The haircuts. There's just something about the haircuts.

Watch out for the try-hard addict look: the filth, the long hair, even the emaciated look may be convincing for a while, but how is their skin so clear, their teeth not yet rotting? Also, short-term stink is different from long-term stink. That's a detail that goes right to the subconscious, and the thing that gives the cop away is no more than "something feels off." Sometimes, undercover cops stand with arms away from their torsos, because they're used to fat utility belts. They squat for dropped items, instead of bending, because they're used to a gun in the back holster. Those are the newbies, or those under shallow cover. The elite ones morph into their targets, ravaged teeth and all. They become shadows, a self from another realm.

"It's like dressing poor to avoid highway bribes," says a South African friend. "You can't fake it. You have to be gaunt. You have to be the fourth person who's worn your clothes."

Quite often, though, even the best spies are betrayed by some simple item of clothing or slang. Both are specific to times, to places, and differentiate in-groups from out-groups. They are full of metaphoric meaning. And if you're on the outside (maybe a cop newly undercover or a refugee girl newly in love), it's easy to see jeans as interchangeable and slide into your usual pair, agonizing instead over shades or a phone (or Rolos), when ultimately the jeans will give you away.

Group-speak can be simple generational argot ("groovy" or "lit" are both metaphors: fire, the grooves on vinyl), or it can be a fully formed subversive anti-language that helps keep the secrets of vulnerable subcultures. Polari, the coded language of gay communities in 1960s Britain, began as a way to identify each other without triggering suspicion. It might have been a nod to your "batts" (shoes) or a joke about the "lilly" (police). Polari was full of images for vital words (police were also "Betty Bracelets," "Hilda Handcuffs" and many more).

For a long time, pretenders simply didn't have the words, though you only needed about twenty or thirty to identify yourself to friends in hostile surroundings. At a time when homosexual acts were criminalized, a proposition without the usual metaphors was risky, and hardly believable. Later, because of the influence of gay artists in creative industries like television, those twenty or thirty words became widely known. Suddenly everyone knew what a "friend of Dorothy" meant, and Polari as a secret signal became less and less useful and, after some social progress, no longer necessary.

A community's private language gives the vulnerable a modicum of power. When new Christian refugees arrive from Iran, my mother grills them for the shibboleths. If you're a "believer" you will have a "flock," you will know the songs, the verses, the images that signal brotherhood to members of the underground church in the Islamic Republic. As the community gains influence, respectability, and aspirants, the code grows more elaborate, exclusive, and subtle. And yet, it takes so little for a more powerful outsider to invalidate it, robbing it of its charm and vigor. Polari faded because mainstream use stripped off its protective covering. After that, many of its words slipped into English slang, used simply to suggest hipness. The hostile gaze cuts through the metaphor, casting a harsh light on the thing itself—powerless, endangered. The undercover cop, when he outs himself in his own time, destroys every metaphor that he used to infiltrate a vulnerable group, who will now need a new set of signals.

There is a famous letter Iranians pass around online. It's supposedly from a local employee of the National Iranian Oil Company written to an English boss, Mr. Hamilton, in the 1950s or '60s. Throughout the letter, the employee begs for his boss's help. "My hands grab your skirt," he says, and he beseeches "to the fourteen innocents." A wily coworker is "putting watermelon under my arms," he says. "I have six bread-eaters."

In Farsi, it's a heartbreaking read: a poor, overworked, frustrated man begging for help. Yet when it first appeared online it was an object of pure ridicule. All those Iranian sayings translated directly to English sounded silly—Mr. Hamilton surely laughed before passing the letter around. Years ago, my friend and agent gave me a gift: the *American Women's Club of Tehran* handbook, printed in the prerevolutionary 1960s. It's a relic from the Shah's Iran, a country beholden to the colonialist West. It lists common phrases of "the local help," requests obscured by Iranian manners. It instructs American women on how to respond. It cracks open the face-saving metaphors, giving instructions on how to lay bare and ignore the raw pleas underneath.

What magic the dramaturge could have performed with those funny Iranian phrases, changing them from a rant to something moving and profound. How many Iranians try to tell their story in precisely this way to stoic asylum officers who have had their own narrative rules engrained since childhood? (*This rings true; that is too insistent.*)

But, as it stands, the Western reaction to that letter is humiliating. I don't know why Iranians laugh along at this wretched man. When the code isn't an explicit struggle against existing power, it reinforces that power. And, given enough time, it isn't the outsider who's at a disadvantage, but the systematically weaker one. The undercover cop may have to learn slang, the local idioms, for a brief time before he casts off his mask and claims back his power, but the manager of Iran Oil never needs to bother with a word.

———

I buried my Noah hurt, throwing myself into my science project: creating a personality test. The next day I showed it to my favorite science teacher, a kind middle-aged man with a pocked scalp and an ever-bemused smile. I told him that my ultimate goal, maybe for later in high school, was to make a test that could create a single metric for a person's potential. And it would combine their talents, education, and—I wanted to say refinement. But I didn't know that word then, so I said, "Their talents, and education, and also the parts of them that are kind of sharpened by the stuff they do all day. Like can they tell if they're served bad meat, or how to eat a taco, or if they're at an American's house for dinner and somebody says something about something, do they know what to say back even if they haven't read much about that thing? And are they wearing pink with red like a moron? You know, stuff like that."

My teacher nodded through my bog of words. "Like a culture test?" he asked.

"Not exactly," I said. "Like, a *knowing* test. Getting by in front of people who're higher, I guess. It's like, do you have taste?" I stopped, embarrassed. "Anyway, this isn't the project I did. This is just to verify the Myers-Briggs. See, I've got questions for each category, and I took it and it matches my results. Extrovert, Intuiting . . . See?"

"Well, the Myers-Briggs would be testing yours," he said. I glared. He continued, "Because *that* was made by experts. You've got a great project, but write it up like it's yours, that's verified or not verified by theirs. See?"

"Right," I said. "Because I'm not an expert at this."

"Exactly," he said. He turned, thinking I had understood how to write my report.

"So," I called after him, "when I'm an expert at something, and a person wants to say I'm wrong, it's always *my* work that's the test for *their* work? So, like, I get believed first as long as I'm . . . or until they're higher, in expertness?"

"*Expertise*," he said, chuckling to himself. "And Lord, if you didn't just explain the whole ugly hamster wheel of academia."

I didn't get the hamster joke. I was too busy having an adolescent epiphany. I'd just been told that when you became an expert, you stood safely on a high rung, and nobody below could plausibly challenge you. You could claim a respectable place among Americans *in that one thing, the subject you knew*. I could wear my refugee jeans to the lab, but if I cure cancer, people have to listen. I could wear a cat T-shirt to court, but if my arguments convince a judge, I win. In refugee camp, lawyers and translators had seemed so vital. They had the skills to knock open heavy doors. Maybe this was a small part of the elaborate code that I'd been sniffing out since my first day in America—and it was everything I already believed in: real, hard-earned expertise.

"Maybe I'll make a test with, like, twenty prototype people," I muttered, trailing my teacher to his desk. "Like, a chef from California, a doctor, or a sporty garbageman, or a chic lawyer from Harvard. Stuff like that. And test the whole class and see what everyone is most likely to become. I'll test myself against the Harvard lawyer for a control—"

"Great, we'll do that and then I'll be fired," he said.

"Amazing! I'll write it up," I said, and bounced away.

I forgot all about Noah for a while, giving my heart entirely to the pursuit of Harvard and of some elusive and precious "expertness." The trouble was, I'd already given my heart to Jesus.

When I was six, on a trip to London, I repeated my grandmother's words to invite Christ in.

"Is that good?" I asked. "Am I saved now?" Growing up in Iran, I'd never heard of Jesus.

She said that I was.

"Will I ever be unsaved?"

She said that I wouldn't, that the only unforgivable sinner was a believer who renounced Jesus, but no *true* believer could ever do that, so it was a merciful paradox: the unforgivable was logically impossible, like God creating a rock so heavy that even he can't lift it.

"So, if somebody renounces Jesus, it means they never really believed?"

That's right, she reassured me, and Jesus would forgive them if they one day decided to believe for real, their first salvation having been proven false.

"Do *I* really believe?"

It seemed so, at least to my grandmother.

"But then, does *this* believing not count, until I die and we can be sure I never *stopped*?"

Well, nothing was decided for anyone, really, not until *those trumpets sound.*

"But I'm *sure* I believe—"

It felt unjust, presuming to tell me that any future disbelief could cancel my current belief. Nowadays, when I question Elena's thoughts, she screams, "You don't know my world!"

For years after that conversation with my grandmother, I fearfully toiled to please Jesus. The Bible reading and the faithful questioning of the text was easy. The good deeds were a touch harder, until we became refugees and had little left to give. I was baptized in a lake near our refugee hostel in Italy. It was peaceful and quiet, ringed patchily by trees. In photos, I'm wearing a black one-piece and shorts, and a pastor bends down to ask me something. That act, too, was easy. Only one miracle of faith proved impossible: despite my most fervent wish, wherever I went, and however earnestly I tried, I couldn't speak in tongues.

"Why doesn't it work?" I whined to my mother, every Sunday afternoon, every Wednesday night, as I flung myself onto my bed. "What's wrong with me? Why can't I do it?"

I had been trying for so long, but this one testament of my faith eluded me. First as a convert in Iran, the daughter of a respected family, then in a hostel in Sharjah where, for Jesus's sake, we had become undocumented migrants, then among other Christian refugees in a camp outside Rome. And it failed me later, in a church full of American believers in Oklahoma, where now and then after church I stood in a circle of prayerful mothers who were convinced that if they prayed with me, they could get me to "receive the gift of tongues." They had already summoned this baptism of the Holy Spirit in so many other young people.

They watched me expectantly, and I thought, *Am I supposed to fake it?*

Sometimes my mother stood in the circle. She didn't pressure me—and each time I failed, she said that it wasn't a question of my salvation, it just wasn't the time. Or maybe it wasn't my gift to have. Or maybe—this last possibility was always just implied, though I knew that some of the other mothers had whispered it—*maybe, deep down, you don't truly believe.*

How was it that everyone around me had this gift? The most puerile, silliest girls in our church seemed to be blessed with it the quickest. And yet I squeezed my eyes shut, gripped strangers' hands (pastors, youth pastors, Sunday School teachers, deacons' wives), and begged Jesus. I reminded him that I had been through things for his sake, that I had given up the life of a comfortable medical family for refugee camps, then a dirty apartment complex in Oklahoma. That I had given up my father. Not that I was ungrateful.

Dear Jesus, I believe more than anybody. If you want, I'll stop reading witch-burning stories in the library. Please make me speak in tongues or give me a sign that Lindsay is faking.

Why couldn't I speak in tongues like Lindsay, who made out with boys behind the church on Sunday afternoons (and performed her spiritual ecstasy, complete with little moans, for the proud mothers watching, her breath catching as if she were about to make literal love to the literal Jesus)? Or Ashley, who cursed whether or not her mother was listening? Or Suzanne, who had a wad of gum in her mouth as she succumbed to ecstatic babbling? It made no sense.

"Well, Jesus doesn't reveal himself the same way to everyone," the pastor told me. I've heard this logic a lot since then:

If I deliberately set that fire, may God strike me dead now.

For some reason, he usually doesn't choose to do that.

I began to doubt. I never *entertained* my doubts, not consciously. Some part of me began to sense the lie embedded at the core of this whole business. There was an easy way into the ranks of the righteous: just close your eyes, move your lips, and fake it.

While I didn't articulate my skepticism back then, I never performed glossolalia either, never even considered it—though, as a fluent Farsi speaker with a pocket full of old nursery rhymes, I could've duped this Oklahoma Sunday School so much more handily than any of the Lindsays with their tired playlist of "shambalalalas." How did these girls stay in character? Nary a giggle or a side glance. Never a whisper across the prayer circle. They were so damn good. How did they avoid dying of shame in front of themselves—or, in front of that other self, deep inside, that's always cringing? I had a constant, scathing internal whisper. Didn't *they*?

But the bigger mystery now, after I began doubting the realness of *every* rapturous episode, was whether my own mother was a tongues-faker or a tongues-believer—or if there was some in between (a tongues-try-hard?). One day, I knocked on her bedroom door as she was studying for some medical exam.

"Do you know what you're saying when you speak in tongues?" I asked.

She looked up from her book. "It's not my prayer," she said. "Sometimes it's God's message for someone else."

"Do you think everybody who speaks in tongues is really speaking in tongues?"

"It's not our place to judge," she said. But then she added something to the effect of, "When it happens, though, we (the faithful) know."

Wait. A. Minute. Was she saying that she knows who's faking, and isn't outing them?

"Do you believe those girls?" I said. "Do you think they have more faith than me?"

"We don't know what's in their heart," my mother said. Then she explained that I should stop making it such an obstacle in my head. I should drain it of its mystery. This was a normal thing, an everyday (but miraculous) communion with God. And it didn't mean a loss of control. You're the one moving your lips, you're the one deciding to stop. But the urge, it comes from somewhere deep, and true. That first time, you just have to be willing, and let God speak.

"That is so confusing!" I said. "Just tell me what to do and I'll do it."

This kind of bullshit assignment was exactly why I preferred math. Math was simple, even when it was hard. There were right and wrong answers, right and wrong next steps. You didn't have to trust in some unseen power. It was all observed things, all tangible, incorruptible, equally accessible to anyone, whatever their language or place in society. It came down to subjectivity and trust: I could figure out a math problem and be right, and if someone doubted me or tried to shame me or tell me to submit to some unknown authority (God or the state or a circle of church ladies), all I'd have to do was show my work and be proven right.

Seeing my frustration, my mother took mercy on me. As it turned out, she had made a tape. As a seasoned glossolalist, she could routinely enter trances during her private prayers, and she had recorded herself. This brought up a hundred questions about my own situation: each time I failed, I'd been told that I wasn't concentrating enough, or giving my thoughts wholly over to God. So, then, how does a person who has moved beyond all earthy thought remember to push the "record" button? When I asked this, my mother repeated (again) that after you've done it for a while, you are more in control. The first time God does it for you, through you. After that, you can get yourself there. The mythology of this is, one must admit, highly sexual. But fine.

"Is this why Ashley sometimes opens her eyes?" I asked, remembering how frequently the girls seemed to decide abruptly that the ecstasy was over, depending on the state of the others around them. "Is it why she can chew gum?"

My mother didn't answer the question. She told me, as ever, that I should have more faith if I wanted to receive the gift. So I listened.

My mother's prayer began in Farsi. It grew louder, then softer, as she forgot the tape and lost herself to her meditation. Briefly I was moved by her prayer, the depth of her belief, her vulnerable, girlish voice. It was the voice on my baby tape, one of the few childhood treasures we had smuggled out of Iran: a tape of me (a toddler) and my mother (only twenty-five then), singing, reciting poems, giggling over the big words.

Then, the prayer on the tape changed. It morphed into four or five strange syllables, repeated as in a chant. I leaned in. What was this? My mother's voice, still, but such unfamiliar words. She wasn't making any strange sounds—no clicking or grunting, as I had heard others do— just new combinations. I felt myself beginning to blush—she was, after all, sitting just there, at the edge of her bed, watching me absorb this the way some parents watch their children open a safe deposit box of grandpa's old watches. This was my weird inheritance, and she hoped I'd treasure it. I tried to make sense of it. Could it be a garbled Farsi? Or lines from a prayer book, in Hebrew or Latin? Maybe the sedative fog of deep reflection had made her slur her words.

I looked away. The syllables sounded fake, redundant, unimaginative. A tightness spread over my chest, a dull, heavy ache. Some part of me, a creature who lived in a deep buried place, was disgusted with the person I loved most in this world—my brave, beautiful, rebellious mother who had cast off the headscarf and whisked me to America. It's impossible to overstate how I had worshipped her before then; how, as my own intellect awoke, I had expected to join her in an enlightened circle of bookish adults who craved rational discourse and academic rigor, adults who had no patience for nonsense. She had, after all, sold her Christianity to me in this way: it isn't dogma, it isn't a religion. It's a relationship with God. As a child, she had encouraged me to question every line of the Bible. This was about *using* our minds, not switching them off.

And yet.

She didn't play more than thirty seconds of that tape for me. In real time, this is a forgotten scene, a minute of her life. She played me her prayer and returned to her medical book, to her own complex inner life that balanced faith with scholarship in proportion to her need, satisfying her heart and mind with her own chosen myths and sciences.

But the kindest thought I could muster was that she was tricking herself. Maybe the Pentecost did happen, and continues to visit the holiest, but most others fool themselves. They're overcome by emotion, pressure, the desire to please. Maybe the fundamental difference between my mother and me was that, somewhere deep beyond all my striving and struggling for approval, lived that other Dina, the one who believed what she sensed and reasoned, and didn't care what anyone else thought. At such decisive moments, eyes clenched shut, squeezing the bejeweled fingers of some pastor's wife, when I might have released the pressure and given myself over, allowing nonsense to slip off my tongue, suppressing the knowledge that *I am inventing this*—in such moments, that other Dina gripped my tongue in disgust.

I stopped trying to speak the language of angels. And I put away the mystery for a while. I had so much school work, so many squats and lunges, before Harvard would even look at me.

Then, when I was fifteen or sixteen, a revival came to our small Oklahoma town. Our congregation was thrumming with anticipation. The revival promised transformation, renewal, communion with God. It promised a spiritual surge. Exhausted from a huge academic load, sports, and all my activities, I decided to make Harvard the focus of my prayer.

Dear Jesus, please help me become an expert, to go to Harvard and become a person who knows something (anything) for sure.

Ever since our conversion, we'd been watching Benny Hinn and Kenneth Copeland and even old videos of Oral Roberts, a 1950s Oklahoma evangelist with slicked hair and a kind voice who told kids they'd no longer stammer. These "prosperity gospel" ministers told desperate geriatrics to "name and claim" anything they wanted from God:

health, riches, love. All they had to do was prove their faith by sending small sums to the minister. As the decades went by, these con artists grew bolder and more theatrical, shouting and jumping, laying sweaty hands on sick men and women who obediently dropped to the ground ("Slain in the spirit!") and claimed to be healed. Benny Hinn lulled his audience with whispered chants to soft music: *Let the bodies hit the floor. Let the bodies hit the floor.* Then he raised his hands and roared into the silence, his voice possessed, as several rows of bodies fell like an ocean wave.

How we loved Benny Hinn, an olive-skinned man from Israel who looked like us, who could have been one of our fathers.

For our hometown revival, I put on a skirt. I prayed quietly and listened in awe to the ecstasies around me. *Dear Jesus, please let a good university take me. Please give me Harvard.* I glanced over at my mother, praying softly. What did she want from God?

Now and then, throughout my life, I'd dig up a math problem or logic puzzle so tough that my mother became consumed by it. Once I told her one just before she went to bed, and she woke the next day, groggy and muttering, "As if a person can sleep after that!" She took a sip of coffee and added, "But I figured it out . . . Get a piece of paper." I'd watch her unravel it, sketching out tables and grids with her messy prescription pad handwriting, her Latin T's and L's always capitalized. When we played logic games, my anxiety melted away. I thought: *I come by my oddities honestly, and I'll survive because I come from logical, analytical people.*

The preacher was ramping up, his voice began to boom, his energy hitting a peak. He was sweating hard. "Name your desire and you will have it!" he bellowed. I had heard those words so often: *Name it and claim it. Name it and claim it.* Crammed in that sweaty throng, the words had a power over me. They were familiar, comforting, my family's trigger words—our slang, our usual metaphors—for empowerment, for taking control of one's destiny. The preacher carried on about sacrifice, hard work, putting your money where your mouth is.

My heart began to thunder. I decided to take another tack with God. I prayed. "Jesus, to show I mean it, I'll give up chocolate and ice cream for a year."

Suddenly, I felt a weight lift. This had been what God wanted, a price. The urgency in my heart had been conviction, and now the lightness there, the relief in my chest, was confirmation that I had been right. I couldn't wait to tell my mother what God had told me. I would have a place at Harvard if I just gave up chocolate and ice cream for a year, as a sacrifice.

Then, a silence, a boom: the preacher threw his hands up. He sensed something. Someone had a message from God—who was it? Across the congregation, a woman's sobs broke the hush. The crowd swelled. The woman began beseeching the Lord in tongues, her voice rising to a holler, a scream. A young man jogged over with a microphone.

Well, look how close he was standing to her, whispered the other Dina, *all ready to go.*

"Who has received the translation?" the pastor asked, his eyes shut tight as he paced the stage (*How many rehearsals, honestly?*). A beat or two of silence, then someone picked up God's transmission. The translation was about the same length and tone, and it was lovely and reassuring. I wanted so much to believe it.

No. Amid the rises and falls, I kept stumbling into hidden beats of time, lucid little pockets in which this highway-grift choreography felt shameful, stupid, and grotesque.

This is embarrassing, the other Dina whispered hotly into my ear. *This con artist can't give you expertise, or even a degree. Zero people in this room, especially and including you, deserve to study at Harvard. And if we could look through a telescope and see the Harvard class of 2001, guess how many will have ever stood in a small-town revival tent? Yeah, that's right.*

Humiliated in front of myself, I shook off all the voices, my own and the preacher's. I tuned out all the prayers. I spent the rest of the service mired in boredom, in errancy and strangeness. I was so out of place here, yet I'd never wash the stink of this sanctuary off me. *It's me or them*, whispered the other Dina, and already I knew who she was. I needed her, my most essential self.

In Iran, when I was forced to stand in a line of school girls and chant "Death to America," my mother warned me never to say the words, never to go along. *Words are dangerous. Don't say rote or hateful things. Don't be mindless.* During the daily Islamic Republic mantras, my mother advised, I should pray to Jesus instead. *Tune it out.*

So, at the revival, I did exactly that. Though I'd give up ice cream and chocolate in the following year (just in case), that night in the sanctuary, with my ears burning from the strident fainting and the shrill tongues of angels, I stopped listening for words or meaning. I was so ashamed. I closed my eyes and did a calculus problem instead.

I understood by this time that a pastor couldn't publicly renounce a supplicant for faking, even if he suspected it. I understood that this was an enterprise, that it was big and important to the community, that the pastors, in seeming to release control, were absolutely in control. But what about my mother? I thought often about that private tape in her cupboard. Listening to it had plunged me into a period of confused disappointment and shame, though I knew she had shared it so we might bond. In her bedroom, I had put on a wretched smile.

"That's—" I had muttered. "I don't think I'll ever be able to."

"We all have our gifts," she had reassured me. At the time I took this to mean *tongues aren't your gift.* Now, I wish my mother might have meant *your skepticism is a gift.*

Most people find it impossible to be humiliated in front of themselves. They're too fused, too whole. They can fake things, forget things. I'm constantly cringing before a smarter, stronger, more capable self who only shakes her head. I think my daughter Elena's scatological obsessions are rooted in this same tendency. She's disgusted in front of herself. It's a comfort to know that my daughter won't easily trick herself to please others. And yet, I know that believing that someone is always watching, losing that boundary between private and public, is a sign of autism. I also know that when people sense this pitiless other Dina controlling things, deciding things, they lose trust in me. But the girls in my church, too, had their own calculating voices. Maybe theirs whispered that to succumb to the performance was to accept their role as carriers of the ritual into the next generation.

Years later, when I told Sam about the rapturous Lindsays at Sunday prayer, I joked that he should engrave on my tombstone: HERE LIES DINA, SHE NEVER ONCE FAKED IT. He laughed. "I don't know if that'll fit in with your McKinsey burial," he said.

"What's *that* mean?" I said, stung. I had recently written a few speeches for my old consulting firm, but only (I kept loudly repeating) for the feminist, socially conscious executives.

"Only that you *have* faked things. Or, everybody does." He paused. "Except you've had real, professional training in it."

This again. Fine, I might now and again fake enthusiasm or patience or understanding—even expertise—but I don't fake spiritual things. I don't fake *ecstasies.* How to make him understand that performing excitement is different from performing pain, that faking affection is better than faking physical or spiritual wounds? That worst of all is mimicking *belief.* Even—especially—when you're alone, with your inner voice, or with your God.

Instead, I said, "So have you! There isn't just one kind of professional deception. We're both trained storytellers." He laughed. I thought, *geez, I have two master's degrees in lying.*

In my youth, I spent so many hungry Sunday mornings wishing I could prove that all the glossolalists were lying. Had I grown up in the time of the internet, I would've recorded them to compare to various modern languages. At the Pentecost, our church taught us, the apostles spoke in "divided tongues like fire." Stories abound of travelers in foreign lands hearing their native tongue in a stranger's fit of prayer. A good portion of the time, we were assured, the gibberish was another earthly tongue—so, statistically, if a well-traveled, multilingual person were to listen to enough of it, one might reasonably hope to recognize a word or two. Had I the resources to compare Ashley's or Suzanne's or Lindsay's eager whimpers and ululations to the world's collected languages, I might have accepted four or five years earlier that the whole thing was a scam.

Now I go looking for scientific research on speaking in tongues. I have a hundred questions, and they've all been asked by academics. Does anyone fake it under pressure? Was my mother in a trance? Was she accessing a real language? I find a paper on early church status symbols, angelic languages as social hierarchy. In every church my family attended, being anointed with an indecipherable tongue wasn't suspicious but a source of pride: God chose only the purest vessels for the language of angels. After baptism in the spirit, young Pentecostals were granted more respect and trust. They were no longer kids. They were part of the Faithful.

In Ron Hansen's novel, *Mariette in Ecstasy*, a pretty, wealthy girl in a nunnery gives her body over to God, then slips into trances and bleeds from stigmata. Having prayed precisely for this, the other nuns should rejoice. Instead, they become petty, judgmental. Mariette is a sinner and a novice, easily drawn into lustful talk. Why would God choose *her*? She's getting too much attention. Is she performing?

Hansen's descriptions are visceral, carnal, and precise, reminding the reader of the physical strangeness of the religious phenomena we call up from a blurry distance. If manifested, stigmata are a mess. They have a smell. When performed, the gift of tongues is cloying, humiliating. No one believes Mariette. Why should they? Deep down, did they not understand that the whole thing was a meditation, a way to remove oneself into solitude and quiet, and still to live as a part of society? Did they believe in the physical truth of the mysteries they peddled?

In charismatic churches across America, sometimes everyone prays together, their rhythmic chants blurring together, changing from English to the sacred tongue and back to English again. And sometimes, during a silence, a voice rises loudly in a strange tongue, no longer praying privately, but delivering a message to the flock. When this happens, the preacher asks if the Lord has sent anyone an interpretation. These displays tend to be prophecies, about individuals nearby, or even about the community, the country, or the world. Glossolalia, I read, is often associated with prophecy.

It seems, also, that linguists have already done what I wished I could do: record many hours of tongues and try to make sense of the syllables. Why do the people speaking in tongues always say the same syllables? Why does each person have their own set of six or seven syllables? (The mothers in my church said it's because each person is given a language. But the same words? Are they praying on the same topic, each and every time?) And why is it that no American glossolalist ever makes the sounds we had in Farsi, like *kh* or *gh?* Likewise, in our church in Iran, no one ever made a sound like *w* or a *th*.

Also, if this is a real and holy thing, why is no one ever accused of faking? Precious things, if real, always compel forgeries. Lindsay, for example, was a faker, and not nearly as good at it as Hansen's Mariette. Why did no one dare question her? Was the whole enterprise that fragile? Or was it simply that the church believed some good came of the ritual, of the gesture toward such a practice, no matter how false?

Or maybe it's that the real thing is so cognitively close to faking. A pastor told me once that the two can feel similar, and only in the deepest places of your heart can you know if this is God speaking through you, or your ego. He never takes away your control; you choose when to start and stop. And that's why we can't judge people like Lindsay, because then we'd have to ask the same question of all the pious older sisters with unquestionable faith, and of the pastor, and of the men and women of the Pentecost, and every saint and penitent who came after.

In 2006, *The New York Times* reported on a University of Pennsylvania study in which five women were given brain scans as they spoke in tongues. Their frontal lobes, responsible for thinking and decision, were relatively quiet, as were the language centers. But regions controlling self-consciousness were active. These women weren't in a trance, or meditating, but the study noted that they did "cede some control over their bodies and emotions." To whom? One cedes control during a rote habit, too. I wonder what a brain scan of a first-time glossolalist would show. In that first time, under pressure, with a few syllables "received" and hanging at the tip of the tongue, I bet a suggestible person's decision center lights up like a street fair. In subsequent performances, it might become rote, like a song or a poem recited a hundred times before. If such a song slipped off my tongue thoughtlessly, without my having to recall the words, wouldn't my brain scan look just the same as those women?

An archived 1971 article in *The New York Times* cited a small 1965 Brooklyn study, financed by the National Institute of Mental Health, concluding that glossolalists have the same levels of mental health as others, but show subtle differences in personality, namely the desire to submit to a higher authority. "The glossolalists are able to develop a deeply trusting and submissive relationship to the authority figure who introduces them to the practice of glossolalia," said Dr. Kildahl, the lead researcher. "Without this complete turning oneself over to the leader, there can be no beginning to speak, in tongues." This ability to relinquish one's ego in the presence of the authority figure was close to being hypnotized, and "existed among all personality types," implying that one "could 'learn' to speak in tongues."

And why shouldn't they learn their community's shared joy, its ritual? Tongues is an in-group rite. After a bout, says the 1971 article, glossolalists feel happier, more assured of God's love. The practice improves their marriages, even their sex lives. "If your theology is such that anything that makes you feel good is the gift of God, then glossolalia is the gift of God."

I found no study or research that showed an adherent unknowingly speaking another earthly language. But the findings of Dr. Felicitas Goodman, who studied glossolalia and religious ecstasy among an array of believers in Mexico, the United States, and elsewhere, sum it up for me: The gibberish has similar intonation patterns and accents as the speakers' native language. Though there are verbal units, pauses, and syllables, there is no link between sounds and concepts, and the glossolalia of Christians isn't that different from that of other religions. Though variations abound, the scientists heard no human language unknown to the glossolalist. Dr. Goodman thus concluded that the glossolalia is a kind of vocalization in simple patterns, without content or meaning. That doesn't mean it's faked—trances, religious or otherwise, are psychologically complicated. But it's not a language, let alone that of angels.

I lingered on those pages for days, my heart aching, refusing to close my internet browsers. *Oh, Mother, how I respected you, how I believed in your stunning intelligence.*

What about the interpretations, then? Where do those come from? And why is a message directed at an Anglophone community delivered first in Dutch or Hindi? Nobody cares. When they speak of their spirit baptisms, believers talk in broad sensations: they are filled with joy, one with the flock, wrapped up in a blanket of love and peace. The repetition becomes collective memory: *In this era, we had a ritual.* Communities need to perform certain acts together.

Still, one aspect of the spirit-baptism mystery left me curious and unconvinced: whether it's ecstasy or meditation or a trance, afterward, how do the glossolalists, confronted by the superego, avoid melting in shame at the memory? The answer: often, they don't remember.

Would recalling the moment you *chose* to lift your tongue, to make that strange sound and the next, beat by beat, be humiliating?

In *The Drowned and the Saved*, Primo Levi admits that he entered the lager (concentration camp) as a nonbeliever. He persisted in his unbelief after he was liberated; the lagers only confirmed that unbelief. "It prevented, and still prevents me from conceiving of any form of providence or transcendent justice: Why were the moribund packed in cattle cars? Why were the children sent to the gas?" And yet, when naked and facing death, Levi prayed. Or rather, in his solitude, he was tempted to deceive himself. "For one instant I felt the need to ask for help and asylum; then, despite my anguish, equanimity prevailed: one does not change the rules of the game at the end of the match, not when you are losing. A prayer under these conditions would have been not only absurd (what rights could I claim? and from whom?) but blasphemous, obscene, laden with the greatest impiety of which a nonbeliever is capable. I rejected that temptation: I knew that otherwise, were I to survive, I would have been ashamed of it."

There's something heroic about Mariette's insistence. Maybe she's conning everyone, but not herself. Levi, I think, would make an exception for the powerless calling society's bluff.

I don't doubt my mother's faith in Christ. But maybe in the midst of her suffering and persecution in Iran, her heart squeezed tight, her tongue dry, she stumbled into gibberish. Like a record scratch or a missed beat, it lasted only an instant. But she startled herself: *Other tongues!* The memory of it, after she survived, might have felt much like the one Primo Levi anticipated—the intellect whispering that the prayer was animal weakness. But couldn't it still be *true*, even if she was frightened into it? She might have been ashamed of the slip of her frightened tongue, of her feeble body trembling before a Harrow, or she might instead be bold and claim it, repeat it, lean in and call it her gift. A person can be entirely mistaken and still entirely sincere. And yes, my mother was changing the rules in a losing round. But hadn't this world changed the rules on her a hundred times? Maybe she wanted a fickle and cruel God to prove himself just once. And if he did, she'd live among a strange new people and learn this strange new code.

Doesn't that, from a certain angle, seem almost the braver option?

3.

On December 15, 1941, the Nazis marched nearly 16,000 Jews out of the Ukrainian city of Kharkiv to the wilderness ravine of Drobytsky Yar. In 5°F weather, they forced men, women, and children to strip off their clothes and to dig pits. Then they shot them in rows, allowing one row of bodies to fall on the ones below. To save bullets, they threw in the children alive, knowing that the adult corpses would quickly suffocate them. Almost three months earlier, in the snaking, mile-long ravine at Babi Yar in northwestern Kyiv, the Nazis shot and buried over 33,000 civilians in two days, the largest single German massacre of the Jews. For two more years, the Nazis continued to use the site for executions and mass burials of another 100,000–150,000 people.

Understanding that these were war crimes, the Nazis tried to destroy the evidence. But two years later, as it pushed the Germans back from Stalingrad to Berlin, the Soviet army discovered the mass graves. Traveling with the army, filmmakers carrying handheld clockwork cameras (to collect images to rally the Soviet people) gathered relics of Nazi atrocities, documenting what they saw in high-quality footage good enough for newsreels.

In 2006, historian Dr. Jeremy Hicks, a professor of Russian culture and film, came upon a trove of unseen footage locked in the Russian State Film Archive in Krasnogorsk. These films, Dr. Hicks realized, were some of the earliest footage of the Holocaust, an initial stage of mass killing preceding the gas chambers, carried out with bullets and mass graves on the Eastern front.

In a 2014 film, *The Unseen Holocaust*, Dr. Hicks shares his shock at finding the films, and their importance to our understanding of the Holocaust. The shootings weren't a footnote to the program of extermination in the gas chambers. Rather, the Nazi genocide began full-throttle on the Eastern front, with hundreds of thousands shot and buried in mass graves. Why was this footage hidden until now? Dr. Hicks admits that it took him a week to get through an hour of footage. I, too, watch the film slowly, in five-minute increments. It's some of the most grueling Holocaust footage I've seen. Investigators dig through the artifacts soberly, examining thousands of bodies for precise causes of death for use in tribunals. They drive sticks into the holes in skulls, measuring the trajectory of bullets. Those are the easiest scenes to watch.

And yet, according to Dr. Hicks, reports of the damning Russian army footage were dismissed at first by mainstream international media, until the British and Americans arrived at Bergen-Belsen and Dachau. Having once assumed the Soviet footage was wholly staged propaganda (the Soviets had, after all, falsified films before), they now realized that the Russians weren't lying about the Nazi mass murders. And now, given the Soviet army's precedent of filming genocide wreckage, the British and the Americans did so, too. "Would they have dared to do that," Dr. Hicks asks me in an interview, "if the Soviet footage hadn't set that precedent? I doubt it." As the Russians had done, these crews subtly staged the scene, inviting locals and authority figures, like the Archbishop of Canterbury and General Eisenhower, to bear witness—and to be filmed reacting.

Even after the British and American discoveries of the lagers, Cold

War mistrust cast the Soviet films into disuse. Their origin tainted the footage, and some broadcasters worried it might alter the way the Holocaust was viewed. Besides, the British had always considered images of real death and its detritus distasteful for hours-long cinema viewing; cinemas were for entertainment, not education, as the Russians believed. Though portions of the Russian footage were shown in the Nuremberg trials to identify the dead, over time these films became a veiled part of the Shoah's video legacy—in the Holocaust's aftermath, the world saw mostly images of the death camps, the lagers, the showers, the ovens. The genocide in the east fell into shadow.

Back in wartime Russia, the films were shown in cinemas all over the Soviet Union, twice a week. With all the raw footage and artifacts that the army's documentarians had gathered, the Soviet government began a program of public education about the Nazis—*education*, I call it, because the footage was true, though according to Dr. Hicks, this campaign to rally the people (and the manner in which the films were shot, edited, and shown) had all the remaining hallmarks of propaganda. And here is another reason the footage fell into disuse: with film a new medium and an uninitiated Russian public at risk of not fully understanding, those who appeared in the films scouting for bodies, finding gruesome relics, and ultimately stumbling onto their massacred love ones were asked (or otherwise compelled) to *perform* their pain.

"They started showing the films, but they didn't just show it," Dr. Hicks tells me. "It had to be understood in the right way. These women, the relatives of the dead, played a role. They portrayed themselves, but they were also playing a role, telling the national Soviet audience and then international audiences how to feel: that here are our compatriots eviscerated. These murdered people are just like us. The dominant image they use to accomplish that is women, elderly women, who could be mothers of grown-up sons, pulling their hair, tearing their clothes, ululating." For Soviet audiences, this was a familiar image of mourning.

Those performances did not age well, and maybe that is why they were kept so quiet: it's easy to see how they could fuel Holocaust deniers. For me, it's heartbreaking footage. I've witnessed many powerless women *trying* to be seen: mourners or court petitioners in Iranian villages, refugee mothers, young women in finance, friendless ex-wives of influential men.

"There's no denying that much of what was shot was staged for the cameras," *The Unseen Holocaust* advises, and that much is apparent. Groups of women and children are escorted to the ravines, where rows of bodies await them. They search. Professional cameras shoot the scene from many angles. Mothers and wives wail directly at the camera. One looks just like an Ardestooni grandmother performing funeral rites. In rural Iranian funerals, mourners are expected to dramatize, to exaggerate their turmoil in proportion to their respect for the deceased. In the silent footage, this Russian grandmother balls her hands into angry fists, shakes them at the sky, crosses her arms and grips her shoulders, then beseeches the heavens and pounds her heart. I know these gestures. In villages, as women age, they must insist more fervently. That insistence takes physical form, traveling up their limbs and spilling out of the tips of their fingers, from the tops of their heads, making them *less* believable. So, they insist harder, until they are absurd. The rawest, freshest grief is melodramatic, and yet we are taught that melodrama is the opposite of art, and truth.

I wonder: What if these women were accustomed simply to being believed? What if, starting in youth, their words were enough and grew sacred with age? They might behave like elegant Western matriarchs, revered and therefore brimming with subtlety and quiet gravitas.

In a stunning moment, as a mourner weeps into a handkerchief, her eye briefly flits up at the camera. For a nanosecond, her gaze asks, *Are you watching?* Dr. Hicks explains that the Russians wanted to show women in headscarves reacting, in order to suggest a connection to the Soviet families watching in cinemas—these were *their* daughters and mothers. The filmmakers felt compelled to take these measures, to direct huge arrows at "the point," because they had no confidence that the people would see, or understand, the gravity of what they were seeing. Without realizing, they injected absurdity into some of history's most solemn moments.

Eyewitness accounts reveal, writes Dr. Hicks in *First Films of the Holocaust*, "that Soviet camera crews deliberately concentrated on filming people who were crying profusely, occasionally even shouting orders to weep when bystanders appeared numbed." They also wanted the victims to be seen as Russian first, not Jewish. "Indeed, as the report on the liberation of Rostov in *Pravda* put it: 'The Germans didn't care whom they killed.'" A ridiculous claim.

For me, the most disconcerting aspect of the footage is the disconnect between what a 1940s Russian audience might have seen and what is evident to modern movie-watchers. The filmmakers had arranged gruesome detritus—frozen corpses, wrecked limbs, clothing, even bones—into piles in front of the camera, before which women gesticulated wildly, rocking, flailing, falling into each other's arms. "They ensured that the images were compelling," says Dr. Hicks. And yet, these are real bodies. A chapter of history's greatest tragedy. Sacred relics. The women wanted to honor the dead, to stamp their memory into eternity. No doubt they were told (by cameramen who truly believed it) that this was the only way to make sure such horrors were never forgotten, that the audience understood.

Often, we're told not to tell a story too soon after it happens, or risk turning it into melodrama, shaking our fists and beseeching the audience to grasp its awfulness, instead of standing somberly back and allowing its visceral details to reveal themselves without fanfare or embellishment. Back then, though, what chance did these women have to hit an authentic note for posterity? It would be a challenge for anyone, however cunning and practiced, to calibrate their raw disgust and sadness. Add to that the standards of the time: in the 1940s, even professionals were prone to overacting; mid-century cinema's iconic moments often make modern audiences chuckle. And yet, these aren't outdated camera angles or filters—there is no going back to fix the footage. The problem is outdated directing, hackneyed storytelling. The guile shows, and one wishes the women were left alone, a camera hidden just out of sight, instead of being asked to work for it in this brutal moment.

Crafting the footage, how much might the cameramen have expected of these women? *The audience won't understand unless we really show them. The camera softens things. You must insist.* Now directors advise that the camera sees all, even a flit of the hand. Subtlety is everything; even a glance at the lens and the take is rubbish. But, moving with army troops though gunfire and other real dangers, these crews were inside the story, not just crafting it with artistic distance. The adrenaline of the advance fueled the drama of their films. Did they trust that they'd be believed? At the time of filming, hardly anyone knew about the Final Solution. What a huge, impossible story they had to unpack for the world—would anyone want to believe it? They must have known that they'd have to *prove* the story, instead of just telling it. And they'd have to prove it far beyond sympathetic Russian audiences. If Cassandra wasn't believed because she was an outsider, unintelligible, telling stories that nobody wanted to hear, what chance did these documentarians have of delivering the Holocaust story to disbelieving masses?

Yet flashes of unvarnished reality sear the heart almost a century later. Families are walked through rows of bodies. As they search, they forget the cameras. Their eyes scan one face after the next, their focus on the grim task. A boy kneels beside his dead mother and sisters. After the Nazis set their house on fire, the boy ran into the woods, escaping death. But now, his baby sister's lifeless head slips out of her scarf, nuzzled in the crook of her mother's arm, her fist balled up against her breast. His big sister's mouth is sweetly pursed, her eyes serenely shut. The boy weeps over their bodies, oblivious to all around, his mouth agape behind a cloud of hot breath, tears streaming to his collar. He is in another dimension, another universe.

An older boy stares at bodies in the ice, unable to react, or even to compute. Locals arrive to witness, signing statements. Women with babies search for their husbands among the dead, their gaze sober, meticulous. When they find their men, they collapse in anguish, bones turning briefly to rubber. Bodies are dug up, Nazi beer bottles scattered among them. A woman hiccups and gasps for breath, her voice breaking as she explains that her son was taken from a factory. Attempts at story shaping and stagecraft aside, there is no falsification here, says Dr. Hicks. "The Nazis committed these crimes, and the Soviets recorded them, and that is the bottom line."

"What is odd is not that so many of the iconic news photos of the past, including some of the best-remembered pictures from the Second World War, appear to have been staged," writes Susan Sontag in *Regarding the Pain of Others* (2003). "It is that we are surprised to learn they were staged and always disappointed." Dr. Hicks tells me that a certain discourse exists that the Soviets staged everything, and so nothing they show can ever be believed. "They're not a credible framing presence." But some events are too important to allow to pass into obscurity. They must be captured ("Narratives can make us understand," writes Sontag. "Photographs do something else: they haunt us."), and harsh conditions don't always allow for journalistic purity.

Dr. Hicks was able to find telegrams from frontline cameramen at Auschwitz who were filming inside the barracks. The cameramen had been shooting outdoors in daylight and didn't have the proper lighting equipment to shoot the barracks. The lighting they had ordered took months to arrive. By the time they were ready to shoot the images of the barracks, the prisoners had left. "So, the Soviet team invited back some local Polish women, asked them to put on striped uniforms, and filmed them at death's door in these barracks." Were they falsifying? "They'd seen the prisoners but had to wait for the lighting equipment." Their choice was to reenact what they had seen, or let that image die. And in the 1940s, reenactment was common for documentary filmmakers.

We want to believe that a photograph is a perfect record of history, an un-staged image, Sontag tells us. But every photo is to some degree created. We want to forget that.

Dr. Hicks reminds me that Joe Rosenthal, Pulitzer-winning photographer of *Raising the Flag on Iwo Jima*, was often accused of staging his photo, but the real "staging" was the flag-raising itself. We like to think of that moment as triumphant, frantic, the euphoric wake of conquest. But it was a ceremony that happened four days after the invasion of the island and a month before the island was fully secure. And they did it twice. The iconic photo is of the second flag-raising. These weren't soldiers just after the final kill, hearts pounding, as they rushed to raise the flag atop the captured island. They were raising it in ceremony, a performance for historians and photographers. No, Rosenthal didn't stage it. They all did—and we *all* do, for history, and for our children and grandchildren who may not remember or care or believe.

When we spoke, Dr. Hicks expressed frustration at the way the documentary depicts his reaction to the footage: without irony, the documentarians mirror the behavior of their subjects. They ask Hicks to repeat and perform his shock (Hicks shakes his head: "I thought we were doing takes of one shot, so they could use the best one. They showed every take!"), focusing on ghoulish details. The documentary presents Hicks's primary reaction as horror at the footage (which is real, but hardly debilitating to a specialist in war and genocide films). In fact, what matters to Hicks is the historical implication of the discovery, that the films verify how early the Eastern extermination campaign began. I laugh. "I can't tell you how many times I've had to perform for television interviews," I say, "clipping old photos to a clothesline, watching trains in the distance, walking up and down a square fifty times, just so I can talk about displacement and asylum. You do the dance, hoping they'll read the actual work."

I worry, though. Will these videos be misused? "I survived, I bear witness," says Primo Levi. But whose word is good enough, whose description elegant enough, whose performance artful enough? Not all testimony is welcome. Even today, such women offer their stories and the world calls them schlock, fake, lies. Critics, artists, and intellectuals say that they're staged, facile, offensive, melodramatic, the stuff of bad movies. Why should these grieving mothers, having lost everything, trust comfortable families in safer lands to sympathize and believe? Stuck across a cultural chasm that grows wider with each decade, they have no access to our tribal tongues, no option but to package their grief as a hysterical theater, a gruesome show. How can their instincts at such a time be explained to an audience accustomed to trust? A sophisticated audience, who, despite the occasional humiliation, has always clung to that bottom morsel of dignity?

Maybe it isn't madness, after a pain just shy of fatal, to perform some of it, to take on an extra helping of disgrace, as in an old-world funeral rite. I hear a whisper of reason in it. It might even mend things, delivering the mourner to another reality: a village where the grief becomes corporeal and can be expelled, like a worm wrapped around a healer's stick and tossed into an ever-kindling fire; where humble lives escape notice, the lofty stakes of youth mercifully vanished so that stories are left to grandmothers to animate according to their wisdom. A place where all grief is farce, a chicken is always roasting, and every suffering is endurable by those who continue to live.

4.

In November of my last year in high school, my English teacher got her hands on my college application essay. "Oh, Dina, this is *bad*. You've got to throw away your thesaurus and tell a good story!" She showed me how, but by then, I'd already applied to Harvard early decision. For months I thought, *It'll be okay. Jesus will get me in regardless.*

I didn't get into Harvard, even after all that praying.

My teacher tried to soften the blow. "Honey, there are so many other good colleges. But what's the life lesson here? What've we learned?"

"The lesson is . . . don't show off."

"Yes, but the bigger lesson is, show your work to other people."

I remembered the conversation with my middle school science teacher, years before, about expertise, and getting your work checked by those who know. "I feel so stupid," I muttered. "I can't believe I thought I could impress Harvard with big words."

"Well," she said. "You can. Just not with *those* words. Not with SAT vocab words. The point is, ask for help. Always, always ask for help."

I tried to hide the tears forming. It seemed in those days, I was always tearing up in front of kindhearted Americans. Six months later, I got into every (other) university because of that English teacher. At church people said, "Jesus saw your faith, giving up ice cream for that long."

I went to the local creamery and ate a triple chocolate. *What a waste of a year*, I thought.

At Princeton, I gave myself up to be remade. I was still no good at faking, but no identity felt any realer than the rest. It became easier simply to transform for short bouts. All through university, I dyed my hair, changed my scent and the cut of my jeans. I did clothing swaps. I felt more and more American, but nothing felt quite right. Some part of me couldn't stop squirming.

I spent much of my final year at Princeton studying for job interviews. I had decided, over my four years, that my best shot at never again repeating my childhood poverty and rootlessness was to be taken in by a top consulting firm in New York.

McKinsey, I dared to hope, because it was the best, the most selective. I put all my energy and talents into that goal. I tested leather folders, suit jackets, hairclip arrangements. To close friends, I signed my emails, "Honed and Sharpened, Econ Dina." Sometimes professors asked if I should broaden my search. "I'm interviewing at investment banks, too," I'd say. But I used the banking interviews like dress rehearsals. Once, in the peak of job interview season, I spent an entire weekend reading old *Wall Street Journals* to understand market trends. I got the phrase "believer in the bubble" stuck in my head, and my OCD compelled me to say it aloud. So one day I did. I said it in an interview for a trading job I didn't want, but was determined to get.

"You mean, you believe it exists?" said the interviewer, an older alum.

"Yes," I said. "It's a bubble and bubbles burst."

"But only that?" he said, nudging me on.

"That's what it means," I said because I was sure.

He moved on, but I had lost my focus, obsessed with how I had misused the phrase. (If you're openly debating insider language with an insider, you've definitely misused it. If all parties use it correctly, it stays invisible.) For traders, believing that a bubble exists is meaningless, like saying the sky is blue: so what? The question is, how you can make money from understanding its traits? I went home and made a note in my journal. *Don't say their phrases unless totally sure.*

For months I practiced my leadership stories, my confident voice, my case interviews—my favorite since they were essentially logic puzzles, so I didn't have to pretend. In a case interview, I could be myself, which confirmed that maybe I belonged in my future job. It confirmed, too, that the adult world was simple (or simplifiable). Humans were rational, just as I had learned in Economics, acting according to the simple logic of riddles.

I got the job at McKinsey. I thought, *nothing can go wrong again.* McKinsey was a masterclass in how to be believed, and that was (still) all I cared about. Though the firm was the gold standard in all kinds of metrics, only one made it enviable: its minuscule job offer rate ("If the odds are good," we used to say about men and jobs, "the goods are odd."). And there were the vast sums McKinsey spent on refining us, making us worthy of immense confidence.

"What's your opinion worth?" a director asked early on. "Everything you do and say subconsciously answers that question." Clients, he explained, are always asking themselves if you're high-quality talent, whether you can be trusted with their livelihood. You can present a genius model full of macros and good data, but if you present it like it's a guess, it's worthless. "They pay millions for your time. You have to be worth it. They have to follow our advice for years after we leave, or the whole thing's just paper."

Right. So, be impressive. But how?

In those long nights and weekends, I learned the trust signals: how to think systematically, how to create workstreams, how to present the same slides in five minutes, in thirty minutes, in an hour. I learned to listen and negotiate calmly, to release sunk costs, to leave a solid voicemail, to look a sixty-year-old CEO in the eye and become a de facto manager to a dozen thirty-five-year-olds who hated me, to hide my youth with no-lens glasses and slim-cut pantsuits, with razor-edge haircuts and control over the pitch of my voice, my eyebrows, my emotions, my reactions to exhaustion and stress. I learned why we priced ourselves high and never gave discounts, how to order table wines, how to choose a restaurant for a client, for a team outing. I was offered careful instruction about how to tailor my clothes, accept a compliment, deflect questions that revealed my age, and when to share data and in what order. McKinsey even kept a stash of free art, to decorate our offices.

One exhausted morning, before anyone's first coffee, a manager looked me over and let loose. "My God, Dina, do I smell hairspray? Have I been transported to the fucking senior prom?" I stepped away. I did spray that morning, because I hadn't had time to shower, and my hair had gone wonky. "Also, while we're here, let me look at you . . . That is a *bad* pink. There are very few good pinks, so just avoid pink." I muttered something. He kept going. "Those are fake. Real pearls or no pearls. Your hair is too long. And the crease in those pants never changes. It's just permanently there . . . That's not a compliment." In a weirdly parental gesture, he knelt down and examined my fabric. His voice softened. "Listen, inside your outer coat, you wear natural fabrics only. Unless you're skiing. Worms, sheep, cows, plants. That's where your inside-the-coat workwear should come from. Not a fucking plastics factory." As he stood, he glimpsed my sunglasses perched between my breasts. I quickly pulled them out, but that wasn't his complaint. He turned the glasses over, looked at the huge intertwined C's I was so proud to afford (on sale). "Did Chanel pay you to advertise, or are you doing it pro bono?"

After an embarrassed beat, he smiled. "You'll learn." Then, unable to help himself, he added. "While we're here, get rid of that class ring." The ring, I later learned, was a *triple* violation because it was a brand, everyone had a degree like that, and it begged the question of my graduation year, thus giving away my age. I yanked it off my finger and put it in my pocket.

That rant has stayed with me for twenty years. In one hangry tirade this guy had solved my pink-red dilemma, my "Why is that fabric bad?" puzzle, pre-empted all brand and fad nonsense, and so much else. Most of the McKinsey instruction, I now realize, was just worldliness, a speed course in having forty-year-old good sense at twenty-two. Once, when I lobbed a fizzy *"bonsoir"* to a French-accented server, my manager rested a hand on my arm. I went silent. The waiter smiled tightly. Later, the manager said that, most likely, that man was a non-European immigrant, like me. He was probably faking the accent for our benefit. "I've never met a French waiter in New York. Maybe once at Daniel."

When I was finally assigned to my first client, I was buzzing with energy, even joy. I couldn't wait to show them what I could do. As we were introducing ourselves to the client team, I bubbled out of my chair. "I'm Dina! First-year BA from Princeton. I'm so thrilled to be here!"

Beside me sat my classmate, Rich. Rich had also graduated in 2001 and joined McKinsey the same summer. We were equals on the project. His introduction seemed a direct response to mine. He said, "Hello, I'm Richard, business analyst on this project." That's it. He didn't say "first year" or his university. And the bastard left out his (very real) excitement, and that crucial article "a" so that he seemed to have said "the" business analyst. For a good month (before I went around subtly disabusing everyone of that notion), everyone thought he was my boss.

The first time I stuttered in a client meeting, I was assigned an expensive public speaking coach who designed weekly control exercises like "Don't say the letter E for an hour" or "Count your *ums* the next time you phone your mom." She taught me not to hide my energy, and how to make it seem like *older* energy: breathe deep, show joy and excitement with your eyes, not your limbs. Hold gazes and hands firmly. The eyebrows of those who are used to respect, I learned, just move differently somehow.

More than a decade later, I still call up my McKinsey training when I give talks, or to control stress. During my C-section, I soothed away my OCD by making a list of measurable outcomes. Each time I'm late for a plane, I recall the manager who said, "The optimal number of planes to miss in your lifetime isn't zero, not even close. If you've missed zero planes, you've wasted too much time in airports." Sometimes when Elena misbehaves, I raise one threatening McKinsey eyebrow, but she sees right through it: "Mummy, stop trying to be beautiful."

Then there was the firm-speak. I learned quickly that "a night off" meant "leave at 9:00 p.m. instead of midnight." If a manager said "Don't boil the ocean," or "Don't reinvent the wheel," they actually wanted their analysts to work all night but hide it from the partners. If you had an appointment at 8:00 p.m., they said, "Sure, go home early." "Awesome work!" with no other feedback meant it was just okay work. After a year, I was conditioned to yawn at the phrase "Off to Chennai!" (the go-ahead to email a handwritten deck to the PowerPoint specialists in Chennai to turn around overnight). At our firm, employees were never fired; they were "counseled out." It was so absurd that it became a joke among my classmates and managers. Once a colleague said about his breakup, "I'm trying to counsel her out of our apartment."

But I found the canned language soothing. I was twenty-two and believed I could never be fired. Besides, my firm took good care of me. They didn't invent the doublespeak, and we all learned to decipher it in time, like the Iranian expectation of *taarof* (disingenuously refusing every offer, even payment for services, three times. In America, *taarof* gets many immigrants into trouble). Regardless, the simple way the doublespeak removed accountability, guilt, and consequence had tempted many in the finance industry, where hundreds of my university classmates now worked, to questionable behavior. It was easy for a weak, stressed-out investor to buy a few drinks for an insider, learn a tad too much, and cover it with "I have a hunch based on a 'mosaic' of 'non-material' information I gleaned using 'standard analyses.'" Mosaic theory is a real defense to ward off allegations of insider trading— it's a pretty phrase that signals to investors how to cheat, a metaphor for mixing metaphors: the less your mosaic looks like the true image when examined up close, the more believable that it's pieced together from public information, and the less indictable you are.

I noticed that the corporate executives who hired us also spoke strangely. In client meetings, senior partners parroted their comforting dialect. At first I just listened. Consultants sell brainpower, not specific industry expertise, so we junior folks didn't hide our knowledge gaps (at first). Meanwhile, our clients flashed blinding expertise signals. Looking back, I'm convinced that the single unifying skill I witnessed from corporate leaders wasn't math wizardry or verbal clarity or confidence building: it was stringing together random metaphors to create a broken but dazzling picture, to imply expertise too deep to probe, and to place the cognitive burden of deciphering each unrelated metaphor on the listener, so that she will miss some galling but central fact. This is a common stalling tactic, a beat of confusion as the audience deciphers a garbled image, instead of reacting to the underlying information. Force the listener to leap from realm to realm so much that he falls behind, trailing, exhausted, never fully making the connection. Then there is the dishonest metaphor. In his public apology for a 2015 roller coaster crash, for example, a theme park CEO compared technical issues to "teething problems." He wanted to make this machine for which he was responsible seem organic and childlike, a natural thing whose growth was out of his hands and required sacrifice.

I know now that a good metaphor conjures a single compelling image; it improves on rereading. The liar doesn't want to be reread. She jams together discordant images, counting on her audience to read fast and to retain nothing, except that something was said. Dishonest and lazy writers survive, Orwell argues, by "gumming together long strips of words which have already been set in order by someone else, and making the results presentable by sheer humbug." Such writing is easier, forgettable, and untraceable. And so, reaching for these convenient word bundles is "a continuous temptation," like "a packet of aspirins always at one's elbow."

Early in our tenure, we newly minted college graduates began mimicking the drivel we picked up in client meetings. The bombastic phrases signaled where we'd been; eventually it would get us into the ultimate destination, the place we were all heading: Harvard Business School (HBS). Hired out for millions per project, we were supposed to be brilliant, so we'd better sound like it, and fast. In training programs of top consultancies across New York, we learned to strategically deploy studiously and aggressively empty phrases ("directionally correct," "achieving granularity," "outperforming at scale") so we would sound credible and confident, like seasoned consultants. In a blog post entitled "How to Sound Like an Expert," a former consultant and CEO of a B2B marketing agency advises to "keep current on expert phrases—whether it's 'best practices,' 'industry benchmarks,' 'low-hanging fruit,' 'quick wins' or whatever the smart-person phrase du jour is, you might want to keep your ears open for what smart people are saying when they speak. If it works for them, it might also work for you." If you do it right, the truth will lurk somewhere behind piles of familiar phrases, scraped clean of thought and jumbled together to create a mosaic, a likeness that holds only from far away.

For us kids, the bad language was like a Sunday morning chant: soothing, unchallenging, and decipherable through context but, if you really looked at it, mostly nonsense. Bullshitting gracefully is such a useful skill. In every meeting, we performed with passionate intensity—a hallmark of our young success—then we laughed over our stories. Once, a business analyst accidentally left the phrase "Source: POOMA" in the footer of one of his slides. When the client asked about it, the partner, cheeks reddening, brushed it aside. Later, he screamed at the analyst for an hour; far too many people knew that POOMA means *Pulled Out Of My Ass*. Lucky that the client hadn't developed a habit of following up on his momentary curiosities, like sources or definitions. He was, as we often said, the kind of guy who wasn't accustomed to doing the math.

How were we expected to resist this culture, this spellbinding cult of intensity and self-belief? Should we have broken away on our own, from this easy passcode to power, to riches, to impunity? And for what? Devotion to language, to truth? So that we'd have to work harder, show truer results, and be held accountable? The system contains no mechanism or incentive for change. We young protected it, fortified it at the base rung.

Nowadays, I warn my students to be on the lookout for lies by simplifying sentences the way you would a fraction. To see the value, find the lowest common denominator: 5000/1000 takes nine characters to type, but contains a single character of substance. If you reduce a sentence, do you find, hidden in the fluff, a groundbreaking thought? Or does it reduce away to nothing? Until you take the time to do that, you may not realize you're being lied to, though you may feel something off, like the drug dealer whose shoes don't crunch with broken glass.

"Truth is most beautiful undraped," writes Arthur Schopenhauer in *The Art of Literature*. The old library copy I've borrowed is full of ghostly pencil notes from a previous reader. Genius needs no linguistic ornament, he says. But it's risky to say something simply, concretely, to have it judged on its content and remembered as yours. Schopenhauer compares stylistic preening to a grimace or a mask, and rages against sentences that read "like a box of boxes one within another, and padded out like roast geese stuffed with apples." These abstracting tricks, he writes, tax the memory instead of the judgment or understanding. They have one purpose: to hide a complete lack of anything new or original to say. By the end of his essay, Schopenhauer sounds spent, despairing. In my library copy, I begin underlining, adding my own pencil checkmarks. Schopenhauer writes about the power of popular music, how moving are the simplest truths. Only the profound can risk a brush with naivete. Beside this, my anonymous notetaker has written, in tiny, careful script, "tell kids."

————

As a foreign kid, I knew that *American* was a performance. So is *refugee, good mother, top manager. Scientist* is harder, but still a performance, inherited and learned. Sometimes the drama boils over; sometimes it's a pot on low simmer. In fields where expertise is harder won, more grueling and high stakes, archetypal expectations fall away—one performs *brain surgeon* as much as *CEO*, but only by completing brain surgeries. Do that well and you're free to smell like bubblegum and wear boat shoes to work. A CEO is all theater, aped and perfected in private, then trotted out publicly to varying degrees of success. There are some excellent fakers out there.

A few months ago, I googled the name of my childhood crush. Noah had won a local business award. He had all his hair, was healthy, with a wife and children. He looked happy. I had imagined adult Noah as an artist, or a doctor. No, a cowboy. Instead he was an executive at a small investment firm.

I was about to close the browser, when—wait, where was he? There, atop his company's leadership page, was the World Trade Center Oculus. I clicked a few more pages. The Flatiron building, Brooklyn Bridge, London Bridge. Something about this seemed off. I clicked on the contact page. The address was a post office box in an Oklahoma strip mall. Was my kind friend running a scam? No, it was a real firm. The big city imagery was . . . decoration?

The CEO, a fast-talking thirty-something from Harvard, caught my eye. She was a familiar brand of presentable Ivy Leaguer with eager eyes and a lot to say. In a video, she pitched her company philosophy like this: "We invest in a downside protected way that reflects what we view as that data-informed reality." Alongside visuals of aggregate firm statistics rapidly rising (against no time frame, just fast spooling), and people running around cityscapes, the firm's executives boasted of "consolidation strategies that are very complex," of "nontraditional approaches" and "rigorous analysis." She kept saying that her firm invested only in *the core* of things. Briefly I thought "core" meant something industry specific. It doesn't. It's another metaphor, like the platonic leaf, for companies whose work feels more fundamental—drilling, for example, might be more "core" than an oil services or supply company. Great returns "always comes down to a cost basis," she continued. "That's what we're students of, and ardently defend." I cringed, recalling my own *"believer in the bubble!"* nonsense.

Now I was hungry for more videos about this Harvard lady with a fast mouth. How easily I could have become her, from that eager Economics student studying case interviews. There was something performative about her quick words, the unrelated metaphors, the practiced way she fled from her listeners, speed-jumping from realm to realm hoping to lose the close-watchers, the thinkers. She was mimicking an American power signal. Her affect was rushed, busy, important. In a minute of talking, she connected images from war, American migration, forensic science, like beads in a gaudy necklace. "We've left this acreage expansion, land grab, manifest destiny era of shale expansion and have gone into a more rate of return–focused phase of oil and gas investment, and we call that smart bombing versus carpet bombing." A frantic lock of hair dangled in her face.

To be believed is to know the signals. *We're operating, investing, creating at the core, the point of perpetual focus. We're not posers. We're quintessential and necessary.* I'd love to say that googling Noah gave me some insight into myself, into the ugly world that remade me. It didn't. I just felt smug, validated—and grateful.

Papa McKinsey had taught me how to be a twenty-two-year-old who knows nothing but is treated like a savior with all the answers: *Speak confidently. Dress expensively. Invest in your work space. Never give discounts; your price is your talent metric. Know when to name drop. Upshot things. 80/20 things. Control your voice, your orbit, your data. Don't make nonsense charts (or videos of bullshit figures spooling). Don't say POOMA on the fucking slide.* I closed the browser. Probably my next thought was typical of older members of any dogma: superiority, relief, a bit of gleeful judgment. *I'm chosen. I'm not her. Nothing to worry about. I'm the platonic leaf, the goddamn real deal.*

———

A year after I graduated from Princeton, one of our professors won a Nobel Prize for punching a hole in the biggest underlying assumption in my Economics education: human rationality. Humans aren't *ir*rational, Daniel Kahneman argued, but rationality doesn't fully describe us either. We have many biases and lazy workarounds. We operate, Kahneman proposed, under a dual system of thinking: one automatic, the other deliberate. System 1 relies on heuristics: smaller, easier observations serving as shortcuts for larger, more complex ones. In System 2, the mind calculates. System 1 "quickly proposes intuitive answers" and System 2 "monitors the quality of these proposals, which it may endorse, correct or override."

Scientists developed a cognitive quiz to test a person's tendency to rely on gut responses, or to override them in a calculated way. The quiz asks three questions, similar to the brainteasers in a consulting interview:

1. *A bat and a ball cost $1.10 in total. The bat costs $1.00 more than the ball. How much does the ball cost?*
2. *If it takes 5 machines 5 minutes to make 5 widgets, how long would it take 100 machines to make 100 widgets?*
3. *Every day, a patch of lily pads doubles in size. If it takes 48 days for*

the patch to cover the entire lake, how long would it take for the patch to cover half of the lake?

An average person answering intuitively (using only System 1) will rush to 10 cents, 100 minutes, and 24 days. The mind substitutes in easier questions, since their answers are in close reach (like 2 + 2). To find the correct answers, one must activate System 2, the kind of thinking that would solve for, say, 124 x 342. The correct answers are 5 cents, 5 minutes, and 47 days.

My first reaction to this test: *My mother wouldn't miss a single one of these. Not even in her sleep.* Fall for a trick worksheet? No way. If there's actual math to be done, she always does it.

I tried this test on a few friends. Wildly unscientific as they were, the results felt somehow informative—my partner, Sam, answered the first question using System 1, but when I asked another, his shields went up. "Hey! Is this a McKinsey trick?" He got the next two right within seconds—this wasn't a question of intelligence, but of his mind sounding the alarm that instinct would lead him astray. I've shown him the old McKinsey interview warmups: *how many degrees between the hour and minute hand at 12:00 p.m., 6:00 p.m., 3:15 p.m.?* An unthinking person would trip up on the last one, reaching instinctively for 0 instead of 7.5 degrees.

Kahneman's findings jarred me. If the adult world isn't rational, as I had all my life wanted (needed) to believe, then what's next? No more meritocracy or expertise? Chaos? How will we make decisions? Who will get to make those decisions? And yet, it was comforting to know something more about my mind: as a refugee, I had given my System 2 far more practice than others my age. For years, I spent every minute distrusting my instincts, knowing that my words and my shortcuts will make me my least desired self, that I'll confuse others and humiliate myself. How exhausting it had been, my vigilant adolescence, and yet what rigor; what a useful skill to develop. Trying to settle into a new country, you don't trust even your five senses. Are Rolos high-quality chocolate? Has this unfamiliar meat product gone off? You look for guidance in everything, stress-testing every observation. You're a throbbing skinless creature, but eventually you grow a second skin. You become a chameleon, unconsciously adapting. It strikes me that many have spent their lives mistaking instinct for thought. I imagine that most of this group has never been displaced. The native-born can trust their signals, their institutions. They can choose never to be uncomfortable, to watch news and read books that reaffirm their instincts.

Can System 2 become so rusty it stops working? Kahneman writes that our frequent observations, culture, and fundamental beliefs grow into our shortcuts; they are useful for quick thinking, and vital to our self-preservation or homeostasis. "For some of our most important beliefs we have no evidence at all," writes Kahneman, "except that people we love and trust hold these beliefs. Considering how little we know, the confidence we have in our beliefs is preposterous—and it is also essential."

We need our instincts. So maybe having them garbled by displacement isn't such a superpower, after all. And sometimes, even with the most powerful override button, we still choose the myth, behaving as devotees. An old story goes: a visitor spotted a horseshoe hanging over Nobel laureate Niels Bohr's front door and asked whether he was superstitious. "Of course not," Bohr replied, "but I understand it's lucky whether you believe in it or not."

———

One morning in 2016, in a conservative part of Pakistan, Mohammad sat in his father's animal feed shop waiting for his assistant to arrive. When he didn't, Mohammad assumed Suleiman was sick. The next day, young Suleiman again failed to appear. Soon, Mohammad was receiving texts from the boy: Suleiman had eloped with the daughter of a prominent local family and needed money. Soon men from that family began harassing Mohammad, demanding to know the couple's whereabouts. Mohammad worried for the couple. What if they were honor killed? He sent them a little money. One night the men returned. They beat him, threatened his life. They shattered his thigh bone. The police did nothing. The girl's father, a local kingmaker, had sent the men, so Mohammad must deserve his punishment. "Tell us where they are," the men demanded, day after day. In 2017, after months of harassment, beatings, and a steel rod in his thigh, Mohammad ran.

In American courts, every tactic was used to deny him asylum. *You can live safely in another city*, they said, though Mohammad's attackers had been savvy enough to know about the money transfer and could easily have found him anywhere in Pakistan. *You can rely on the police*, they said, though the kingmaker held the police in his pocket. Such illogic baffled Mohammad, as it has many others: It seemed that in America and Europe, from whose bullhorns spills the rhetoric of fairness and rule of law, the asylum office is the one place where the word of Pakistani police is gold. In the end, DHS's primary argument was that Mohammad was persecuted for information, which isn't a protected ground for asylum. Were he to give up the couple's whereabouts, the men would leave him alone.

If Mohammad returned home, they admitted, he could die—just not for the right reasons.

His lawyer, San Francisco asylum attorney Maleeha Haq, pressed her client, pen in hand, ready to take down every word. "What *exactly* did everyone say?"

"Why does it matter what everyone said?" I interrupted Haq's story. For most migrants, she explained, credibility isn't the reason for rejection. In fact, the issue of credibility is cleverly avoided by using the claimant's own lack of knowledge about the definition of a word. What is a *refugee*? Before he is believed, an asylum seeker must choose the right story out of many, the relevant part of a complicated life. It's like being asked to cut a circular disc from a cylinder. You have many stacked circles, but if you cut at the wrong angle, you have an oval. You've failed to present the desired thing.

Ahilan Arulanantham, senior counsel at ACLU Southern California, explained this using "the classic Central American example": Imagine you're an ordinary citizen in El Salvador. A gang threatens to kill you unless you pay. You run. At the U.S. border, the screening officer will demand your specific reason for refusing the gang. If you don't have training in asylum law, you'll likely say, "I didn't have money." This is a damning response, because a refugee isn't just any forcibly displaced person in danger. According to the 1951 Convention Relating to the Status of Refugees (or "the Refugee Convention," a multilateral UN treaty the U.S. joined in 1967), a refugee is only somebody who can't return safely home because of a credible fear of future persecution *based on race, religion, nationality, political opinion, or membership in a social group.*

The U.S. (like the U.K. and many European countries) interprets the refugee convention such that the motivation of your persecutor matters alongside your own. Asylum seekers must show a nexus between the persecution and one of the five protected grounds. Take my mother's case. She was a Christian convert in Iran. If agents of the Islamic Republic were harassing her for money, corrupt as that is, her persecution would have had an economic motive, not a religious one. This would be true even if the court acknowledged that my mother was a convert and that the state persecutes converts. Her specific harassment would have to be *on account of* her Christianity. In a country where LGBT citizens are hanged on fabricated drug charges, that is tough to show; the host country can choose to believe the ludicrous drug charge. If the host's sole aim is to show that it's done its legal duty, then that drug charge is plausible deniability.

This makes testimony incredibly important. Your fate turns on this fine point of memory.

Did the gangster say, "You traitor, you'll will get what you deserve"? Now it's political.

Did he say, "You Muslim, you'll get what you deserve"? Now it's about social group.

Did he say "You cheapskate, you'll get what you deserve"? Now you're not a refugee; you're just a migrant. You will likely be sent home.

Many lawyers and humanitarian agencies have argued that this hairsplitting violates a core principle of the Refugee Convention, *non-refoulement*, the notion that no one should be sent back into danger. Only a particular kind of danger, the U.S. Department of Justice seems to say. But how can we assign a single motive to such complex things as resistance, escape, fear? Families running from Central American gangs, for example, may be motivated by many things. But at the border, they are coerced into attaching a simple, universal, non-qualifying motivation to their story before they talk to a lawyer, so they can be rejected as economic migrants. When you apply for asylum, either at the border or in an embassy (often before access to representation), you're given a "credible fear" assessment. *Why didn't you pay the gang?* Many choose one simple reason. If the reason they choose is "I didn't have the money," the asylum seeker does not qualify for refugee status.

Nor does he qualify if he's trying to avoid gang recruitment. What they need to show is opposition of belief—to use the coded words. "Because I don't believe gangs should be running my country," or "My faith doesn't allow me to kill for the gang." These are difficult admissions. They require more self-knowledge and bravery than reminding the officer that you have no money or that you wish to avoid gang recruitment—reasons that are usually also true, alongside deeper reasons that would qualify. Good asylum lawyers dig for hints of political motive—and for a well-founded fear of future persecution—in early interview transcripts, hoping for a qualifying reason that they can then corroborate with their own research into the country, into the family.

I think back to my family's asylum interview. Our Christianity was our family saga. It was the truth, and also the story we were itching to tell. We didn't suffer shame over it, as an LGBT refugee or a torture survivor might. But what if we had *also* wept about lack of money, or how my parents fought? Would they ignore the many Bible stories I had learned and say that my mother was running from personal issues? Would I be an American now?

Back in 2017, Haq listened to Mohammad's story for hours, pressing for every detail. Where did the young couple elope to? What information did the men ask for? Did Mohammad know where Suleiman and his new wife were? If he had, would he have given in to torture? Finally, a small exchange in the story caught Haq's attention: in a frustrated moment, Mohammad had said to the men, "What is your problem? If they're in love and adults and want to get married, you people shouldn't be acting like this." That had fueled the men's anger. Haq latched onto that.

"What he said is both religious and political opinion," she argued. The men targeted him *further* after he said that. "It was tenuous," she said. "I could have easily argued the other side. And DHS tried, but not as well as I thought they would, or I could have done." The judge accepted Haq's argument. "It's so arbitrary and requires such nuance," said Haq. "Without a lawyer, how would a shopkeeper running for his life know to mention that he had once said *let them choose!*"

"Your eligibility for asylum turns on small distinctions that don't seem relevant, or things that are relevant but impossible to verify," says Arulanantham. "If you can prove you're from a city in El Salvador that is riven with violence, as part of conflict between gangs and the state, and you're a fifteen-year-old boy, those facts alone are not enough. You have to show you suffered past persecution and have a well-founded fear of future persecution. Courts won't accept your membership in relevant targeted group. They have to have targeted you."

It reminds of me a story from Ahmed Pouri, founder of PRIME, a Dutch NGO, about a Kurdish woman who was raped when soldiers came through her village in Turkey. The village was full of Kurds, a target group. But the asylum officers in the Netherlands asked her if the soldiers took her to a room, if they targeted her, or said they'd be back for *her*. They decided it was just a random mass rape. She was unlucky, in the wrong place at the wrong time, not a refugee. "But would it have happened if she wasn't Kurdish?" Pouri asked. "Of course not."

Matters complicate further for the last of the five protected grounds: membership in a social group, a vague distinction created in the wake of the Holocaust, when large groups with characteristic similarities were murdered simply for that identity. With such a broad final category, the framers of the Refugee Convention likely intended to protect any remaining targets of persecution as they imagined them in 1951. But the social fabric of the 2020s is much more intricately woven—now people belong to all kinds of groups, with ties sometimes central to their identity, sometimes loose and intermittent. And yet, since WWII, the interpretation of "social group" has narrowed again and again. In 2018, in a move to curb Central American immigration, U.S. Attorney General Jeff Sessions challenged the social group designation for battered women and gang targets, since they don't share inherent characteristics outside their persecution (the United Nations refugee agency, UNHCR, has been unequivocal that gender alone should qualify). In 2019, the next U.S. attorney general, William Barr, ruled that a nuclear family unit is no longer a social group, because members of one family aren't inherently socially distinctive from another.

"But the Ninth and Fourth Circuit federal case law has already established family as a social group. An agency can't just say it's not," says Maleeha Haq. A few years ago, she won a case for a teenage boy. His father, a barber in Honduras, was extorted by gangs who threatened to kidnap and kill the boy. "You'll see his body," they said. The boy fled to America and found his way to Haq. "We were able to say that the child was at risk as a family member of his father. That family is known in the area, it is a quintessential social group. But now, [the DOJ] have caught wind that people are succeeding [so they will crack down]. What are we going to do with these children?" And what about this boy's father, left alone in Honduras with a murderous gang who has been tricked and still wants its money? If he is killed, the government agencies will wash their hands; what could they have done to help? It was extortion, not an asylum issue.

For many Hispanic clients, says Haq, the decision is that "We believe you'll get killed, but not for the right reasons." Or sometimes you have the right reasons, but because the Refugee Convention also defines refugees as those who can't return safely home, they claim that your own country's police can protect you, sometimes in cases where the police are widely known to be corrupt. Iranian communists, for example, are often sent back from European countries with the claim that Iran doesn't persecute communists, when it is well known that many are hanged on trumped-up drug charges. "You hear horrific stories of multiple rapes, children kidnapped, family killed," says Haq. "Everyone has a story like that. Believable. But they say the gangs are recruiting you. It's personal. No reason for asylum. Lawyers then have to spin gang recruitment into one of those five categories. Without a lawyer . . . there's just no way."

Fine legal distinctions can disadvantage the poor and uneducated—people who don't have the savvy and skill to google the Refugee Convention and hire lawyers before they arrive, or at least before saying something damning. Educated asylum seekers are also better trained in storytelling, in logic, in reading someone from another culture. They may realize that admitting their crimes at home might actually help them, if those crimes put them in political or religious danger. Ana Reyes, an award-winning immigration lawyer, wasn't the first attorney to tell me that asylum success correlates with representation. This is partly a selection issue: lawyers vet clients for credibility before accepting a case. But much of it is about refining a story—telling it again and again until memories return, inconsistencies are worked out, dates are double-checked. "If we find someone believable," says Reyes, "I've always been able to find something. A newspaper article, expert report, someone from home who can testify. The real issue isn't credibility versus non-credibility. The real issue is whether you have an attorney. I'd say that the biggest predictor of whether you will get asylum is whether you have attorney."

Yet representation is patchy. Legal aid and charities alone can't meet the need. Poorer, less educated refugees are expected to navigate an intricate system, governed by a mid-century protocol and constantly changing by statute and case law, on their own. Without a lawyer, failure is likely. Asylum lawyers and activists have made the right to representation one of their primary reform goals. "It is critical even if you have a straightforward, legitimate claim," says Reyes, "especially now in the U.S. when all the rules are changing."

Arulanantham argues that the most urgent fixes to the asylum system are equal and fair representation, reducing variability in judging standards, and quicker use of Temporary Protected Status (blanket entry for people from a particular place, during a particular time) as a tool in situations of massive state breakdown. "Too much depends on individual credibility. If something like Nazi Germany were happening, you wouldn't be asking people 'Did the Nazi come to your door or only your neighbor's door?'"

At some point, war, famine, or violence becomes so extreme that individual targeting starts to matter less to judges. A Rwandan refugee in 1994 wouldn't have to show that militias came after *her*, only that she was a Tutsi—they came for everyone like her, and that is a well-founded fear of future persecution. Though errors of judgment do happen. In 1999, while running an emergency errand in town, a young woman named Sabine was raped by Congolese soldiers in a makeshift detention center. She was Tutsi. While the rape was medically proven and the identity of the rapists (as soldiers) accepted, she was rejected by the U.K. Home Office for lack of proof that the rape happened *because* she was Tutsi. The case was later overturned since crimes against Tutsis are widely documented.

Until war on the streets compels the West to offer some kind of blanket protection, your testimony is everything. Who gets believed? What if your story fits, but is dismissed as a lie? When they can, judges and asylum officers prefer to reject on credibility because those are almost never overturned on appeal. Whether you're telling a true story is a factual determination, in which appeal judges are wary of overturning lower court decisions. Whether your credible story fits the definition of "refugee," on the other hand, is a legal interpretation, which is what appeals courts are for. To get a case out of the system, it's easier to say "I don't believe her" than to try to dig out precise motivations.

And so, asylum seekers are rushed through credible fear tests as soon as they arrive, before they speak to lawyers who refine and practice stories, working through nerves, memory, shame, and bad calculation. On a first telling, every storyteller will trip up. And once a refugee has said the wrong thing in a credible fear test, she'll find it much harder getting a lawyer to sign on, because lawyers like to win, and they look deeply into motive and credibility before they take on a case.

From the asylum officer's point of view, if your only goal is to reduce numbers, why not do a first cull this way? Discredit a refugee within minutes of arrival and cut them off from potential help? And yet, for the knowledgeable and the lucky who find their way to an attorney, this first hurdle in the system—*will I be believed?*—is surmountable. Though true stories are patchy, inconsistent, and full of random detail, a lawyer can make yours fit the asylum officer's skeletal notion of truth: perfect consistency, no orphan details, identical recall on each telling. I wonder if there are many unopposed asylum cases—if we are honestly carrying out the terms of the Refugee Convention, why does our government argue against nearly everyone?

Though it's rare, Reyes tells me that she's seen an asylum officer convinced on the first try: a client confessed to damaging information and the officer believed her. If the officer hadn't, then she'd have to prove credibility—which isn't hard if you have a degree from

Harvard Law, as Reyes does. "I've never lost a case on credibility grounds," she says.

———

Never lost a case on credibility grounds. The way she said it jolted me back by a decade. She wasn't only telling me she was a good attorney—I already knew that. At McKinsey and in business school, we learned to present ourselves in this same way: direct, humble, but not remotely humble. *I am the best. If you doubt that, then you haven't done your research.* I imagine Reyes in the courtroom, the effect of her reputation. The judges look at her and think: she isn't some bleeding-heart activist lawyer who wants to swing open the doors. She is ruthless about her win rate, about legal minutiae. Therefore, she only represents bona fide truth-tellers. She does the vetting. The judge can do the approving. She never loses on credibility, so her time is freed up to argue legal points: *Is that cohort a social group? Does this belief count as religious?*

I consider the client who offered damaging facts about herself and cracked the iron-hard shell around the officer's heart. Had she moved him? Maybe. But arguing against yourself is also a business school trick. Within the Western dogma of personal power (a belief that other people's potential is enriching, and their need toxic), arguing against yourself is a signal that, to survive, you need nothing from the other person, even if they hold your life in their hands.

Aso, a refugee working with the charity Freedom from Torture, wrote three lines that chilled me. He too understood how much to expect from comfortable Westerners whose feet have never left native soil. "I knew this from the beginning," he wrote, "when I was inside the lorry, thinking about truth. If you are a good storyteller you will be trusted, get a life, and escape from hell. But what do you need to do to be trusted, if telling the truth is not enough?"

The truth *isn't* enough. Most people aren't even listening for it. They're listening for something else. It took me a long time to admit that

I, too, listen to stories differently. I size up each person, waiting for familiar signals. When I was a kid, I listened with my heart, with my curiosity, longing to be moved and surprised. At ten, in my refugee camp outside Rome, we spent most of our time telling our stories to each other over cheap cups of tea, comforted by the instant bond of a shared life story. We were also practicing, tailoring our stories for asylum officers, knowing that our lives depended on what that officer found credible.

But somewhere along the way, I had picked up the instinct to be on guard against other people's despair, against their need, thinking only of their potential. Where did I learn this?

Alongside many McKinsey classmates, I did end up in Harvard's MBA program. There, I listened as my colleagues wove stories around their business pitches, without worry, confident that they would be believed, that their audience craved to believe them. After a few months of case discussions, every "takeaway" on integrity, leadership, and negotiation struck me in the deep tissue. *Why didn't I know this before?* The refugee in me fumed: these lessons exist, have long existed, and have been handed to those who need them least. The rules were, in fact, created for the children of the (native *and* colonizing) rich. I just happened to be in the room.

Over time, I learned how to listen at the negotiating table. One day, I sat across from a friend and listened as he described a fictional business venture. We were in a mock negotiation, each with information we could share or hide, plus any backstory we wished to add. I listened hard, searching for qualifiers that might tip his hand. How much was he willing to give up? Which contract terms were vital to him but less so to me? On which were our incentives aligned? Later, when the professor revealed the negotiating position of both characters, I felt triumphant; my friend felt betrayed. Not because he had lost, but because I had listened to his story in the unkindest way, digging for vulnerability. I hadn't seen *him* at all.

Despite all the talk of leadership and change-making, what you actually learn at Harvard Business School is how to be believed—how to be the ones people *want* to believe, feel safe believing, given their heuristic shortcuts. Some of that, we were taught, is achieved by developing a reputation for honesty, for precision. Some is communicated through signals and codes, the kind that exist in every profession. My classmates and I had privileged upbringings: not all wealthy, but from educated families (like mine, who were doctors), or trained at prestigious firms and universities. We knew how to dress and had internalized the language of the trusted classes. Over hundreds of case-method discussions, we taught it to each other.

Before we decide how to listen to a story, we put people on a spectrum. Do they come to us with need or with potential? Should we listen with our guard up or our imagination on? Will aligning with this person benefit or drain us? How does the storyteller signal, even before that first interaction, that they are worthy of an unguarded, imaginative listen?

Anyone with a boss knows the basics: lock eyes, shake hands firmly, under-promise, over-deliver, repeat. At Harvard Business School, we picked up other ways to affect the need/potential calculus.

Dismantle skepticism by arguing against yourself.

If a narrative lacks complexity, put it into an intellectually satisfying framework.

Let the other side make your most important point for you.

Say it with charts! Charts are familiar, comforting. And they can lie. Use the wrong one and confusion sets in. Bars where you need a scatter plot and people wince; they start rolling your data around in their mouths, trying to figure it out, like a rogue bean in your bouillabaisse.

Precision implies accuracy (round to 89 or 91 percent, not 90 percent).

Figure out a person's best alternative, then label each and every one of your concessions. Find small ones and make them seem huge.

Embedded in these tactics is a self-belief that works only when it's ingrained and unconscious, not mimicked: *You don't need them; they need you. Your value lies in your vast potential, so walk into every room potential first.*

Later I went through the list and tried to figure out what it would be like if a refugee in an asylum interview had this same education. Most refugees try to win the interviewers' affections by praising the host country, but what if a refugee argued against herself, making it clear that she didn't want to be there and would rather be back home? Asylum lawyers have told me that this works: officers are taught a precise definition of *refugee*, and a real refugee has no choice.

An anonymous Home Office Presenting Officer (HOPO) told me about an Iranian man she cross-examined who had studied the specific burden of proof. He didn't play nice. He knew his audience—he knew the code. He had found the rulebook. "He was framing his answers that way: *If there's even a slight risk, you have to give me asylum.* He'd gone through the requirements and covered everything." The HOPO was impressed. The man wasn't selling himself; he was signaling that he knew the legal burden of proof. The judge believed his story.

The code works; it's just that only a few are trained in it.

"When you're in a situation that requires you to be effective in ways that don't come naturally," says Herminia Ibarra (an organizational behavior professor and leadership guru for Harvard Business School, McKinsey, London Business School, and others) in an address to aspiring businesswomen, "you can't solve it by being yourself. You actually have to try out behaviors that are quite unnatural." In the West, specialists like Ibarra teach our children how to be believed—we codify truth for them. We tell them that they can fail and try again, wipe out their shortcomings and become credible. Refugees come with need, so we tell them that there is no room for human error or flaws. Their stories are shorn of trivial oddities, stripped of color, subjected to absurd burdens of proof.

"The most confused, the least cooperative, these are the ones who are most credible to me, the most vulnerable," says Dr. Elizabeth Clark, who has written more than a hundred refugee medical reports in the last five years. "These discrepant people who don't answer well, who are assumed to be fabricating . . . they need the most help. We do such damage to people in limbo."

————

In Primo Levi's *The Drowned and the Saved*, an SS officer says to a prisoner: "Even if some of you survive, the world would not believe him . . . And even if some proof should remain and some of you survive, people will say that the events you describe are too monstrous to be believed: they will say they are the exaggerations of Allied propaganda and will believe us, who will deny everything, and not you. We will be the ones to dictate the history of the Lagers."

The officer's words reach deep down to the survivors' worst nightmares: that their trauma will run afoul of someone's sacred myth, their essential truths and lazy workarounds. Levi writes of a recurring dream that almost all survivors share, from their nights in captivity. "[T]hey had returned home, and with passion and relief were describing their past sufferings, addressing themselves to a loved person, and were not believed, indeed were not even listened to. In the most typical (and most cruel) form, the interlocutor turned and left in silence."

The known world is too precious; we devote ourselves to protecting it. We try, most urgently, to bind our myths by some tendril to reality, a fraught scramble back to the steady state. After a lifetime of faith in God, country, and human goodness, if thousands of emaciated prisoners stumble out of ghettos claiming to have suffered monstrous atrocities, believing them requires a Herculean override of instinct— the mind is trying to explain away the plainly visible.

And so, the survivor is constantly terrified that the marks on her body won't be enough, and her story will be deleted from history; that even as the listener takes in each awful detail, he's racing to calculate the likelihood of embellishment. And when believing is too hard or threatens his vital assumptions, his subconscious will do the dismissing for him.

Levi's description of the recurring nightmare reminds me of Elif, a Turkish rape survivor who, after nine years of torture in prison, fled to the U.K. "I was like someone thrown out of the world," she said. But she wasn't talking about leaving home. She was describing the memory of her asylum interview, when two men forced her to relive every beat of her rapes.

"How did the police rape me? How many men raped me? Could I give them any evidence proving this? Could I give them any evidence about the torture? It was as if my body was shedding its skin. I wanted to say, 'Stop it! I can't go on, I can't, I can't!' Why couldn't they have been women? . . . I felt dead explaining about my rape to those men."

Elif gripped her papers, proof of her long years in prison. Realizing it wasn't enough, she lost her words. *Oh god, they want proof of the actual rapes.* She ran to the toilet and washed her face. "I didn't yet know that they were robots . . . I wanted to die. And then the interview was finished."

I spoke to Marc, a McKinsey friend turned angel investor. I asked him how he listened to entrepreneurs. He talked about the grandiose slaughterhouse CEO, the CrossFit scammer, the visionary Broadway producer who sold him on two shows, the friends and family who trusted him when he invited them to join him. As he spoke, I realized that his every investment decision was based on believing in somebody, not the stories or business plans. Only people. Why did this seem so right to me? As a writer, I know that good fiction is populated with complex, surprising characters. Maybe the same is true of good investments.

"Well, that, and diversification," says Marc. "Be sure whatever money you put in, you're willing to lose it all."

This, too, makes sense. A good investment is about finding an opportunity before it's obvious to everyone else. So, you bet on a dozen and hope one pays off, freeing yourself from the constant calculation of each individual's place on the spectrum: potential or need. As long as your portfolio is diverse, you can gamble on a longshot—you can hope.

Do I listen with this much hope and excitement? Or do I listen with my guard up because I'm afraid of a wrong call? Do I, too, yearn to believe only soaring tales of spectacle and obvious vision? When my daughter tells stories, I dig for signs of what has happened in school. I am afraid of a single wrong call in her upbringing, and that fear momentarily outweighs my hopes.

As a young consultant, barely out of college, I listened to client stories for inefficiencies I could fix so I could prove myself a star. I couldn't stomach a single mistake. When I read novels, though, I am generous, looking for subtext, artful language. I want to be moved, surprised. Though I have a finely tuned bullshit detector, in the end I'm itching to believe. When reading, my motives are empathetic. I'm paying attention, delving into other people's mourning, humiliation, need. I accept that one book will drain me, the next will bring me joy.

I don't expect one story to fulfill my every literary need. Because I want to grow my body of experience, I read literature the way Marc doles out capital: with imagination on, ready to believe every promise, expecting half to flop. He saves his scrutiny for the portfolio. I care about my intellectual resources as he does his financial one. Comfort with risk enriches us both.

Why don't we apply such wisdom beyond our places of abundance?

In 2019, I explained the difference between a migrant and a refugee in a segment on PBS—the simple definition from the Refugee Convention. I gave Arulanantham's "classic Central American example." Preparing for another take, a lighting designer whispered to another, "Should we be airing this? Aren't we telling them exactly how to slip through the door?"

I came home from the trip and collapsed into bed.

"What's wrong?" Sam asked. I glared at the covers. He had them tucked all wrong.

"These fucking people," I said. "I mean . . . in movies they say they like misfits and oddballs and quirky people. It's a lie! If they catch the slightest whiff of bad luck on you, any failure or errancy . . . if you've ever been anything but visionary, you don't have a shot in hell." I called up Dr. Clark's beautiful words, *"These discrepant people, who don't answer well . . ."*

"But Dina," said Sam, returning to his book as I obsessively kicked and straightened the blankets. "Do these discrepant people have a shot with *you*?"

Performing

5.

The hilltop village in southern France where we sheltered during the pandemic isn't on a tourist path, so it's remained cheap and well hidden. We stay in a comfortably worn-out house that belongs to Sam's parents, and before them his grandmother. A rogue chicken appears sometimes on the square. Most of the villagers have lived here their entire lives, sending their children to the local school whose enrollment varies depending on birth rates. Some years there are seven or eight children, some years fourteen or fifteen, all learning together in two rooms of the mayor's offices. We have an inexplicable *brocante*, a restaurant, and four of the sixty-plus residents are Sam's aunts and uncles. Sam grew up here, summer after summer. I spent a lazy second trimester here, eating forbidden raw cheeses and, in fits of remorse, getting tested for toxoplasmosis. Elena had her first ripe peach just there, in the square, where she drove her soft, hot little belly against her walker and clapped along to a circle of singing neighbor girls. All our shoes are caked in sheep dung.

Over the years many of our friends have visited this secret spot. They're surprised at first, having to adapt to the hot nights and scratchy sheets, the spiders that crawl up the oil drains, the many inexplicable bug bites (because I sleep on my side, my right ankle is ringed with years of scars, like a tree stump), the squat shower inside the kitchen, the hard beds, the constant work of getting wood, clearing insect carcasses, collecting water from the source, fetching canisters of gas. But memory erases the small inconveniences, adding a certain magic, and the friends return: for bookish chatter at the big wooden table surrounded by cooling stone walls and low wood beams, for endless carafes of local wine from just down the hill, for roadside cherries, heavy pots of homecooked ratatouille, chicken roasted in red wine, or daube with bay leaves from the garden, filling the stone house with the smell of winter.

I can relax in this village. It's taken me a lifetime to figure out that despite immigrant cravings for security, I actually don't like money and don't need much of it. I can live in an old jean skirt, stretch a shampoo bottle to a month and a haircut to six months, but as long as I have good coffee beans, some roasting chickens, a view, and enough for books and laptop repairs, I'm happy. And Sam cooks sumptuously, builds, gardens, paints, and repairs things expertly. A conversation with him is as good as theater. He makes a rich life far cheaper. I like that.

I need village life, with elders and children connected to me scattered within hopping distance, rushing in and out of my home, never knocking, taking pots, bringing them back full, nipping firewood, dropping off children you hadn't realized were out. This isn't a craving for community, which might be satisfied by a residency or a commune. Those arrangements end; they're weak links forged by unhampered adults who, however eager, can sever them in a day. This is something more fundamental, blood connections made long ago, in deep time. It's a way of living that demonstrates to children the entire arc of life, their role at every step.

A village is what I had in Iran. After a lifetime of chasing the sparkle of cities, this pandemic, I thought, might return to me the dung-splattered, mud-caked boots of my girlhood. And here was a place laden with Sam's history, a community of resilient villagers, like my father's family in Ardestoon, sheepherders and lavender growers that COVID had largely spared. When in October 2020 President Emmanuel Macron ordered France to hunker down with family, all the neighbors nodded, taking for granted that their "family" was the entire village.

That week, we'd had five guests from Paris—literary ones who made me nervous, having read the right books in college, back when I was digging out of an imagined pit, terrified of poverty. For our week in the country, we had borrowed a dusty house across the square. Neglected for years, it was covered in cobwebs, but it had a woodburning stove, piles of good books, and a sitting room overlooking a little road and endless hills. We had all brought small bags, enough clothes for a crisp week in the country, hiking to the market, crunching pine cones and needles on rocky forest paths, inventing vegetarian dishes. A week of this, and we'd return to the city.

But a few nights in, after dinner, as Aleks (a mathematician) cleared the plates and Jennifer (a writer) swept the floor, we huddled over a laptop watching Macron announce a second French lockdown. The president gave all vacationers two days to return to the cities or settle down, and prepare to repeat the spring lockdowns. After we closed the laptop, we were all silent for a minute or two. We didn't want to relive that bleak April, a dead Paris, cold and silent.

"Let's stay," I said. "I'm serious, everyone, stay."

The next day, after enrolling Elena in the village school, Sam came home stunned. "Dina, you won't believe this. There's an Iranian family there, from the next village. They're refugees."

"No," I said. Then, a terrifying thought. "In a class of seven? How long have they—"

"I don't know," he said, left eyebrow already cocked.

"Did they just show up, like right now?" I said. "Were they in the school last year?"

The eyebrow went off. "Are you serious?"

Yes, I know. The Islamic Republic has a lot on their plate right now, with a megalomaniac rekindling nuclear hostilities and a pandemic pummeling their unprepared agrarian population, among them my father and our beloved village. Iran is too busy to send spies to a French village for my sake. But these are marrow-deep subconscious fears—deeper than marrow, they're good and mixed into my DNA and every morsel of my tissue. I don't get to tell them to go away.

"Fine," I said. McKinsey Dina, though, was already analyzing (*can I trust them?*), itching to ask about the wife's physical traits, and her behavior. Did she keep touching her temple, as if she's been recently militant about tucking in every strand? Did she have fairly even biceps and triceps, the kind you get doing regimented training, or are her biceps and upper back weirdly built, with flabby triceps like farm women? Was she wearing chunky jewelry, big enough to hide a camera? Did she sound like she'd read Western books? What color was her hair? Next time maybe wave around a copy of *The Satanic Verses* and see how she takes it?

The pandemic darkened everything. I had nightmares. My dad sent bad news from Iran of villages ravaged by the virus. "They pour so much rock and cement over the bodies," he said about a COVID burial. "You think, even his soul can't get past that, let alone a virus."

Sam's local family adored our friends. When they dropped by, we slipped into French and became Luberon villagers, our connection to the land, to this country, appearing like iodine in sleeping veins. Then the family would trickle out, and we'd return to our comfortable in-between culture, chameleons returning to our resting shades: Laleh and Aleks, singing and dancing with Elena like elephants and giraffes. Charlie, trying to sell people on his ginger and turmeric morning tea. Jennifer and her partner, a French filmmaker, Manu, singing the Divine Comedy's "A Lady of a Certain Age" to Manu's guitar.

We bought a lot of firewood and negotiated a roster of chores. Having packed only two light sweaters each, we soon ran out of clothes.

We searched the basement, raided the cellar in the bathroom, Sam's mother Flo's closet under the stairs, for clothes the family had left behind. Sam's youngest brother, Josh, had lived for a while in nearby Manosque, and had stored a number of beautiful coats in the house. We found winter dresses, skirts, and Flo's many fitted vests and jackets. In the following days, I kept finding crusty vitamin pills in my skirt pockets, and six euros in ten-cent increments in the shawls and sewing kits. We took walks. While the others had long literary debates, Aleks indulged me in logic games and a campaign to watch shows that others called unthinking, uncomplicated television schlock.

Sometimes in the middle of dinner or a movie, Sam slipped away to answer a distress call from Josh, who was struggling in English lockdown. For most of his life, Josh had suffered from manic and delusional episodes. Even in his bouts of medicated stability, Josh's singular focus was finding a cure, whether in mindfulness, Judaism, or drugs. Sometimes, without telling anyone, he'd board a cheap overnight flight somewhere. He'd wander the streets, call a friend from a decade past, be refused lodging, and after a day of homelessness return, dejected. Once, he flew to Israel, where he ranted about finding his spiritual home. Israeli police, alarmed, questioned him and put him on the next plane back to London. Years ago, Sam had to rescue him from Peru, where he had escaped to an ayahuasca retreat. He went hoping to open his mind, to clear out conscious thought and escape into a beautiful oblivion, an ecstatic trance; when he returned, he might see more clearly what was invading his body.

After Josh's calls, Sam would return quietly to his chair, chewing his lips, his face wan.

"Is everything okay?" I'd ask. We had this conversation a hundred times.

"He's saying things," Sam would whisper.

I'd sigh or shake my head. "He needs work, not all this coddling." Sam would nod.

Sam's insomnia worsened. Often, he'd wake at 3:00 a.m. to pace, read, and write, like a sentry for some imminent disaster. And he threw himself into caring for our friends, cooking, shopping. He was becoming a communal resource, portions of him handed out like stew helpings.

Sam first told me about Josh at the MacDowell artist residency, soon after we met. An enigmatic lost soul who ran away, drove away friends, appeared in and disappeared out of his two-year-old son's life. "He has schizoid personality disorder," said Sam. "I'm always waiting for some stranger to call from Israel. He finds last-minute red-eyes for a hundred euro and takes off without luggage."

Sam showed me a photo of Josh, of his son, Raffa, who already had Sam's big grin and tight curls. Josh, too, looked like Sam, his features subtler, smaller and less severely cut.

In those early days at MacDowell, Sam and I talked often about obsessions. What possessed Josh, Sam told me, was his body, and faith. Did he have lodged in his DNA some foreign thing destroying him? Did he have a disease? Could the Judaism of his grandparents save him? Could he connect, somehow, to their tragic history? He read the Torah and Holocaust histories. He consulted with a rabbi, who found him reflective and spiritually insightful.

My first instinct, on hearing about Josh, was to keep my distance from Sam. *This isn't the right man. His load is too heavy and unwieldy, and inextricably fastened to other people's.*

Yet I wanted to know more about the family. Sam's father, Sheldon, a human rights lawyer, started his family in South Africa, having devoted his early career to fighting apartheid. He was a professor now; he made dad jokes and tested out moral dilemmas at dinner. Sam's mother, Flo, an artist, once on the cusp of fame, donated her most celebrated painting to a tiny Christian charity and gave up her budding career to care for her family. Sam's older brother, Ilan, was a human rights lawyer; his wife was a human rights watchdog who spent half her career negotiating with warlords and the other investigating corporate abuses against African workers. "Anneke's mobile," said Sam, "is full of Congolese warlords. She could text one right now." Sam told me that, because of the conformist atmosphere of his school in Suffolk, Ilan had changed his name to Daniel.

"My brother changed his name to Daniel, too!" I said. He thought I was joking. "I'm serious! When we were refugees, because 'Khosrou' was too hard for Anglophones."

"That's a bizarre thing to have in common," said Sam.

I didn't have a family. Newly divorced, I had only my mother, and talking to her, all her fretting about my ex-husband, her religiousness, her organic farming schemes gave me literal hives. Two doctors said, "If something triggers these, get away from that thing."

Sam's family seemed devoted to each other. A scholarly father who came home for dinner. A mother who, though she was an evangelical Christian like mine, didn't harass her children to believe, or mythologize her own story. Brothers and sisters who loved each other, and worried about the tormented youngest. At MacDowell, Sam gave a reading of his work, a piece about his grandmother who had recently died. Twenty-five artists left in tears.

One day, Sam appeared in the MacDowell kitchen as I was soaking herbs for a Persian meal. "I came to help," he said. His sleeves rolled up, he scrubbed his hands and got to chopping.

"You've worked in a kitchen," the chef said. Sam grinned.

That night he left a note in my mail cubby, along with a sculpture he had fashioned out of the metal capsule around our wine cork—a nervous habit. Now, I've seen him make hundreds of spiders, flowers, ladybugs, tiny coat hangers and such out of cork capsules.

"I love this man," I told everyone on the retreat. "He's my person." When my words reached him, he'd mutter noncommittal things, but a small smile would linger for a long time. Sometimes, at dinner as he carried on other conversations, he placed a huge, rough hand over mine. I had never so openly pursued someone, not since Ali Mansouri on the playground, and not after Noah. Maybe the problem with all those other times, the friendships or loves that had slipped away, was that I didn't believe. I didn't stand on roofs and shout, *this is mine*. You tell the universe what's yours, and then the universe will have to wrestle you for it, right?

But every night, Sam would excuse himself early from the dinner table to call a woman in New York—a painter with high collars who never smiled in photos. One night, Sam and I snuck into town for dinner, and he showed me her picture. She had exquisite taste, he told me, and I responded that I knew the type. *Sam isn't mine*, I told myself, not because of his sick brother, or his relationship, but because he admired this aloofness, this elegance, the air of artistic exclusivity. I'm a goofball, always with an inexplicable stain, or crumbs in my hair, a person you can read like an open book—an easy one. In my bed, I listed all that this mysterious other woman would find mainstream, ordinary, and small about me: my highlighted hair, my Iran panics, my department store jeans, my stories with their beginnings, middles, and hopeful endings, the way I cry at bad movies. Most of all, I'd be judged for the two great dogmas in my past, both so reviled by artists: evangelism and McKinsey. I'm the girl who eats a second slice of cake. I laugh too loud, talk too much, say awkward things. I imagined that I'd understand Sam's parents better than Sam's severe, discerning girlfriend could. That she'd yawn at dinnertime logic games, that they'd need my protection from her judgment. Sam's father, Sheldon, seemed born of my tribe. I would know his language. Sheldon, I thought, would get me.

For days I sulked. Why couldn't I be casually elegant, a person you take seriously? Why wasn't my word gold, my love hard-won and precious? Why was I this misfit, a village grandmother who just hadn't gotten old yet? Already, I loved Sam with such a big stupid love.

On those sad MacDowell nights, I'd wander through the woods to the library and spend an hour setting up the television system. Then I'd watch old episodes of *Gilmore Girls*. Once Sam passed by and chuckled. "But you write such good short stories," he said, as if one had anything to do with the other. On our last day, Sam bought his artist a signature MacDowell basket. After two months off and on, he and I said a last goodbye. I imagined him flying home for Christmas to his big family, his errant brother on his best behavior, his continental parents in matching sweaters, cutting a chocolate yule log to corny holiday music; his girlfriend, sharp-chinned and hungry, with her severe bun and trimmed fingernails, quietly watching.

———

Once a refugee finds the one correct story of her many stories, her battle changes. With home receding into the horizon, she must now *persuade*, though her performance (of the story, of her grief and fear) is tainted by a hundred cultural and trauma-born factors. Sontag was right: cynical modern audiences will fight to remain unmoved. When my family first arrived in the U.S., I thought of Western asylum officers as enforcers of humanitarian right and duty. Empowered by the Refugee Convention and a unified global response to the Holocaust tragedy, these gatekeepers were listening to understand, to rescue, to fulfill a historic mandate—they listened to us with the same care and horror as they had to those mid-century Russian mothers stumbling out of a decimated Europe, reaching for a hand. As I grew up, I shed some of this naivete, but the officers changed, too. Their incentives, their training, their ideologies transformed with the governments they served. They became cynical, miners of tiny contradictions.

Today's asylum officers are instructed to dig out inconsistencies. Trained to disbelieve, they demand a perfect performance and accuse survivors of inventing details, of passing off unrelated injuries, even of inflicting scars on themselves. In the U.K., a few years ago, a fifty-year-old asylum seeker was told that she was too old to be plausibly raped. Imagine performing in a show in which the stakes are your life. Now imagine an untrained, exhausted heckler sneering in the front row. Now imagine he is your judge.

In a 2016 report called *Proving Torture*, doctors and researchers working on behalf of Freedom from Torture (FFT) wrote that in some torture cases, U.K. asylum caseworkers were blithely dismissing expert opinion in favor of their own judgment of a victim's performance: they didn't seem depressed or sick enough, their bones seemed unbroken. One caseworker made the absurd conclusion that if an asylum seeker was in such bad health, he would have been identified at the airport. Another said a bribe seemed too high. In a maddening refusal letter, the Home Office contradicted itself, calling it impossible that an Algerian hate crime victim would tell the police about his sexuality without being arrested, *and* that Algeria is safe for a gay man.

The study found that caseworkers even substituted their own "clinical" interpretations for those of experts, on matters far outside their training or knowledge: "In any other court or tribunal setting, a similar pattern of such practices would be scandalous." More troubling still, caseworkers showed a poor understanding of the 1999 Istanbul Protocol, the international standard for assessing torture injuries, and were applying incorrect burdens of proof to a wide range of asylum stories. Though the law requires a "reasonably likely" burden for refugees, officers were using something closer to the criminal standard, "beyond reasonable doubt," rejecting strong asylum claims based on the mere existence of remote other possibilities. Sabine, the young rape survivor from Congo, for example, had proven that she was Tutsi and that the rapists were soldiers; she was still rejected despite the probable link.

In one case, a survivor was put in detention and tortured, then escaped. After that, he was recaptured and tortured again. A U.K. officer writes in his rejection of this claim:

If it were accepted that your injuries were so severe that it was believed you would die, it is inconsistent that these injuries would permit you to escape detention by jumping over a wall.

All right, one might think. You don't believe the wall part. What does it matter? The man was in detention at least once and has torture scars characteristic of that facility. But the rejection letter follows one logical fallacy into another:

As it is not accepted that you escaped detention it is also not accepted that you were detained a second time . . . It is concluded that the scarring described in the medico-legal report was not suffered in the context you have described.

It took an appeal judge to see the stupidity of this logic. Aside from the considerable expertise of the doctor who wrote the medico-legal report, this survivor's many deliberate scars, the judge said, point to "really only one possible conclusion, which is that the appellant has been subjected to sustained torture or acute ill-treatment . . . I suppose it is theoretically possible that such treatment could have been inflicted on him by people other than the [country] authorities; but if so who were they—no one else has been suggested or identified; and why would the appellant himself not identify them, since it is likely that the outcome would be the same?"

Ana Reyes (the immigration lawyer who wins on credibility) wrote a memo with similar conclusions as the FFT report in America. Common errors in adverse credibility findings included repeated failure to correctly assess testimony, rejection based on mere speculation, and even rejection based on failure to disclose facts that were never requested. In one case, the applicants were called "religious zealots" whose religious practice was "offensive to a majority." This might, of course, be the very reason they'd need asylum, as do Christian converts from the Islamic world; but if the logic is to reject because their faith isn't appealing to *Americans*, we have here a gross misreading of the Refugee Convention. In another case, the interviewer wasn't satisfied that the applicant described his own bleeding head without including the depth of the wound. Reyes cites cases where applicants were both denied for not having medical records on them, and denied because "it was implausible that the applicant would have immigrated from China to the United States carrying a copy of his medical record for no apparent purpose."

In 2020, Freedom from Torture published another report called *Beyond Belief: How the Home Office Fails Survivors of Torture at the Asylum Interview,* including verbatim exchanges:

> *Claimant: I fear the government and their troops in the army because I was neglected and discriminated against. I remember my youth and childhood. I noticed that during the school years, shall I tell you the story of what happened?*
>
> Caseworker: I want to know why you are specifically claiming asylum, not things that have happened 190 years prior to this.

Or in another case, where the claimant begins weeping at the memory of a rape:

> Caseworker: Were you raped during the 5 days?
> *Claimant: Yes, beaten and raped and left naked, I don't like to think about it.*
> Caseworker: How many times were you beaten and raped over the 5 days?

Again and again in the report, torture survivors described being cut off as they told harrowing stories, instructed to give short answers, told that their answers were irrelevant, only to find themselves later rejected for not offering enough information. "He doesn't give me a chance to explain why they have arrested me, where and how," said one refugee. A caseworker said, in response to a refugee's struggle to tell her story as it happened: "You need to start listening to my questions and answering them correctly, as your inability to answer the questions I am asking you is causing delays in progress, do you understand?"

In *The Human Condition*, Hannah Arendt describes public life as a way to cement reality. The opportunity to have one's story heard, to bring it to the public sphere, is to make the story real, and so storytelling is a necessary link between public and private. "Compared with the reality which comes from being seen and heard, even the greatest forces of intimate life—the passions of the heart, the thoughts of the mind, the delights of the senses—lead to an uncertain, shadowy kind of existence unless and until they are transformed . . . into a shape to fit them for public appearance. The most current of such transformations occurs in storytelling."

To stumble to the door of a new nation with nothing but a story, a gruesome torturous story that has altered you, and to be told "you're not correctly answering my questions" is a violence, a removal from the public sphere, the end of a reality, and a kind of death.

———

Four months later, MacDowell was long over and Sam was gone. I was hurt, but I wasn't the terrified wife I'd been. I didn't need anyone to accept or return my love; my story with Sam might have been finished but it was still entirely mine. I lived without binds or tangles in New York, a city full of distraction.

Sam came back to me that spring, after our MacDowell autumn. His elegant relationship was ending. He told me he missed the way I said every thought aloud, and liked what I liked, and so publicly loved him that I wasn't ashamed to be alone in my certainty.

If I had become pregnant just a month later than I did, we might have cemented things, so that I might never have doubted that he loved me that much, too. Sam suspected it first, because I had changed birth control pills, and because my cheeks were tender, my breasts growing.

He made me take a test, which I left in the bathroom. I ran back to bed, hiding under the covers as he read it.

"You're pregnant," he said, astonished. I was about to assure him that it was *my* problem when he blurted out, "It's a great thing! We'd be in this position in a year anyway." We were both divorced, in our mid-thirties. We knew what we wanted—and that *we* were it—and shouldn't lose this chance for a family. "Can you imagine the kid we'd have?" he said.

In minutes we were dressed and downstairs in my local Lower East Side café. Sam bought me a decaf cappuccino and said, "Let's call my parents." Just like that. They were hiking in the English woods with two grandchildren.

"Mum," said Sam, "This is my girlfriend." Flo looked delighted. "We're having a baby."

Off screen, Sheldon cheered. Neither took even a moment to be shocked, or scandalized, or confused. They transitioned seamlessly, in a nanosecond, to news of us both, me and Elena.

Did they not wonder if I had money? Or a passport? Did they not question my motives, this stranger who had come into their lives? Where was their suspicion, their survival instinct? Now I worried for them. Who was keeping this innocent couple from being routinely scammed?

Later, my sensible business girlfriends divined that I was pregnant. I wrote to thirty people to change my birthday party from a Russian vodka bar to a Central Park picnic. People got suspicious. "Let's go to hot yoga," texted a friend. I made an excuse. "Wine bar?" she said. "Sushi? Sauna? Turkish coffee? How about a long soak in a public tub?"

"What are you getting at?" I replied. *I'll miss her.* I knew already that life was ending.

"You know exactly what I'm getting at." Then she forced me to ask myself: Would I have this baby if I were alone? *Yes, I would; I don't need Sam. I love him, though.* "Okay, let's call a doctor. Don't you need folic acid injections or something?" When I told her there's no such thing as folic acid "injections" she said, "I think there is. I think if you pay for it . . . "

For days, Sam shopped for pregnancy books, vitamins, then an astonishing procession of prenatal food offerings: rollmops, smoked salmon, pickled herring. He got a lot of pickled fish. It moved me that he was bringing me food from his culture, as if to invite me into his family. One morning I woke to an omelet so chock full of chopped herbs and garlic, it barely held together.

In those early days in my New York studio, Sam told me about his family. His parents had such rich history: she was born to strict parents in Vichy France, he to a family ravaged by the Holocaust. Neither side had been all that happy when they married. She was a beautiful French artist and he was a Yale undergrad, and they fell in love, bought reasonably priced houses in artsy villages in Essex and Provence, threw open their doors to houseguests, moved all over the world fighting abuses of power, had four children, taught them ethics and logic over big French dinners, sent two to Oxford. They were my ideal family. In New York, when I mentioned Sam's family, people would say, "They're not rich but they know how to live in a way rich people don't," or "They surround themselves with the most fascinating people."

We skyped with his sister, Anna, who told me about childbirth in London, under the NHS. "How's . . . everything now?" I asked, tentatively, mortified at the thought of childbirth.

Sam told me about Josh's trip to Peru. About the time he'd just shown up in New York, expecting the city to welcome him.

Sometimes I worried, imagining what would happen if we broke up. "I'd never keep this baby from its real family," I said, "even if we don't last." And I meant it. Sam's family was so rooted, so artistic and curious.

For months, Sam showed his love for me and for our baby with food—shaved Brussel sprouts with cashews, zucchini ribbons in vinaigrette, plump cherries from the roadside bleeding into a crate, yogurts lumpy with chopped almond, chickens roasted brown in onion and wine, crunchy sour salads, and enough pickled fish to brine my stomach lining. He performed the ritual of preparing our day's food in New York, then in his family's village outside London where my belts pinched my belly, then in Provence where I grew into airy summer dresses, in this same village where I now sit, listening to the crackling embers of the fire he built.

And yet, a suspicion bloomed: Does Sam love me, or is he devoted only to his child? Am I artistic enough, clever enough? Does my work matter to him? Does he privately believe that I'll never be as creative or original as other women he's known? Are we capable of love, after divorces, after watching our most innocent attempts end in sorrow and ugliness?

"Why doesn't he marry you?" my mother kept whispering, though I'd told her often that I will never marry again—never. The institution is nothing to me, only legal shackles.

After some time, I came to believe that meeting Sam wasn't some fluke, that I had gone to MacDowell expressly to find my person. This complicates things, the going to find someone, because it means that I made things happen that might not have happened on their own. But does that make them less real? That has been my struggle in this dusk of my youth. In younger days, the ability to wish a romance into being was something to flaunt. I felt powerful (for this small, universal gift). Now I think, did I rob myself of the chance to be seen and pursued? But why should I have done that to myself? The young have this one chance to go out and seize what they want. Then that chance is gone. Then you're a lady of a certain age, unseen, every word dipped in grains of salt.

One day, early in the pregnancy, I saw a therapist. Does Sam love me, I wanted to ask, and if so, why can't I believe it? I had such an easy time believing this about other men. This isn't some deep-seated inability to accept love, or my own worthiness. It's something else.

"It's possible to believe you're no longer worthy, you know," the therapist said. "You don't have to have always *been* suspicious of love to *become* suspicious of it."

"Why would I suddenly do that?" I asked. "With a man who decided the instant I got pregnant that he wanted to spend his life with me?"

"Maybe you think you don't deserve long-term love anymore," she said.

I rolled my eyes. "Why would I think that? That's twenty-five-year-old nonsense."

"You also seem to think that turning thirty-five has made you some kind of robot."

I shifted in my chair, lobbing nervousness in her direction. "Thirty-five and a mom . . ."

"Is that it, then? Maybe you think Sam's love is reserved for the baby?"

"That's also nonsense." It wasn't. That's exactly what I thought— exactly.

And yet, she moved on. "Maybe . . . because of your divorce from Philip?"

"Well," I started. Then stopped. That wasn't it. Sam was divorced too. I like divorce.

"Well what?"

"I feel bad for Philip. He loved me guilelessly. I erased his wide-eyed love of the world."

"Time did that," she said, with enough certainty to sting my ego. "Not you."

"It was a little bit me! He was guileless, and I thought he was boring."

"You keep using that word." She wrinkled her nose, like a teacher catching an error.

"What, guileless? That's the best word for his character . . . or the space between our characters, I guess. You know, he cried at Pixar movies. Not *cried* cried, but you'd look over and he was all enchanted eyebrows and dimpling chin, a little smile, eyes brimming."

She smiled. "There are worst things in the world than guile."

"You think so? Other people don't think so. It's what they try to hide the most."

"Also, 'boring' . . . it's a trite word you're using to punish yourself. Break down boring."

"Okay . . . he wasn't into literature or stories that are actually good—he had a huge heart, but it was wired with all the easy buttons. He was very literal. Very sincere. He didn't have morbid fascinations with things, like Sam does. He couldn't laugh at himself, or the world. He was into money and image. And he wanted me to bury all my cool strangeness."

"That's not boring. It's incompatibility."

"It's not guile, though," I said, unaware that I was starting to sound obsessed.

"Does Sam have guile?" She sighed, which irritated me. *Is this boring to you?*

"Yes. And that's why he's interesting. And also, why he maybe doesn't love me."

"Is it possible for someone to have just enough guile to interest you, to keep you from being bored, but not so much that you tell yourself they're running a long con?"

"Oh, God, maybe not. Actually, maybe the opposite . . . maybe those two circles overlap."

"Why overlap?" She was scribbling notes now.

"Because some people are boring *and* running a long con. A clumsy one, maybe, but—" I kept thinking, don't I want a man who is capable of deceiving me? A high-quality one with enough artistry and cunning to fake me out for, say, a decade? Wouldn't a less capable man be boring? And isn't all art about bewitching and enthralling hard-hearted people?

She looked up from her notes. Then, a gong: "You have a problem with trust."

I got up. *You*, I thought, *aren't a real doctor.*

———

Arriving at Gatwick airport, jetlagged and nauseated, I looked in the crowd for Sam's parents. Sam and I were on different flights from New York and they were collecting me first. Even if I'd never seen their photos, I'd have recognized Sheldon and Flo in an instant. Of the four siblings, Sam most clearly resembles both parents, having inherited their most striking features—Sheldon's dark skin and long nose, Flo's curls and Viking build ("Sam has legs like a Spartan!" I bragged to the girls. "Or the Spartan's horse."). Briefly, I lingered, watching Sheldon and Flo scan the crowd for me, and I marveled at the magic of it. Would my child look so like me? If a stranger had to pick Sam's parents out of all the parents on this earth, she would choose these two. It was as if Sam had split in two right there at the airport arrivals gate. I wouldn't be as easy to spot. They had learned my name only days before. I took a breath and headed toward them.

That night we had drinks at a river pub. Sam's parents asked about me, and shared their stories. With their degrees and humanitarian careers, this family was everything I admired. At dinner, Sheldon posed moral dilemmas, delighting in logical leaps or intellectual risks; the weirder the question the better he liked it. An older progressive, he was intrigued by his children's opinions, by former certainties that crumbled in the age of technology and inclusion. Still, every conversation eventually turned to Josh's dramas. The family was consumed by his most recent mental health scare. Josh was in and out of treatment facilities. Would he be sectioned? Often, after a few hours, he was dismissed, sent home by unconvinced mid-levels. I kept thinking of the therapist who said I had trust issues. She may have been right, but I was free never to see her again. Josh kept having to persuade the same people over and over.

Every day, I prayed secretly that Sam's genes, his big heart, would overcome my scarred and selfish ones, that this child would be kind, talented, engaged. I imagined Sheldon teaching her ethical reasoning, logic puzzles, moral dilemmas; Flo teaching her to paint from deep in her imagination; Sam reading her poems. And I'd teach her to suffer more than other people, to build skin like suitcase leather. I'd give her roots, but teach her to try like someone who has none.

Meanwhile, Josh was the family's central question, its narrative drive. Were his troubles genetic or born of adolescent trauma? Did he have an innate addictive drive or had he fallen into the wrong crowd, smoked the wrong thing? Newly pregnant, I pounced on the latter options. I resented that Sheldon, an anti-apartheid hero, was having to think about whether his kid smoked too much weed. One night, I said to Sam, "I don't get why your parents stopped parenting with him. I mean, with the first two sons at Oxford, and their daughter this talented artist—"

Sam sat up, eyes like two-euros each. "It wasn't their fault, Dina," he snapped.

"I didn't say that," I muttered. "I wasn't suggesting—"

"They did nothing wrong," he said. "They were such good parents. Totally devoted."

"I know. I'm just saying they were strict and disciplined, and you and Ilan did so well—"

"Everyone did so much!" he said. "And who said Oxford's the measure of everything?"

"It's not! And I never said that," I spat through tears. "I just . . . he's not a refugee or poor or— Not everything is genetic. That's too easy an answer, just blame it on the genes—"

"Well, sometimes, that's what it is," he said.

"Not this time! Not in this case! It sounds like he doesn't try. Like he's just a—"

"A what?" said Sam. "Just some loser?"

Now I was weeping. I had no idea how to defend myself, so I just said, "It's not genes."

Sam opened his mouth to speak, then his expression softened. Pausing to think, he said, "Of course it's not the genes." He pulled me in and kissed my hair. "Our baby will be perfect."

I told him I loved him. He said, *I do love you.* For years, that extra "do" grazed my heart.

Stung, I threw myself into my work. I wanted to write stories of *real* suffering people, refugees trying hard to work and build lives, not lucky English boys who were obviously lying.

On to more important things.

———

There are many reasons honest asylum seekers might behave like liars. Asylum officers routinely focus on contextual detail. *What was the date? The time? Who was in the room?* But torture survivors have had periods of starvation, sleep deprivation, and extreme fear. They've been submerged, branded, beaten. Some memories are gone. Others never formed.

Which of life's most traumatic stories does the memory store? I ask Dr. Katy Robjant, director of national clinical services at FFT, which operates one of the world's largest and most respected forensic torture documentation services. During a fight-or-flight event, Dr. Robjant explains, the amygdala, which is responsible for quick associations, physical reactions, thoughts, emotions, and sensory information, goes into high-performance mode. Survivors remember strange physical details: the smell of blood, their own heartbeat, the dread of imminent death, the fear in their fingertips. These sensations are stored for years, emerging in creative pursuits like writing, or in vivid recurring nightmares wherein the victim believes she's back in that moment.

On the other hand, the hippocampus, which is responsible for contextual data—time, place, how the event started, why it was happening, distances—loses precision during danger, failing to store crucial contextual detail. It goes into high-contrast mode, storing only huge pieces of context (e.g., identity of a rapist the victim already knows, as in Christine Blasey Ford's "indelible in the hippocampus"). Each time the memory returns, stored vividly as it is inside the amygdala, that crucial, reassuring piece of *context*—the knowledge that this isn't happening *now*, but is locked in the past—momentarily disconnects from that memory, causing the terrified reactions we know as PTSD, the sensation of reliving the trauma. Huge as that piece of context is, it's slow to arrive. The *small* contextual stuff, meanwhile, is gone.

Yet Home Officers hang their belief on these same contextual details. "How can you forget how far you ran?" But that is exactly the sort of detail the hippocampus in high-contrast would fail to store. The officer wants the day, the hour, the street name. All you recall is a city, a year. And the blows, the vomit, the dirt. "The disconnect doesn't happen completely unless the trauma is repeated, severe, or in early life, as with child soldiers," says Dr. Robjant. "When the story involves several traumatic events, the memories are even more confused and jumbled together. We would *expect* them to give the wrong time, date, order of events. It's normal."

Even in this, officers and judges substitute their own judgment, knowing nothing about contextual versus sensory information. "Sometimes the details feel too on-point for them, and that can damage credibility," said San Francisco asylum lawyer Maleeha Haq. "Clients will describe the way they were beaten. The car was white, it looked like a jeep, it had a sticker. The number of bats. The judge says if you're being beaten by seven guys, how do you remember the detail about the car?" That is sensory detail, Dr. Robjant might point out. All kinds of weird details are vividly retained by the amygdala. It's context that disappears.

Expert (written and oral) explanations of PTSD, even training sessions offered by charities like Freedom from Torture, seem to have no effect on the questions the officers ask. "The asylum interview itself can be traumatic," says Dr. Juliet Cohen, head of doctors at FFT. "If they don't answer well, the questions come more fiercely, which drives up stress, so they have more difficulty recalling. The feeling of not being believed can trigger memories of being interrogated and tortured and being told *that's not true. We don't believe you. There's more you're not saying.*"

In both the United States and United Kingdom, asylum interviewers use the technique of repeating a question at various intervals to catch an inconsistency. On hearing the same question, most would believe they've said something wrong, or that their answer wasn't enough. Often, people alter their answer to be helpful. They elaborate, inconsistently. Most human conversation is inconsistent, and inexact. This is how the trap works. It takes discipline to repeat an answer again and again, in the precise way you said it before. For torture survivors, fear makes consistency even less likely. They fall back on a survival tactic from home: if your interrogator keeps asking the same question, he wants to hear something else.

One imagines that children might be spared this kind of questioning. They're not. "A child won't tell you anything about themselves right away," says Arulanantham. "It takes time to learn, to be comfortable describing what's happening to them." So, they're stunned into silence.

In the initial screening interview, applicants are often told to keep their answers short, that they will have a chance to speak more later. Sometimes the interviewer fails to ask a follow-up question to a puzzling initial answer, so the Home Office "finds" a discrepancy.

"What were the aims of this political party?" the interviewer asks during the screening.

"The aim is to get justice," says the asylum seeker, remembering to keep it short. The interviewer will move on without warning or exploratory questions. The asylum seeker isn't given a chance to explain.

In a later interview, he might elaborate on the three aims of the party. Someone else will read the transcripts and call this mismatch a discrepancy. It's impossible to know which details are too crucial to leave out in that first interview. And confusing matters further, screening interviewers don't signal when they're about to move on from a topic. No one says, "Is there anything else you want to say now before we move on?"

In such a hostile environment, there's little room for nuances like cultural shame around rape and homosexuality. Many rape victims don't want to disclose to men. And LGBT asylum seekers take months to admit that their sexuality is the reason they ran. Only recently has the court of human rights declared that late disclosure is normal and should not be taken as a contradiction. "Even when they do understand the seriousness of disclosing everything, it's not possible for them," says Dr. Robjant. When they finally do confess, it is a huge milestone, an act of trust. To the asylum officer, it is nothing. The leap of faith is met with a cold response.

"A woman talks of three men raping her and starts crying," says Dr. Robjant. "If the first response is, *You just said there were four men in the room. Were you raped by only three of them?* she is shocked. She expected some emotional parity." And, of course, asylum seekers are often frightened of authority. "If your whole life your people have been bullied and tortured by authorities, the Home Office interview is terrifying. You're told they won't harm you. It's a nice building. But maybe the place you were tortured was nice too. We say, *Of course you won't be tortured by the British authority*, but how would they know that?"

On occasion, victims give false information for reasons we can't understand. In trafficking cases, they are taken across borders, given false documents. They've been dragged into slavery under threat of death by traffickers who seem omniscient and powerful, who have access to their families, even their children, back home. Can they be expected to reveal a name, a secret route? They have endured rituals, spiritual abuse, oaths, and clever manipulations. Some are tattooed as reminders of what happened. In one case, Dr. Robjant tells me, a woman was told that if she broke her oath and told her story, her heart would race, she would grow hot and sweaty, and she'd have memories of the trafficker she was betraying. That was how she would know she was about to die. This woman struggled to tell her story because each time she did, the trafficker's prediction came true, because he had taken the symptoms of PTSD and turned them into omens of death. The traffickers say, "If you tell that story, I'll find your children. And no one will believe you." Often, they're right.

Meanwhile, the asylum officers' country knowledge is patchy at best. Dr. Robjant tells me about a lesbian woman from Uganda whose stories of abuse were believed, all except for the last. She left Uganda because she was subjected to reparative rape—a well-documented practice. In her rejection letter they wrote that it was inconceivable for her rapists to believe that they could make her straight by raping her. And so, her entire story was disbelieved.

I met Josh later that summer in his mother's French village. He had an easy smile, a handsome face. He'd gained weight from the lithium. He chatted about exercise and music. One morning I made Persian tomato-egg scramble. For weeks after that, it was all he wanted to eat.

"He seems like a perfectly charming person," I said later to Sam.

"He *is* a perfectly charming person," he said, shoulders tensing.

"I need to get back to work," I said. How did Sheldon fight apartheid with all this noise?

Now and then, we forgot Josh's troubles. He would play us some new music, or clean the kitchen after a meal, or sit with Sam out on the balcony, small coffees in their hands, two ordinary brothers on an ordinary summer afternoon. Sometimes, Josh lashed out: when Sam scolded him for his slapdash dish washing, or when Flo and Sheldon refused to buy him entry into some absurd healing program. Each of these outbursts sent Sheldon quietly to his corner to grieve. It pained me to watch this dignified, kind man brought low—this good father who spent his youth battling injustice, his old age teaching humanitarian logic, who read every article we recommended, who looked up each child's interests and asked informed questions. That he wounded Sheldon, when some grew up without fathers, made Josh unreadable to me.

Josh's search for meaning, for a faith, was agony for his family to watch. He looked up therapies, meditations, drugs. He followed Hari Krishnas, rapt as they explained their philosophy, and came home gushing about new roads suddenly lit up and beckoning. He wanted to understand his Jewishness. Maybe that was the way to be free of the turmoil, to devote himself to his grandparents' faith. He kept asking for money, though he never looked for work.

It didn't take long for me to decide that Josh wasn't sick, but grifting. I knew the kind of nightmares that kept him awake: dark, itchy tentacles you want to rip out of your brain with your nails. I also understood the temptation to manipulate besotted parents; that's near universal. And the drudgery of trying for uniqueness with two formidable brothers up ahead; I got that too. But all this was rational. The cure wasn't therapy; it was work. Just hard, exhausting, meaningful work. "Josh isn't sick," I said to Sam, "and it's not about genetics or my fears for our baby. He's a privileged white boy. Safety nets beneath his safety nets."

I thought: these beloved children of successful parents, they can never do wrong, are never allowed to suffer. Not just consequences, but everyday discipline, too, the kind that toughens you, sculpts you, so you can fit and function in your slot.

"What do you want them to do, Dina?" Sam said. "He's their child. You'll understand in December when the baby comes."

No, I won't, I thought. *I'm going to make my baby toil until her back is strong and her skin is thick.* "How about tough love?" I shot back. "Show him the family loves him, but this bullshit won't work. Josh has talent! Why can't we get him a job or a project to work on?"

"Dina, you're new to this," said Sam. "We've tried. We've tried everything."

I started to wonder what would happen to someone like Josh in Iran, with the revolutionary guard in charge. How much detritus could a family sweep under a middle-class rug? I don't know what the Islamic Republic does for the mentally ill, but this was a coddled boy misbehaving. I was certain that no Iranian doctor would believe him, or tolerate such indulgent self-diagnoses. One or two bouts of serious misbehavior, and he'd be put to work, the kind that numbs mental itches. But I didn't say such things aloud, not in front of Sam, until years later.

————

Many refugees draw suspicion by fumbling over dates. Not everyone has a birth certificate, or looks at a calendar each morning. A day in a foreign land will turn up a thousand strange things. "A common consistency problem is the Persian calendar," says Natasha Tsangarides, senior policy advisor at Freedom from Torture in London.

When my family landed in Dubai from Iran, the first leg of our asylum journey, we calculated my Western birthday. I was nine years old and my birthday was in *Ordibehesht*, the second month, which roughly equaled May, the fifth month. I scrutinized my mother's calendar and converted the date. But here was a confusion that frustrated us. In the Persian solar calendar, the leap day is added on March 20, just before the equinox. In the Gregorian calendar, it is added on February 29. So, the leap day adjustment happens twenty days later in Iran than it does in the West. What does that mean for people born between March 1 and March 20? Every leap year, they have a different birthday in the Gregorian calendar. They must translate their birthday from a calendar *of the year they were born*. If they check this year's calendar, they could be off by a day.

It strikes me as ironic that those who bother to recheck the calendar year after year (thus creating a discrepancy) are the diligent ones. Others would simply choose a date once and be consistent. Without a good interpreter, the precise would be dismissed as liars. Another irony is that the Persian calendar is the most accurate solar calendar in use today, each year beginning at the precise moment of equinox rather than at midnight, off by only one second a year, while the Gregorian is off by twenty-seven seconds—but let's not quibble about merit, culture, or who invented math.

Do asylum officers know about the calendars? Several lawyers laughed at the question. "Discrepant dates are common," said Tsangarides. "They use that one inconsistency to throw out all credibility." Want to know what else counts as an inconsistency, they ask me? Sit down.

In Kenya a husband has a religious conversion. He tells his wife that she will soon be cut, along with their daughters. Female genital mutilation, or FGM, is common in Kenya and the wife understands the risks. She tries to change his mind. "This is going to happen," he says. "You should accept it." She knows that sometimes people arrive in the night to perform FGM. She has seen women who resisted, whose thighs are a patchwork of scars. She runs.

In London she finds a charity connected to doctors, lawyers, and survivors. There is no mark on the wife's body showing attempted FGM—the charity workers believe her. But Dr. Elizabeth Clark tells me that asylum workers often disbelieve incomplete FGM. A recent patient fought so much that the mutilation didn't complete, but she had cuts. Clark had to write a medical report testifying to the possibility of FGM, but the authorities didn't understand the 1999 Istanbul Protocol: of the five levels of corroboration ranging from "not consistent" to "diagnostic," hardly anyone uses diagnostic; doctors don't work in absolutes. A cut clitoris with labia sewn shut is "diagnostic" of FGM. But scars from metal bars can only ever be the fourth level, "highly consistent" of torture. Asylum officers take that as reason to doubt, applying a standard of certainty far higher than legally allowed. Who is to say what cuts on upper thighs mean? Those who've worked in Kenya know that a woman in such circumstances very likely got those cuts in an FGM struggle. Are we to punish her because she didn't let them finish the job?

Each culture has their own ideas of what a "real" victim sounds like. Does she cry? Does she dissociate? "In some cultures, people don't answer immediately on the point of the question like we do in English countries," says Dr. Cohen. "In Turkey and Iran, it's more formal. A number of sentences for setting scene, some gathering of thoughts, then an answer. If you are interrupted before you arrive at your answer, you can seem evasive." As an Iranian, I know just what Dr. Cohen is talking about. You can't interrupt an Iranian in the middle of a story, especially an important story. If you do so with an older person, you will lose their trust and respect. They will tell the story meagerly, through gritted teeth. "Iranians have an enormous amount of time to tell a story," said the Dutch asylum lawyer Marq Wijngaarden, whom I interviewed for my previous book. "They'll never answer a question with yes or no. It'll always be a story." Iran is a country of double meanings.

Just as grief performance is shaped by culture, so is all storytelling. But it is also singular. Stories worth telling are created by our relationship with culture—they are strange, unrepeatable. That's what makes them worth telling. According to Dr. Cohen, the U.K. Home Office claims to discount medical opinion only when there's a credibility issue in another part of the story—but who designates an unfamiliar detail a "credibility issue"? Is it someone with global knowledge and understanding? With a love of strange stories? With appreciation for the vastness of the world? Or someone with a checklist? Life is full of singular events; a particular baffling story (like KV's) might happen one time, but one-time stories happen all the time.

A young Mungiki woman from Kenya came to one of the doctors that I interviewed. Her attackers had tied something around her clitoris and pulled. The pain was so excruciating, she kicked and fought until she was free. Then she ran. After that, she didn't look at her body again. She was too afraid to find some unthinkable horror. For years as she healed, she bathed and dressed without looking. She never used a mirror. She avoided sexual contact and all medical examinations. She felt deformed, and removed herself from her body. When her hearing date approached and she finally allowed a brief exam, the doctor gave her good news: she had gotten away in time. But now she had another problem. After all that strange behavior, and given that she still had a clitoris, would that English asylum officer believe her story?

In 2012, before joining Freedom from Torture, when she was working for Medical Justice, Natasha Tsangarides made a Home Office subject access request on behalf of a client. She paid the ten pounds and expected to receive a heavily redacted file of interview notes and a reason for rejection. The Home Office accidentally sent a file without the usual black marks covering the page. The annotations revealed an interviewer so hostile, he heard nothing of the man's fear and misery, or his desperation to return home. *How stupid is this guy?* he wrote. When the man wept, the interviewer wrote: *App is crying. For 1 minute. LOSER.* The asylum seeker tried to explain his tears: "I think about my wife and children." The officer wrote, *You wouldn't have to, if you just went back to SLA.*

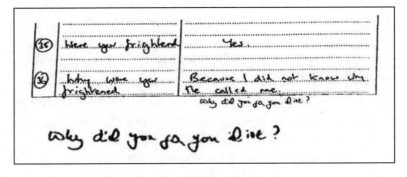

Why did you go, you idiot?

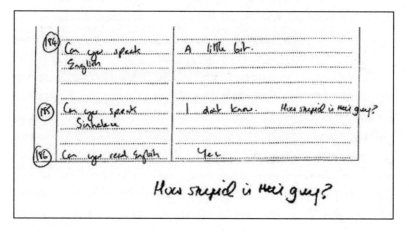

How stupid is this guy?

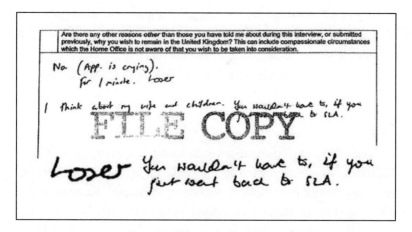

Loser.
You wouldn't have to, if you just went back to SLA [Sri Lanka].

Tsangarides wrote a report about it for Medical Justice, called *The Second Torture*. Nothing changed. This callous, inhumane culture was deliberately created. It is rewarded. In lunch rooms across Europe, asylum officers compete to catch out the tiniest inconsistencies, inventing codes and rules of thumb. There are quotas.

According to the American Psychological Association, "Research has consistently shown that people's ability to detect lies is no more accurate than chance, or flipping a coin. This finding holds across all types of people—students, psychologists, judges, job interviewers and law enforcement personnel." Former FBI agent Joe Navarro said that this was the conclusion of "every study conducted since 1986," adding that "while it is true that a very few people are better at detecting deception than others, they are barely above chance . . . Unfortunately, many people have come along and declared themselves deception experts over the years and that has influenced professionals and society in significant ways. I have listened to jurors post-trial comment that they thought a witness was lying because they had 'heard somewhere that if you touch your nose you are lying.' . . . there is no single behavior indicative of deception." Even interrogators trained in micro facial expressions don't reach much higher than 60 percent accuracy.

Yet asylum caseworkers have been known to say, "I can know by looking in their eyes." What do they see? Class signals. Marks of a good education. Western politeness. Our gatekeepers carry these biases into the interview.

The catch-out culture can affect the work of interpreters too. Narges Kakalia, a New York asylum attorney, told me about a Christian minister from Pakistan whose first language was Punjabi. He spoke it in a dialect specific to Punjabi Christians, but his interview was in Urdu, the national language of Pakistan, conducted through a telephone interpreter. When the minister struggled for a word or two, the interpreter interrupted (though his sole job was to interpret). "He's not a native speaker," the interpreter told the officer. "He doesn't speak the national language natively." Kakalia was appalled. "Already there was the presumption that he was lying. They saw Pakistan as a monolith without understanding the nuances." Then, the client began speaking of being apprehended by Daesh. It became clear to Kakalia that neither the interpreter nor the officer knew that Daesh is ISIS. "I had to stop and explain that he's talking about ISIS. They asked, "Why isn't he calling it ISIS?" I had to say, "Because ISIS is an English acronym."

An asylum seeker, "Joy," recounted an interpreter who spoke so little of her language that his translation no longer matched her story. When her lawyer tried to send a corrected version, she was dismissed. Even Joy's birthday didn't match, but her birth certificate was rejected as proof that the interpreter had translated everything wrong. Joy's lawyer asked, "Why did you tell the Home Office one thing and me another?"

"Even if you woke me from a deep sleep," said Joy, "and asked me there and then, I would say what I said to you before . . . it's the truth. It's the only story I have ever told anyone."

Because of the discrepancy, she was sent to detention.

———

For long patches of time, Josh disappeared from my orbit. We moved to London. Elena was born, a beautiful, healthy girl. We threw ourselves into domestic life, and our writing.

Our first year of parenthood was a pitiless slog. One day, as I was leaving for a job interview, Sam slipped a disc. His ex-wife ran to our rescue, baby strapped to her chest, as I pumped my breasts in an empty classroom. That year, both Sam and I were hospitalized. Josh was in and out of the country, on and off his meds. Because talk of him spiked my anxiety, Sam hid his calls from me. Once, on a long drive with Elena, Josh called Sam every five minutes for an hour, frantic, nonsensical, and Sam calmed him. That night, I was tempted to block Josh from Sam's phone. Instead, I changed the contact name to HMRC, the U.K. tax authority, then, ashamed (*Why wouldn't he answer that?*), I changed it back. Sometimes Josh tried on new accents. Suddenly he was Scottish or Cockney. It mattered little; I had never understood him.

Why didn't Josh try to save himself with work, rather than snake oil? I'd spent all my life battling anxiety, OCD, tics, nightmares. My response was to neurotically, religiously *try*. Why was Josh giving up? He had real artistic talent, an adoring, capable family, passports from France, England, and the U.S., a degree from a terrific university. The passports alone made it impossible for me to tolerate a nanosecond of complaining, a single bill dropped at his mother's door, a single drinks tab he walked away from. I had cruel thoughts involving refugee camps for soft white boys, or Iranian solutions to this privileged nonsense. *Wish I could schedule tea with the crankiest mullah in Isfahan.* Discipline imposed by a strong hand, I believed, was what Josh needed. Nothing else. I had no patience for Ilan's dogged handholding, or Sam's coddling voice on the phone, his insistence that Josh's problems went too deep. Josh was smart, competent, charming, capable of guile and manipulation. Now and then, deep in a conversation about a book or a movie, I forgot that Josh was troubled. *Look, everyone,* I wanted to shout, *a clever, engaging person. Maybe the biggest gift we can give him is to expect more.* His doctors, too, warned his family not to enable him. The trouble was, Flo loved him too much. He was her baby. I get that now. But then—

"Imagine if it was Elena," Sam kept telling me. And often I closed my eyes and tried. It was too hard to sit still and allow the heartbreak to take hold, to imagine my baby so desperate, so cunning, so lost, her little chin trembling, her sticky hands asking for something. I, who can't even allow this child to finish a five-minute time-out, who looks away when she strikes me, I'd never have the strength to follow the doctors' advice to hold strong, to say "no" to enabling.

What was Josh searching for? What spiritual answers did he crave? After a bout in France, he called his parents and begged them to participate in a performance therapy called Constellations, a program based on the idea that all our decisions, successes and failures, are rooted in our family's past, in traumas and joys that we've inherited. Nothing stands on its own, and we unlock the links between our life and our inherited history by role-playing certain scenarios. Josh had found the program in rural French artistic communities, and believed it held the answers. The family saw it as another desperate grab, one that would cost money and lay blame at their feet. They rejected it kindly. I rolled my eyes so far into the back of my head, I had to put Elena down. "Somebody get that boy a job," I said. "If this was Iran—"

"Yes," said Sam. "*We know* what would happen in Iran."

"Sometimes the Iranian way is better, Sam. It's not always worse."

He glared. Meanwhile, Josh tried to sell Constellations to the family. When they refused, he showered them with rage. Sheldon mourned, and this deepened my anger. Who wouldn't want to please a father who's so eagerly waiting for you to take a single step forward? Sometimes when I published essays, Sheldon texted to say they were clever, that we would discuss them at dinner. This would light my duskiest days. *Didn't Josh see what he had?*

I found a confidant in his sister, Anna, the third-born whose philosophy was closest to mine. Despite pangs of pity, she was having none of Josh's antics, and believed in the doctor's recommendations that we hold a tough line on money, and on enabling his fantasies. "Why can't someone just take his passport?" I said. Because, Ilan explained, that's not legal, and Josh knows exactly how to enforce his rights. When feeling confrontational, I'd respond that that was proof he could handle himself in the world; that, demons aside, if left alone, he'd find his way, even thrive. When I said such things, the family looked at me as if I was in the wrong story, misunderstanding everything. And maybe I was.

To me, Josh was unintelligible, the ultimate bad glossolalist, his act too raw. He sought out and parroted the faithful and the dogmatic, trying to diagnose himself with medical and psychological nonsense, a vocalization of familiar syllable patterns that, though meaningless, were tragic to witness. Do glossolalists sometimes try on other accents? Scientists have shown that their intonations, syllable patterns, and pronunciation are consistent with their own native tongue. So maybe Josh (in Cockney or Scottish) was more aware of the performance than most. Once, as the family talked, eager to include him, he quietly recorded us on his phone. What did he plan to do with that recording? Play it over and over, pressing his earphones as he analyzed it for loyalty, betrayal, maybe for arrangements of words, the intellectual bundles that gave his Oxford brothers their power? Sam and Ilan were so easily believed, so welcome. On such nights, when Josh lashed out and blamed his brothers for their advantage, Sam cooked in grave silence, his thoughts far away, and it took two or three tries to pass him a dishtowel or ask for a high pot.

Josh vanished and returned, creating messy dramas. Sometimes he was kind, funny, his family basking in the warmth of his good days. Still, he made me feel always a little conned.

I bought an apartment in North London. We moved. We were robbed. Elena spoke in a pretty little English accent. We made an office space. Sam taught himself carpentry. He designed and built an elaborate treehouse for Elena, two trees shooting up through its roof. He built a broom shed, a laundry nook. For long hours, he measured and drilled in silence, mourning his father's health, a dazzling light now fading. I traveled to refugee camps and wrote a book. For a time, we were able to forget Josh's misery—or maybe the truth is that I left Sam alone in it.

———

Few instincts are less ignorable than one that you're being deceived. For refugees in the U.S. and Europe, legal aid and expert opinion are scant and variable. In America, without massive charities like the Helen Bamber Foundation, Freedom from Torture, and Medical Justice footing the bill, medical reports require private funds. And even when it's available, each judge weighs expert opinion differently.

This variability in judicial standards is one of the greatest flaws of the American asylum system. Why should the weight of any kind of evidence vary by judge? Should one's fate depend on the compassion or politics of the judge one is assigned? Should it vary by administration? "Like cases aren't treated alike," says Arulanantham, the ACLU lawyer who gave me a tutorial on refugee law, the one with the classic Central American example. "We need to guarantee people legal representation and make immigration judges structurally independent. Those are big fixes. Asylum grant rates go up and down based on who the attorney general is. That's not just at the judge level but at the screening stage. The number of people found to have credible fear and entitled to be seen by a judge depends on political pressure." Spare a thought for the Refugee Convention—if the definition of a refugee is fixed, it shouldn't alter by administration.

What if one of the fussy grandmothers from my village in Iran had to run for her life? A functionally illiterate Iranian villager from another era, with undiagnosed autism and a head full of superstition, is unreadable to an American. What if she gets an officer who's never known a rural grandmother? That officer's empathy shouldn't matter, but it does. She won't know what she said wrong. These women don't look at calendars, they look at the moon. They can't fire off the names of the last three presidents. They talk in riddles. I don't know a single one who would seem honest to a Western-born millennial with a two-year degree and a 700-case backlog.

In job listings, caseworkers on both sides of the Atlantic are asked to be detail-oriented and comfortable under pressure. I spoke with a former U.K. Home Office Presenting Officer (HOPO), a British woman of Afghan descent, about how she listened to stories. Her job was to argue cases on behalf of Theresa May's Home Office. She was young, with a law degree and six months of training and shadowing. She described caseworkers so overworked, under-skilled, and badly trained that they were buckling under the intense pressure. They were indeed required to hit targets based on rejections, not acceptances. The Home Office's training and incentive structure was focused entirely on how to reject human rights claims, with no emphasis on humanitarian duty or the Refugee Convention.

Many caseworkers and HOPOs, my anonymous officer told me, are people of color, from migrant, working, and middle-class families, often living in communities with asylum seekers and new refugees. "Having to work on cases that are like my family members', it was difficult. There was a tension." She told me that the more cynical senior decision-makers, older, more conservative officers, often without degrees, are suspicious of stories, facts, or documents that are too similar. "They see these patterns and assume they're false. You can see why all we ever got were rejections." When she saw a bad decision from a caseworker, she'd try to change his mind. But if the caseworker sticks to his decision, it's the HOPO's job to argue the Home Office's case before a judge. "Caseworkers won't withdraw because of their quotas. So, I'd go to court and roll over."

An understanding HOPO and a kind judge may not be enough. For certain kinds of cases that don't go their way, the Home Office will try to appeal every time, regardless of individual details. During this HOPO's tenure, caseworkers were reviewed monthly on various metrics. For meeting their rejection quotas, they were offered a store voucher. For weeks of overtime, a £200 bonus. Some officers were run so ragged they ignored protocols and asked applicants for inappropriate details. One lashed out in a training session. "I was in court more than I should have been," the HOPO told me. "Sometimes I had to prepare four or five cases the day before."

I asked her about her duties as a presenting officer. What was her job? "To draw out the inconsistencies. That's our job. We have to prove they're lying." Despite my shock, she was unequivocal. "No one questioned what our job was: it was to catch inconsistencies. That was our training. Some HOPOs will be very pedantic . . . Oh, you said 6:00 p.m. here and 7:00 p.m. there. If you get a hard judge, they'll love it if you go to town on those tiny discrepancies."

I asked the HOPO if she ever tried to imagine her way into the refugees' stories. It wasn't her job, she said. But it helped to be Middle Eastern. Once an interpreter was speaking the wrong dialect of Arabic. "I could hear the misunderstanding. I had to stop the proceedings.

"I thought I could learn from the inside, but I found myself saying *he's lying, he's lying* . . . I know from where I live that sham marriages are happening. Men from Afghanistan and Pakistan marrying women from Poland, Lithuania, Romania, whatever. There's a whole system. There are accountants, caseworkers, solicitors, landlords. So, when I'm at work and see these individuals, I know what questions to ask. I know they're lying. Many of these guys aren't the brightest. They get stuck in their own web of lies."

The women stumble on their husband's prayer schedule, the name of his mosque. Their wedding photos seem staged—his male friends, none of hers. Rehearsed details but no thought to the religion of future children. "Part of me knows they just want a better life, but part of me is angry that they're abusing the system. And it's very easy to catch them out."

If you can win an intellectual battle, and it's your job to win it, then human instinct will make you try your best. Still, now and then, despite her training, a story roused her imagination and she was transported, the truth of a situation apparent only to her. Once a caseworker refused to believe that a two-year romance could happen in the streets, in cars, leaving no trace, not a single photo, note, or text. "But I know that in Afghanistan, you have to have relationships in secret, because if our parents found out, they'd kill us! For me it's so familiar. To another presenting officer, it's suspect. So, I'd tell them, 'It's completely normal to meet like this.' I'd tell myself, 'At least you were there to provide that nuance. At least they had you instead of some white English person who knew nothing.' That's how I'd comfort myself. 'It's okay that you're working in Home Office.'"

Would an English person have tried to understand Afghani youth culture? Absolutely not, she answered. You'd have to teleport to Afghanistan to understand.

During a moment of silence, she took a breath. "It's not a crime to apply to remain," she said, "but . . . on the ground, that's how it is . . . if my parents had tried to come in this climate, there is no way they'd get any sort of stay. I wouldn't be here."

Other asylum professionals of color were troubled by the obvious preference for white, Westernized refugees, or the call for "meritocracy," when the asylum system is intended for those in danger, regardless of their perceived value. "There's a huge bias for people who look like they belong here," said Narges Kakalia. "When I went for my own green card, I brought stacks and stacks of evidence. I walked in, spoke perfect English. The man asked me one question, stamped my form, and said, 'Welcome to the U.S.' All around me people were sobbing hysterically and speaking other languages. They were asked about their husband's brand of shampoo."

For the well-meaning asylum officers of color, good students who want to do their jobs better than their cynical predecessors and to show they are worthy of their place in Western society, this is a painful dilemma. Over years of working shoulder to shoulder with colleagues who write interview reports peppered with *Loser* and *Go back home*, you worry about something vital changing in your heart, your mind.

"Twenty-something men traveling alone don't get as much sympathy as families," says Haq, the asylum lawyer. "As they say, *your judge is your destiny.* A case that might win in San Francisco may have no chance in Atlanta. I had a case with a family from Nepal. They had several businesses; the wife used to be a model and national athlete. They had a studious son." They were assigned a former criminal court judge whose appointment to immigration court was heavily condemned by progressive lawyers and advocacy groups. "I thought he's going to be the kind of white guy who will say, if I'm benevolent enough to give you permission to stay I want to make sure you belong in this country. He's a racist. That became part of my strategy. I told my clients, this judge will want to grant you asylum if he thinks you deserve it, if you're upstanding people. We have to emphasize your socioeconomic status, that you had a great life in Nepal and wouldn't leave if there wasn't danger." Haq asked them to dress upper class—a suit, a skirt, and blouse—though in America they were working in a car dealership and a nursing home. And it worked. The judge asked the couple about their work, their income. "I've never been in front of a judge who asked for that information," says Haq. "I have a client now who was a vegetable seller in Pakistan, has never been to school. If he had that same judge, I'd be very worried for him."

Haq paused just then. We both sighed. Not wanting to end the call, I told her about a strange quirk: as a new immigrant, I was constantly afraid of looking shabby to Americans. In those early days, classmates taunted me for repeating outfits, for owning only one pair of jeans. At Princeton, I wore skirts and makeup every day. Later, I corrected the other way. I'd take a base pleasure in having them see me in my pajamas. The fancier the witness, the bigger the surge of weird satisfaction—*I win, because I don't care.* Haq laughed. Performing for the Western-born makes us bizarre. Conte, a London refugee, told a story about waiting in a line with other refugees. "English people are passing by," he said. "They'd ask, 'Why on earth are you queueing in this weather?' As though we were mad. But you didn't answer. It was too shaming, too humiliating. We'd all just wait in silence, not replying. Your heart is always in your mouth."

———

Josh disappeared and appeared again, sometimes heavy, chewing his nails and making playlists and helping with dishes (on meds), sometimes gaunt and far too quiet (off meds). He seemed too fragile to approach, but at Anna's fortieth birthday, after two glasses of wine, I asked to see the playlist. I joked that no one would notice if we put on something with dirty lyrics. His face lit up. We giggled as bougie parents in heels chatted politely to the Weeknd's "High for This."

The family, Sam told me, had become camel-like in savoring Josh's good moments. Each had developed a practice of grasping the smallest such offering, fattening it with childhood anecdotes. "I wish you had known him then," said Sam. "He was so funny, so kind."

I tried to practice this, though I didn't have their stores of memories. At Elena's birthday party, we watched as the children whacked a piñata. Standing a little apart, Josh muttered, almost to himself, "Did anyone remember to fill it?" Everyone looked up.

Sam whispered, "You're supposed to *fill it?*" I slapped my forehead.

"Can't you see there's no candy in there?" said Josh. The adults snorted into their palms.

"Okay, a little break!" Sam announced. "Cupcakes in the living room!" Meanwhile the adults scrambled for anything sweet—cooking chocolate, gummy bears left from Halloween.

Josh found a bag of marshmallows. "Open all the bagged stuff," he said. He figured that being showered with loose candy would impress preschoolers. As we scurried around, filling the piñata, Sam and Josh laughed together.

All night, Sam couldn't stop delighting in the memory. "Wasn't it a great idea to open the bags?" he said, smiling as we prepared for sleep. "Funny nobody noticed but Josh . . . good idea, the little marshmallows . . ."

Four months later (or was it the year before?), in the same London flat, we threw Josh a birthday party. I took a photo of him smiling at his lit cake. Then, within an hour, he walked out.

In 2019, the family started inviting me to meetings, a daunting milestone. I sat in on a medical consultation and many kitchen table brainstorms. Soon, talk at every meal transitioned to Josh's illness. I bit my lip through most of it, until one day Sam came running into our apartment and said that Josh had been sectioned, having threatened to kill himself. He said not to worry, though. Josh was in the hospital, and apparently the threat hadn't been credible, something along the lines of

If you're going to cut me off, then I have no choice. The kind of threat one hears in romantic melodramas; not a true intention but a display of intensity. My father's marriage proposal to my mother included a similar threat, so I suppose owing my life to such hysterics may have primed me to discount their reliability as a predictor of actual death.

Sam had Elena when he got the call, so he rushed to the hospital with her in tow. He planned to stay at Ilan's until the situation was re-solved, keeping Elena awake long past her bedtime. I flew into a rage. Sam and I didn't speak for a few days. When we finally did, he said Josh was better, that Josh had made this kind of threat before, tied to money. The doctors, he told me, whispered assurances that it wasn't a credible intention of suicide. One night, I got up at 4:00 a.m. to google what suicidal people say. I didn't do it out of concern—I already knew what I believed—but out of rage.

The family met at Ilan's house to talk options with their cousin David, Josh's friend and a doctor. Sheldon and Flo weren't invited this time; we were discussing Josh's impact on them and how they might be persuaded to follow a strategy. Sheldon had just finished chemother-apy; everyone was terrified for his health. We had all recently heard his warm, gravel voice over the phone, every syllable unsure and mourn-ing, worrying about what Josh might do. The thought angered me. Could Josh not leave his poor parents alone to take care of themselves? Why didn't he appreciate what he had, these parents who had given him a lifetime of love and care?

I was the first to say aloud that I didn't believe. "Don't people try to hide it . . . if it's real . . . so they can carry it out?" I said, using soundbites from suicide websites. "If it's attached to a threat . . . if it's future-focused or focused on some end result . . . isn't that—?"

David nodded. "That's a guideline." He explained that, while it's impossible to write a script for suicide, planning for the future signals a desire to live. As does trying to get something with the threat. It's the ultimate trump card. Anna mentioned the medical advice again. The

NHS doctors and nurses seemed unconcerned. I backed her up—tough love was what Josh needed, not coddling. The parents shouldn't enable threats by giving him money or a place to stay.

"So, what do you suggest, Dina?" snapped Ilan. "Should we let him sleep on the street?"

"That's not what I said! I think he's capable—"

"Dina, Josh has a mental illness," said Ilan. "It's a real thing. It's not an act."

"Well," I muttered under my breath. "He seems perfectly capable—" I didn't finish. *Of taking huge logistical steps for stuff he wants.* Anna shot me a weak "we're all just tense" smile.

"Any time someone threatens suicide, you have to take it seriously," Sam's aunt said.

I wanted to say, *Well, in that case, anyone could just—*

I stopped, ashamed in front of myself. "Of course," I muttered. Across the table, Anna breathed out. Someone asked why they kept sending him home instead of to a real doctor.

"It's incredibly delicate," said David. He began explaining strategies that didn't require us to arrive at some definite stance on the threats. No one gets to decide that, he said, because only one person knows. And so, we go forth in all seriousness and we believe.

I shrank back, and for the next few days, Sam and I were silent. *He's going to leave me,* I thought. *Or I'll leave him.* One morning in the shower, I found a stress hive on my thigh. My best friend met me at our favorite wine bar for burrata and smoky reds. She asked me if Sam was close to finishing his novel. I shook my head; he wouldn't let it go till every word was perfect. Besides, he was spending all his time on Josh, sometimes secretly, hiding his phone from me.

"Of all the things that could break us," I said, "I'd never have guessed his baby brother."

6.

To be fair, we took long breaks from Josh's troubles. In October 2015, seven months pregnant in a bureaucratic and stern U.K. national health system, I developed a whole new (but completely the same) obsession: *Who gets the benefit of the doubt on the exam table?*

As a girl, my mother had told me not to worry about giving birth. "In our family we have C-sections." The trouble was that in 2010s London a dogmatic "normal birth" culture prevailed, and midwives were the first point of call. I'd heard stories of women having their labor pains trivialized or dismissed, and I wanted a surgeon. So, since I had no birth plan and a lifelong fear of labor, I decided to dabble in some medical theater. My reasoning went like this:

As with all medical innovations, C-sections were invented to answer a need, and so must be better for some. Do you hear anyone insisting we go back to medieval ways of treating dog bites or broken bones? The nearly universal Western dismissal of C-sections as a lesser outcome strikes me as suspicious, accustomed as I am to hearing the propogandist's whisper in accepted wisdoms, particularly when wealthy or knowledgeable insiders quietly choose the opposite. Gynecologists recommend vaginal birth to their patients while quietly scheduling cesareans for themselves, without medical justification, at far higher rates. Even if something is best in the aggregate, individual factors may alter a crucial variable. I didn't want to risk the fecal incontinence rate that the NHS finds "acceptable." For me, worst case data is more relevant than aggregate data. A patient can summon disaster by believing in its inevitability, with fear and tension. I know my body's limits. I was raised by an OB-GYN who had C-sections.

Other arguments, too, compelled me. Globalization means that half-Viking men like Sam can impregnate tiny Iranian women, and after a few generations, the cesarean makes itself necessary. If the procedure enables enough big-headed babies and small-hipped women to survive childbirths that might otherwise have killed them, those traits (big heads, small hips) pass on, making "un-survivable" births much more common. That's enough to frighten some of us into failure: I don't want to enter a Darwinian cage-match with my pampered twenty-first-century birth canal. Besides, why should only rich women have access to innovation, while the rest of us are pacified with natural-living memes, lest we demand equal time from the most capable doctors—the ones who can unbreech a baby with one hand and know which needle to stab into my dying heart three seconds before I flatline?

So, here was my problem: I'm not rich, and the National Health System only allows elective cesareans for women who have a physical or clear psychological need for one.

"You can't just demand a surgery," said Sam. "My brother's spent his whole life having his *actual* psychological needs dismissed by the NHS. It doesn't work this way."

"It's a bureaucracy, like an asylum interview," I said. "You give them what they want for their tick boxes." Sam's eyes grew wide. "What?" I shrugged. "This is *my* normal."

Now I had to spend the final four months of my pregnancy convincing a professional that I had a medical-grade fear of vaginal birth. It was time to perform my fear, an act that, though true, felt like a lie.

It also felt mean-spirited, because my opponent was Astrid, a sweet, doting, grandmotherly midwife who kept rubbing my palm. Performing my fear for Astrid, learning the tongues of frightened straight-to-cesarean mothers, was humiliating and technically difficult. But I needed her to see my most alarming hysteria—my direct and literal fear from the womb—and either to convince me that I could give vaginal birth, or sign me up for a section.

———

Last year I called up Adam, an old college friend who's now an emergency physician, to talk about pain performance. "As an ER doctor, you pretty much expect people to try to fool you," Adam joked, his playful dad grin and jaunty Princeton cap belying the sheer ghastliness of his days. "It's like wearing clown shoes in a minefield."

Lately, I've been reconnecting with the quietly extraordinary classmates I should have befriended in college, the tribe of skeptical misfits and nerdlings in plain sight. Every night during our senior year, I greeted Adam in the Tower club dinner line. I was twenty-one and already in a suit jacket and fake pearls. Adam was witty, kind, into hard sciences, and conversant in social issues. As a Jewish student, he was prone to conversion targeting by baby evangelicals. And he was one of twenty people at whose table I felt comfortable.

Here's a story that vined and bloomed outside my field of vision: now and then, when Adam was missing from the dining room, he was visiting his father in prison. I never knew of his routine, or that his father was sick; if I had, I might have told him that I've visited my father in prison, too, and that mine was an addict, and often ill. Like Adam, I was eight when my father was locked away. I might have told Adam about the day I was carried on the back of a moral police officer's motorcycle, across a prison yard, to a strange man, sheared bald, smiling broadly in white pajamas. I asked the guard who that was. He said, "Don't you recognize your Baba?" I didn't. My Baba had lustrous hair;

he was known for it. Who was this stranger? Getting off the motorbike, I felt desperately lonely and confused. Now, I think, what if on that same day across the globe, Adam was visiting his father, too?

At some point in our last semester of college, Adam would have told his father that he was accepted to medical school. His father would have chuckled; with each bout of illness, he was offered a cursory glance and kicked out of the ER. After every begrudging doctor visit, the clear but unspoken attitude was: *You're a criminal. You are wasting my time and the state's money.* I imagine that after he learned of Adam's medical school acceptance, his father advised Adam to listen to the patients nobody believes, because don't they, too, have bodies that can break down?

One day, while Adam was in medical school, he received news that his father had died of heart disease, the culmination of symptoms he struggled to prove for two decades in prison. Adam became an ER physician. The day he witnessed his first clumsy pain performance, all he could think of was his father. Now a man sat on an exam table, his eyes imploring. Adam knew this stranger's pain was real. Its manifestation, though, was so laden with need, motive, and circumstance. He thought, *These poor people, how the hell are they supposed to get treatment?*

Over time, Adam formed a soft spot for the prisoners who were shuffled in and out of the ER. They would arrive in their orange jumpsuits, shackles on their arms and legs, flanked by two guards. It wasn't rare for a guard to make a derisive or dismissive comment right in front of them, ignoring every wince and dropped gaze. "This piece of shit just wants a turkey sandwich," they'd say, or "Don't waste too much time, doc," or "Sorry we're taking up a bed." Adam would rush to these cases, and he'd give them real time. Though it wasn't in his nature to scold the guards, he did his best to soften the shame now creasing his patient's face. Almost every prisoner that Adam treated over the years was meek, appreciative—movingly so.

The patients wanted Adam to know that they understood the

secondary gains of an ER visit. You get a few hours of jail. You get to sit in a soft bed, eat a turkey sandwich. You get to ride in a car and see free people. But these small comforts weren't the reason they had come.

One day, a forty-year-old prisoner, incarcerated for something small and nonviolent, came in with a terrible cough. "I've brought him in ten times for this," said the guard, "it's always bullshit." ER records called the man *a histrionic patient*. Despite no workup, no blood work, and a year since his last chest X-ray, the doctors kept writing: *no findings to support complaints*. If the patient is overreacting, Adam asked, then why did the guard bring him back? "He has a fever this time," said the guard. "The jail thermometer's shitty, probably broken."

The guard's naked cynicism reminded Adam that the job requires an almost daily sensory recalibration. Too much exposure and you become desensitized to pain; your radar falls out of whack. It's an age-old problem; every pain is only truly felt by one person. We are programmed to intuit our own suffering, to salve our own wounds. "To have great pain is to have certainty," writes Elaine Scarry in *The Body in Pain*, "to hear that another person has pain is to have doubt."

Adam listened to the man's lungs. When he was finished, the patient muttered something strange. "Thanks for listening to my lungs."

"Don't we always listen to your lungs?" asked Adam.

"Nobody actually listened before," he said. "You were listening."

Adam did a full workup with an ache in his chest, because he had already heard what the X-rays would show: the worst pneumonia of his career, a mass, and multifocal opacities covering all the lung fields. The man had stage IV cancer, and little could be done for him now. At the very least, Adam got to talk to him for a long time, not about the disease that would kill him a year later, but about being believed. What was the man in for? Adam asked. Taxes.

I don't know what else the two men said to each other. I imagine Adam spoke of fate, of the unpredictability of life and our most vital outcomes; maybe he hinted about God's hand in things. The truth was, though, that the man was in jail at the wrong moment for his cancer. When the warning signs came, he was wearing an orange jumpsuit.

In our forties now, Adam and I laugh about our college days over Zoom. I tell him about my prenatal theater, Josh's struggle to see a doctor. He tells me about the ER minefield. People come in for all kinds of secondary reasons, besides the apparent emergency: a dose of painkiller, narcotics for a party, a doctor's note. Frequent fliers know every nurse, doctor, and PA by name. Some are homeless, desperate to escape the cold, to be fed; they come in with a new ailment daily. A jaded fifth-year intern will say, "Oh that's just Lenny. Give him his sandwich and send him along." To that, Adam says, "Let me tell you about the day the last ten Lennys died." There is always the day when the frequent flier dies. When the true warning signs come, the frequent flier knows just where to go. But after all those turkey sandwiches, he is rarely believed. It's a classic wolf cry. At the end of the story, Adam reminds his interns, the wolf always comes.

Adam tells me about a sweet lady, partially blind, who came in once a week. "Every doctor's seen her fifty times. ER doctors are cynical schmucks. We knew ninety-nine percent of her visits were for nothing. But you don't want to miss the one time it's something. Clown shoes . . . " He glanced down at his hands. "We knew her," he says, "and one day she died."

Who is hardest to believe, I ask Adam, and who does most of the disbelieving?

Of countless medical biases he's seen, Adam describes three notable ones: the Google bias (used to dismiss teens and the elderly), the poverty bias (used disproportionately against poor people of color), and the you-*should*-be-healthy bias (a quick way to disbelieve women).

"Two weeks ago," Adam tells me, "a precocious fourteen-year-old comes in with appendicitis." The boy arrived in urgent care vomiting, with extreme belly pain. He told the nurse, *I have appendicitis*, explaining that the pain began in his umbilicus (he used that word), then moved to his right hip, and that, in the car, the road bumps gave him sharp aches. "A first-year med student knows this is a textbook presentation of appendicitis." The nurse chuckled. "The patient's been googling!" She told him it was probably gastroenteritis and gave him food and drink, delaying his surgery by three hours. Eventually, the boy ended up in the ER, but the appendix might have burst while he was waiting for surgery, and because of his full stomach, he might have vomited, aspirated, and ended up on a ventilator in the ICU for a month.

The more seasoned the medical professional, I've noticed, the less frequent their eye-rolling over patients who research. Maybe because that knowledge isn't threatening; they don't need to distinguish their medical degree from Google results. "But nurse practitioners don't have even ten percent of a physician's training," says Adam. "They don't know what they don't know." The most effective mid-levels understand that and guard for blind spots. Adam says his best PA is cautious. "He says, Doc, eyes are super risky. Can you back me up? That's how it should be. I trust him because I know he'll come talk to me the second anything gets confusing."

The poverty bias happens when patients without health insurance or access to primary care use the ER disproportionately. They come in for ailments that they understand aren't emergencies, because the ER is the only place that will see them. They become frequent fliers and quickly labeled non-serious patients, rushed through the system with the assumption that they're "in for bullshit." Adam tells me about a hypochondriac who's often in his ER. One day, he arrived in tears and was assigned to one of the more compassionate PAs. A triage note warning of dramatics left the PA unconvinced. "Either this guy is a huge pussy," he told Adam, "or this time it's an aortic dissection," a deadly tear in a main artery.

Adam went in to see the patient. "Here was this 250-pound burly guy crying like someone knocked over his ice cream. And he was sweating!" As a resident, Adam trained under Amal Mattu, a world-famous physician and author of many books on emergency medicine. "If one of us ever came out saying 'this is just another whatever,' he'd sit you down for a thirty-minute chat. He'd say: Nope. You're going to kill someone." Dr. Mattu used to say: you can fake a lot of things, but you can't fake sweating. If a patient is sweating, you better be sweating.

Like many poor patients, the burly frequent flier had often used the ER as primary care; this time, though, he did have an aortic dissection. He received a bypass and a graft. Later, the PA confided in Adam. "He was so dramatic in there. And he's in here *a lot*, and was being so loud. The triage report wasn't good." The PA sighed. "I guess he wasn't a pussy."

When he'd recovered, the patient returned to deliver Adam and the PA some bone-crushing hugs. Sometimes, drama (the tears, the hugs) is just a part of someone's singular nature.

The first piece of data a doctor or PA receives isn't a patient's symptoms, or whether they're sweating or crying. The first item that pops up on a triage note is the number of visits that year: if they've been to the ER twenty times and never admitted, that's bad. This first fact shapes a caregiver's judgment; it might anchor an opinion, even before they enter the room. "Every medical record has bias. This guy, his triage note said 'very dramatic' but that doesn't reduce his chance of a catastrophic illness. I do a lot of medical malpractice reviews. If a triage note says 'very dramatic' and the patient dies, that's a settlement. You won't recover from that in court."

A court judgment, though, isn't Adam's worst fear. He tells me about the third bias.

Meredith shouldn't be sick. At thirty-three, she's active, healthy, with no medications or history of serious illness. "People like her," says Adam, "they have trouble convincing even seasoned doctors that they're sick." It's easier to believe that they're hypochondriacs, hysterical, or stressed out. But Meredith had good reason to worry. She had a long family history of breast cancer, and wanted to be tested for the BRCA gene. "You're probably fine," said her doctor. "You would've had cancer by now." When Meredith insisted, though, he agreed to test her.

Meredith tested positive for BRCA. The typical recommendation for women with her diagnosis is a double mastectomy and removal of the ovaries. But Meredith was unmarried, childless. She wanted to date, to be attractive, to fall in love and start a family. She decided, with her oncologist, to wait. "But we're going to be aggressive with the monitoring," he said, outlining a plan that included checkups every three months and imaging every six months.

A few years passed. Meredith was vigilant about her routine. As the pandemic swept across the country, Meredith began to worry about access to health care. She worked, ate well, exercised, and kept healthy. When lockdowns made brisk Atlanta dating schedules a thing of the past, she wondered how much longer she'd hold on to her breasts and ovaries. These parts of her body that she'd hardly thought about before, now seemed by turns luxuries and time bombs.

Meredith threw herself into work, and soon she received an offer for a job near her parents in Colorado. The pandemic seemed a good time to leave a once-bustling Atlanta. A few months before her scheduled move, she woke with breast pain. She went to a university hospital and was assigned to a nurse practitioner at the cancer care ward. The NP read through her chart. "You just had your MRI, your 3D mammogram, ultrasound. All fine." The nurse had a kind smile, a reassuring demeanor. "There were a couple of spots we're monitoring, but totally fine. I'll see you again for the next one, okay?"

Though she liked her NP, Meredith left uneasy. A few days later, she made another appointment, moving up her scheduled check-in by a month. "Your breast pain is probably just nerves about the move!" said the NP, her voice empathetic. "And, hey, your BRCA result. Maybe that's making you nervous?"

"Well, yeah, the BRCA result makes me nervous about the breast pain," said Meredith.

The NP chuckled, patted Meredith's hand. "You're young, healthy, so pretty, look at you! And you have all these years of negative tests. Stop worrying. Come back in three months."

After each previous visit, her nurse's warmth and certainty had given Meredith a few hours of relief from the worry. She nodded, squeezed her nurse's hand. Three months later, she arrived promptly to her scheduled visit. "It's hurting more," she said, before her nurse had a chance to ask.

"Still nervous, huh?" said the nurse. "When you get to Colorado, go to a doctor, okay? Next time, Colorado. Okay?"

In the meantime, Meredith's scheduled imaging fell on a day during her move. She asked if it could be done earlier, before her move, but the nurse reminded her that the staff were dealing with a pandemic, and told her a small delay wouldn't hurt.

Meredith knew that a BRCA-positive woman with unrelenting breast pain should be scanned. The only reason not to investigate is believing that the pain doesn't exist, that it's in her head. "But I'm supposed to be vigilant," Meredith argued. "These are *symptoms*."

As soon as she arrived in Colorado, Meredith had her scans.

She had triple negative breast cancer, the vicious BRCA kind; and it had reached stage IIIB, meaning it had spread just outside her breast tissue, but not yet to distant sites.

What did that nurse hope for, when refusing to test Meredith? That she could freeze her in her unblemished body, just by looking away? Maybe she hoped that this tragic young beauty would move and become another nurse's problem. The nurse had all the information to know that her wishful thinking might delay a young woman's cancer diagnosis, nearly killing her. But who can see a hidden mass of lethal tissue under all that female hysteria? During her chemo sessions, Meredith explained to her new oncologist that her follow-ups in

Atlanta had been with an NP filling in for a doctor. Meredith believed that her caregiver had done her best, and maybe she had. "But you know what?" said Adam. "A doctor wouldn't have done this to her."

Adam had mentioned nursing credentials a few times—I became curious. I know I'm prone to educational elitism. Now, after researching Western immigration policies, I'm wary of racism and sexism disguised as meritocracy. Many nurse practitioners are like me, ambitious women of color who want to use their gifts. Not everyone has the luxury of spending years in medical school. And nurses have done so much heavy lifting during the worst global pandemic in a hundred years. "What's wrong with having another path into a medical career?"

I call more doctors. They rave about "old school" nurses, or "super nurses." Brick-and-mortar nursing programs still produce stellar NPs, but in the last decade, two dangerous trends have emerged: scope creep (nurses being asked to do far more than their training) and degree mills (shoddy online programs speeding up and muddying the credentialing process). Still, I worry about the roots of such talk, all those wealthy white doctors doubting the abilities of underpaid nurses of color.

I call Dr. Natalie Newman, an MD with nearly thirty years of experience in both medicine and institutional racism. "People never think I'm a doctor," she says. "They think I'm housekeeping. They think a Black woman can't be a doctor."

"So, is this a real problem?" I ask. "Or is it classism? Are doctors just being degree snobs?" I remember a kind nurse practitioner at MacDowell who drove me to a pharmacy for my antibiotics. I remember others, like kind aunts, taking time to check out old scars.

"Those are the old school nurses," Dr. Newman says. "No one wants to lose them. But this is a new problem in the last ten years. It's huge, it's real, and it's ubiquitous."

She tells me that when the nurse practitioners under her supervision started making basic mistakes, she looked into their education. The problem cases weren't the experienced Florence Nightingales of old, or even the newly minted ones with solid degrees. These were a new crop of online nurses with barely any clinical hours, many letters after their names, and no understanding of even the most basic medical terms, procedures, or protocols. "If I wanted to become a nurse practitioner now," Adam told me. "I could do it entirely online, at a school with one hundred percent acceptance rate. Then a few days of shadowing, and boom."

Alongside that trend, there's a national movement to increase NP autonomy in primary care to free doctors for more complex specialized work—a push that wouldn't alarm doctors if all the nurses in the national pool were the rigorously trained kind. A study often cited by Dr. Mary Mundinger, a nurse independence advocate, only uses data from brick-and-mortar nurses. Dr. Philip Shaffer, a vocal figure in the debate, showed me several major data flaws in the study, but the biggest one was this: it ignores the sham degrees fast polluting the pool.

Dr. Newman recalls telling a new NP to put in vertical mattress sutures. The NP stared, so Dr. Newman explained, "with the edges everted so the wound doesn't indent." The NP went away confused. Then she decided to fake it. Later when Dr. Newman checked in, she found the skin sutured like a piece of cloth, with the edge tucked in to look neat. Dr. Newman smiled for the patient's sake. "You know what? I'll just do this over." Later, alone with the nurse, she couldn't contain her shock. "It's not fabric! If you tuck in the skin, it'll die and infect!"

In America, the rapid buy-up of medical practices by private equity firms is creating a market for degree mills: programs with no rigor or screening process, run entirely online. These programs barely require clinical work, and nothing beyond shadowing. With a zero rejection rate, they attract the lowest quality students and leave them woefully unprepared for their first day. Then, hospitals run by profit-maximizing businessmen (instead of doctors bound by the Hippocratic Oath) snap up those graduates. Nurse practitioners are cheaper than doctors, but it's impossible for businesspeople to differentiate the excellent ones from those churned out online. As I write this, twenty-eight American states allow NPs full authority to treat and prescribe with no formal supervision. Meanwhile, alarming questions like this one are popping up on mid-level Facebook groups: *I'm a pediatric ICU NP . . . does anyone have primers on pediatric oncology?*

When another patient's oxygen was dropping, Dr. Newman told an NP to detach the patient from the breathing tube and put them on a bag, a manual resuscitator, to see if the oxygen continued dropping (the problem might be the tube). When the doctor asked, "Did you ambu bag her?" the NP didn't understand. Later, Dr. Newman saw that the NP had put an ordinary face mask over the old apparatus: the breathing tube was still in, the oxygen still dropping. Dr. Newman was stunned, then livid. "What the fuck is that mask going to do?" she said. "That's like putting a fourth wig on someone with three wigs on! It doesn't do shit!"

Dr. Newman threw out that NP and requested another one. But the same thing kept happening. When a patient came in with heavy discharge, the NP decided to skip a pelvic exam because the patient was a lesbian. "She kept giving the patient more antifungals," Dr. Newman told me. "Guess what? Lesbians fuck men sometimes! Maybe she had an urge. Give her a pelvic exam."

The role of the mid-level medical professional has always depended on understanding that you don't know (and cannot guess) what you don't know. The best nurses know when to call in a doctor. But what if the private equity firm that runs your hospital is hiring far fewer doctors?

Now, many online programs have created academic or administrative doctorates: DNP (Doctor of Nursing Practice) or DMS (Doctor of Medical Science). The worst essentially sell the title "doctor" and encourage their degree-holders to call themselves that in a clinical setting. Would *you* ask the person in the lab coat to clarify what she means by "Doctor"?

Is there some way to measure the harm? You can't rely on patient satisfaction as a metric, since niceness doesn't equal good care. As for health outcomes, Dr. Julie Vieth, MD, tells me that finding stats is difficult, because medical malpractice data lags years behind the actual harm, and often only the physician is named, so the mid-level's role is wiped from the record. Or the physician fixes the mistake before any harm is done. "The data hasn't blossomed into something we can make meaning of."

I ask the doctors about suicides. They all say they take every threat seriously, but it's a tough calculus. What do you do with a patient who has been asking for oxycodone for hours, has been sitting with a nurse for three hours, and has never once mentioned suicide, then as soon as you refuse them the drug, they say, "I'll kill myself"? Sometimes you send that person home because everyone in the room, including the doctor, reads it as a tantrum, or a manipulation.

The U.K.'s national health system is similarly overburdened, but at least it's not run for profit by finance people. Many skeptical nurses and exhausted doctors have turned Josh away. Maybe, years ago, someone wrote "very dramatic" in his notes. This unreliable Josh—with his religious obsessions and theories about his body, with his threats and manipulations and rages—has cemented into his medical files, has become the only Josh on record.

Dr. Newman explains to me that anger from pain is often misinterpreted as drug-seeking anger. All kinds of people get dismissed when they get angry. People of color, mental health patients, inmates. They're always suspected of wanting drugs. They tell the NP their insulin dose and they're not believed. "Guess what?" she says. "Even if you're doing meth, you know your insulin dose. You take your insulin, and you take your meth. People are complex."

I chuckle. Dr. Newman sighs. It's been a frustrating decade, trying to get the world to listen. She has made a habit of tossing out the bad caregivers, supporting the good ones, and always telling the mistrusted and unheard patients, the misfits and foreigners and addicts that no-body else trusts, "I believe you. I'm sorry no one listened to you."

For weeks after I finish talking to the doctors, I feel angry, duped. I spent my whole life trusting in expertise, in education, in credentials. Where is the Western meritocracy I was promised? I know the word "merit" is vague and largely meaningless, that it's often used to shut out the vulnerable and the marginalized. But I will never be okay with watering down sciences, with slapping an "expert" badge on anyone with a joining fee. This is medicine, and lives. Or rather, *poor* lives. A few nights after we talk, Adam emails me a tweet: a young NP from an unknown institution asks where to look for work. An older NP re-sponds: "correctional facilities."

Are patients ever compelled to perform their pain? Depends, Adam tells me, on who you are and what you want. Race, gender, and income have a profound impact on how you're treated.

"If you want to talk performance," he says, "let's talk about sickle cell, a genetic disease that almost exclusively affects Black people." One in twelve African Americans carries the sickle cell gene, mean-ing that their red blood cells are shaped like crescent moons (or sick-les) and there aren't enough healthy ones to carry oxygen around the body. "I've never seen a white person with it," says Adam. "It's painful. Symptoms start when you're a just little kid, and it kills almost everyone who has it." My heart sinks.

People with sickle cell require high doses of narcotic pain medicine from an early age. In childhood, they're treated with compassion. *Poor sweet kid with sickle cell*, the nurses say. "But the second you turn eighteen, and go to the ER for your painkiller, you're a sickle cell drug seeker." These children become dependent on narcotic pain medication at five years old, and to deny them their medicine is literal torture. "It accom-plishes nothing," says Adam. "But you hear nurses say, *I'm just not going to give them this drug. It's all they came for.*" In a racist Georgia county, it's even possible to add an undetected racial slur, secretly, in tribal tongue. *All those sicklers finding their way to our county.* Translation: *All those Black people moving too close.*

Sickler. Remember it. It's a racial slur.

Since 2016, Adam tells me, smoldering racism has sparked up in new ways. If a mother comes in with an iPhone 11 asking for a prescription for children's Tylenol (covered by Medicaid when prescribed), some nurses resist. *A person with a phone like that doesn't need a prescription. Why should my tax dollars buy her kid Tylenol?* But you don't choose your phone if it comes from a local assistance program. A new iPhone is pure luck. And yet, there are stories of nurses giving half the doctor's prescribed dose, or pushing saline to deter patients from returning. Even after a verified diagnosis of sickle cell, they sometimes whisper, *I wonder how much Dilaudid he'll want today. Let me guess, he wants it with Benadryl* (to get a bit high).

"This is an actual diagnosis," Adam will remind them. "These people are suffering real pain that they didn't ask for. Can you not see that?" What he wants to say is: you're racist. You just don't think they deserve this drug. "Amal Mattu used to say he'd rather give a thousand drug seekers a dose of Dilaudid than to deny one suffering patient adequate relief."

Anyone caught lowering a patient's dose gets fired, but the troubling part is that to these medical professionals, young Black people with legitimate diagnoses look like addicts and criminals. Yes, these patients *are* addicted to Dilaudid—their addiction is an inevitable outcome of their disease. Dilaudid is a powerful opioid that, in the long term, is only recommended for cancer pain. An addict's behavior might look similar to that of someone hooked on a street drug: the desperation for the next dose, the cagey demeanor from a lifetime of being suspected and side-eyed, the performative affect that comes from realizing that your dosage isn't set in stone but is determined by a nurse's attitude, or even politics. None of this changes the truth that a sickle cell patient is entitled to consistent access to her established drug.

Nonetheless, some behaviors make caregivers suspicious, even with a verified diagnosis.

They come in nervous. They show their histories. To make things easier, and to prove an established pharmaceutical regimen, they name their drug and dosage. Later a nurse might whisper, *Ugh, he told me exactly how much Dilaudid he wanted, dosage, name, everything.*

"Of course he knew it!" says Adam, throwing up his hands, even in the retelling. "He's taken it for twenty years! It's his tenth time in the ER this year! That same nurse would criticize a cancer patient for not knowing the name of his chemo. But if it's sickle cell and you name your medicine, you're a drug addict. If you're a cancer patient and you forget it, you're an idiot."

While with sickle cell (and cancer, and other painful, diagnosable diseases), no performance should be required, even Adam is trained to spot drug-seeking behaviors in others. A patient comes in with chronic abdominal pain; many specialists can't figure out what's wrong. They order many workups. The patient continues on, *Oh doc, it hurts so bad. I need that medicine.* If a doctor promises them pain relief, they're adamant about what kind: *What are you giving me for the pain?* Then they begin to argue, eliminating every option. The red flag is when they get to this one: *Morphine doesn't work for me.* Then comes the most irritating part of the routine for Adam, the protracted "I don't recall the name of the drug" rigmarole. *There's this one drug that works . . . I don't remember . . . it starts with a d . . . Delo . . . delay . . . delaba . . . dolo . . . Can you look in my chart and see? It's there. Starts with a D.*

Sometimes Adam smiles, plays along. "I have no idea what drug you're talking about." He pretends to wrap it up, and the name of the drug suddenly manifests in the memory or in a pocket where it was written down and forgotten: *Oh, it's called Dilaudid, that's it!*

If it's not sickle cell or cancer (verified lifelong pains), that's when

Adam puts an end to the insulting theater. "Look," he says, "I know you know it's called Dilaudid. You know because you've had it fifty times. Let's talk about how we can actually get you feeling better." If you survey a thousand doctors, he tells me, every one of them will corroborate this scene.

But what if the patient arrives, without pretense, without games, and simply asks for Dilaudid? That same doctor will call *that* drug-seeking behavior. There is simply no correct way to ask for this drug. Knowing too many of the usual words is a sign of drug seeking. Pretending not to know the words is a sign of drug seeking. Saying, *I don't want you to think I'm a drug seeker, but . . .* is a sign of drug seeking.

In the end, Adam says, drug seekers try to direct their care. He believes the ones who give up the hunt for that particular drug, the ones who want freedom from pain, not Dilaudid or any specific treatment. Those who don't try to steer the ship get believed, but they also get more conservative pain control. With each new doctor, they repeat the steps: the mild medicine, the slightly higher dosage, and so on— because saying *I've been through this a thousand times, and this one doesn't work for me* is a drug-seeking red flag. Better to say, *I know I'm here a lot. And I know I'm being loud and crazy and hard to understand, but I have this horrible pain. I just want to feel better, so I don't have to come in again. I don't care how you do it. But I am feeling frustrated, because nothing works. Please find me something that works.*

Of the thousand things a suffering person might say in an exam room (with competing instincts to beg, to act, to explain, to weep), good luck stumbling onto that one perfect paragraph: vulnerable but not theatrical, forthcoming with information but not directive.

In my last book I wrote that melodrama makes stories unbelievable, and that refugees, while prepping their stories for asylum officers, are forced to wait indefinitely. This wait rubs away at their sense of proportion, and they slip into a kind of frantic unreality. Just before having to perform their stories, they become melodramatic, impossible to believe. Those who are systematically disbelieved always come out defenses first. In hospitals across America, there is almost nothing a pregnant Black woman can do to convince a racist doctor that she has the wrong kind of belly pain. The direness of it, and the importance and urgency of making herself heard, will cause her to behave badly. There is nothing she can do. It will take a generation of implicit bias training in nursing and medical programs to give her the credibility she is owed.

My absurd C-section theater began with a birth plan. I thought about how to craft a believable voice for days. Then I remembered a man I had dated who would insert misspellings and lowercase letters in his emails to make them seem casual, uncalculated. Until I figured out the trick, I believed that everything he said was his most unfiltered thought, straight from his deep psyche.

I decided that I must give Astrid the impression of seeing too much, a hastily scribbled birth plan. I spent an hour watching movie scenes of female hysteria interspersed with up-close vaginal birth videos, and when I was sufficiently worked up, I gave myself five minutes to write the damn thing and press send. No editing. No second-guessing. This was supposed to be my raw fear on display. This is a portion of the birth plan Astrid received later that afternoon by email:

> . . . *If there is so much as a paper cut on my vagina, I will go into psycho-logical trauma . . . I don't want forceps, ventouse* [ventouse is French for plunger. PLUNGER!] *or any vaginal aids in the room. I want all those instruments removed . . . If the baby isn't clawing its way out, we go straight to C-section. *I want epidural as soon as I arrive**

She replied with surprising calm. We made my next appoint-ment. Before the NHS would sign off on a scheduled C-section, I was supposed to confide my fears to Astrid three times. One of those meetings would include a tour of the "normal" birthing rooms. We couldn't visit the operating rooms, but Astrid thought the sinister baby-blue birthing tubs and vomit-pink throws would comfort me more than an icy-cold operating table: a suction machine, a tray of knives, an anesthetic chart, items that screamed *science*, *pain management*. *Oh, Astrid*, I thought.

During the birthing room tour, my breath started to catch—for real—and I excused myself to sit in the bathroom for a few minutes and breathe. I splashed water onto my face. Why did I have to do this? Why could Astrid not simply believe that I am unable to push a baby out of my vagina? That I'd freeze? That I'd faint? That I'd push myself to exhaustion and end up in an emergency C-section anyway, the worst outcome whatever your birth politics?

After my second visit, I received a call from the hospital's mental health unit. Astrid had decided that I should speak with them. The call caught me off guard. What qualified Astrid to tell me I needed a mental health assessment? Briefly, I dropped my guard. I became unhinged, and I told the woman on the phone a lot of ugly truths. "I don't believe in midwives," I said. "I want a real doctor with a medical degree. I believe in medicine, in training, in science. I will submit to being sliced open, if that gets me a surgeon. Otherwise, I'll faint or die. Do you get it?"

There was a pause on the other end. "I know Astrid has explained to you the details of a cesarean." She started to talk about how many layers of tissue the surgeon would slice through.

"Save your spiel," I said. "My mother was an OB-GYN. I watch C-section videos with my lunch. What scares me is fecal incontinence. And vaginal tears. Sometimes I have nightmares about my vagina and anus becoming one giant irreparable hole, just this permanent wound. And . . . and fecal incontinence! FECAL! My God, is *that* not enough? I want a surgeon."

"All right, take a breath," she said. "We'll schedule you in for a section. That seems best."

What had just happened? Becoming my mother is my greatest fear, yet here I was spouting one of her dogmas. Though many things irritate my mother, only two things can make her snide: asylum seekers pretending to be Christian, and Americans who, upon hearing stories from her OB-GYN days, see only an Iranian grandma and ask, "So you were a midwife?"

Had I just earned a reprieve with my excellent acting? Or was I deluding myself about my own mental health? Maybe everyone in my position goes in thinking, *I'm going to put on a show until they give me a C-section.* Maybe they're fooling no one, just proving that they check the boxes. That they are, in fact, exactly the thing they're pretending to be.

––––––

There is a saying in hospitals, not even whispered—an open joke. "The Idiopathic Hysteria of the Hispanic Female." There are variations around the country, like HHS, "Hispanic Hysteric Syndrome." It's widespread enough that it's addressed in the bias training at many hospitals. Nurses and doctors feel that the joke is justified, because they've seen it so much. It's not a lie. After every death in a Hispanic family, the family comes into the room, wailing, crying. They perform their grief as ritual, as respect. Like the older generations in my village, or the Russian grandmothers in the videos, identifying their loved ones in the pits.

After every display, hospital staff show outward respect to the family. Behind closed doors, though, they make jokes. There is a medical term: "status epilepticus," a long, unstoppable seizure. Adam told me about nurses who change this to "status Hispanicus" to refer to families' mourning. It's so common, there are even Reddit threads and an Urban Dictionary entry for it: *When a large Hispanic family gets together at a hospital to support a member of their family with a minor injury and have a sustained freak out attack to show the support.*

I've lived my whole adult life away from my closest family. Right now, I live in a French village where Sam is rooted. I try to imagine my own family coming to visit me in a hospital bed, making a theater of their worry. I'd feel so loved. The more hysterical the better, kinder.

Many doctors and nurses understand, of course, that this behavior is cultural, and a ritual. They know that to my family or to a Hispanic family, white customs are equally strange. "You know what's weird?" says Adam, who is Jewish. "A Southern Baptist who loses his father and he just sighs and says, 'Well, I guess I'll call the funeral home now.'"

This talk of melodrama takes me back to my writing education, the hierarchies in the artistic world that so closely mirror those in the corporate and academic worlds. Those at the top are subtle. *Did Chanel pay you to advertise?* asked my McKinsey manager, because subtlety was rarefied, expensive. In asylum interviews, heartbroken sobs are branded as melodrama, a style of performance that's outdated and false. Somewhere in between are those with passionate intensity, with "potential" (or fire, drive, faith). Before now, I had really only seen two of the tiers: need and potential. But there is a third, hovering over them both: a kind of aristocratic nonchalance.

I have a friend who writes subtle stories for *The New Yorker*. Her brother jokes, "I feel like you're always winking at me." I love her stories, because sometimes subtle gestures do reveal an avalanche of pain, and she sees and understands those gestures. She drops them in, like grains of sea salt. She'd have no problem communicating her pain to a serene, reflective doctor from Princeton or Yale. But Western readers are taught that it is always more dignified, deeper, to swallow your drama, because they've been fed on a canon of white writers aiming to please one man, one school, one journal: Gordon Lish, the Iowa Writers' Workshop, *The New Yorker*. They pass down the same lessons. Drama is bad. Big emotions are lowbrow, and to understand events complexly, one must be emotionally unsure. Subtle pain is deeper pain. Better to show a trembling hand, though even that is too much.

Where, then, does that leave survivors whose pain is as uncontainable as it is true?

And what if your pain isn't some worrying tremor or some invisible old-age cancer hardening over your heart, but a horror that you witnessed with your senses when you were young? What if you saw a friend's arm blown off? What if you watched your child die?

Show me a grandmother with furious fists, demanding that God explain himself. Show me a wife beating the chest of the officer who delivers her to her husband's body. Show me a Hispanic family performing their love for their broken son or daughter, loudly, unashamed, sweating and cursing as white people watch, judging. Show me a withered, tired mother, standing beside a staged mountain of skulls, staring directly into the camera and saying, *You don't understand how bad this is and you never will. But I will make you understand.*

One day I'll write a story about a woman who, giving vaginal birth, tears from bow to stern. She lies there, an open wound flanked by caramel thigh flesh, blood-speckled. Her grannie batters the sky, demands that God explain. A sad midwife sighs at a nearby desk, loads a dose of morphine onto a cart, and studies a discount sushi menu streaked with dry hand sanitizer.

Adam tells me about the medical theater that most saddens him. If the Dilaudid memory-slip is a comedy, this one is its tragic twin. He sees it most often in sickle cell patients, and in Black or Hispanic women with uterine fibroids, burst cysts, or other painful ailments that can be mistaken for run-of-the-mill menstrual frailty. "They'll come in very stoic," he says. "They know how the system works. They think, *I need to be laser-focused on the facts and utterly unemotional, or I'll be called hysterical.* The problem with that is, then it doesn't seem like the pain is that severe. The doctors use that same bias in the other direction. Where with a loud patient they said, *Oh my God, these people always exaggerate, it's probably nothing,* Now, they think, *These people tend to be dramatic when they have real pain, so this must be nothing.*" The more people snicker about the "Idiopathic Hysteria of the Hispanic Female," the louder the baseline for getting any attention, and the louder any woman of color has to scream in order to be heard. After a few succumb to the pain and crank it up a notch, the baseline moves up, and the next real pain requires a new kind of ultra-hysteria.

"What's a woman of color have to do to get treatment then?" I ask. "What's the code?"

Adam thinks for a moment. "Be honest, but, if you get someone who's not listening, behave as his mother would: learn and mirror the doctor's social norms, as exhibited by the most sympathetic woman of his community. A physician faced with his mother, or sister or daughter, will remember why he became a doctor. Familiarity breeds empathy.

I understand now why the Russian cameramen told the women to scream louder, to wail harder, to punch the air more—this was maternal mourning in 1940s Soviet villages. It's mourning to me. What does the doctor consider a true performance of pain, and of female pain?

Maybe my C-section theater worked because I acted like Astrid's daughter or sister. We relate to singular, memorable details in stories. Though the strange ones thrill us and awaken our curiosity, we are constantly seeking out the familiar, the signposts from our own life. We latch onto those, attach more weight to them. Everyone has a terrible movie they love beyond reason and argument, because it happened to them *just like that.*

Meredith loves her new doctors in Colorado—both are young breast cancer survivors. She feels she's getting better care, because they understand her every ache and worry. A teenage boy with testicle pain shifted in a chair in Adam's office. "Ever accidentally sit on one of them?" he asked. Having once been a teenage boy, Adam will viscerally recall every ailment that boy describes. He'll be moved by an instinct deeper than his medical knowledge.

"It's like crying for a speeding ticket," says Adam. "There's a right way to do it." You read the officer, what he finds manipulative or sincere.

Susan Sontag observed that we search for signs of trickery. One set of acts makes you a good patient, a worthy refugee, a penitent sinner. Other acts make you genuine in your grief. We want others' pain to mirror our own; sensory recall removes our doubt. Subtle or not, we want our truth manifested, embodied, and dramatized. Truth is trembling hands, hot fingertips, sweaty waistbands. Corporeal. We crave to feel the pain for ourselves. Or to remember something like it, so we can be persuaded that it exists now in another body. Make the pain tangible.

Performance therapists told Josh to reenact his ancestral stories. Sam's grandfather's grandfather dug his own grave in a ravine in Eastern Europe, beside his wife, his friends. Their names appear on genealogy charts, adults and children, all dead in one 1941 day. His grandson (Sam's grandfather, Lewis) was already in America on the day a large segment of his family was massacred. It's strange to think of this man, who had a hand in the life of my daughter, digging, knowing what was coming. Without him, Elena wouldn't exist. Sam's grandpa Lewis looks just like Elena. Their baby photos, a century apart, are uncanny. People joke that Elena is a reincarnation and that, like Lewis, she will be relentless, ambitious, and bold. Lewis became that way, Sam thinks, in part because of the slaughter of his family, and his wife's family: that he lived in America was unearned luck, and he had to atone. Or maybe it was the opposite: he had to suck the marrow, now that he understood that goodness is rare and fleeting.

That photo of baby Lewis hangs in our London flat, and each time I pass it, I shudder at Elena's face, ghostly and out of context, in a century-old photo. Lewis made and lost a fortune. Sheldon rejected the profit chase to study human rights. Callings, I think, are inherited.

This year, we celebrated another of Ilan's courtroom wins against Shell Oil. Though Ilan has spent his career fighting corporate human rights abuses in Africa, we joke that he's relentless against Shell because it shares his father's name. Sam's unfinished Holocaust novel, Ilan's late-night procedural battles against Shell, Sheldon's fight against apartheid, and Lewis's empire-building, they all started in that ravine in 1941. Maybe so did Adam's vow to believe all pain.

Josh grew up obsessed with his Jewish ancestry, and with Judaism as a faith for himself. He thought something of his grandfather had leaked into him. "It made him reject nine-to-fives," said Sam. "He thought he was destined for greatness or death."

Greatness or death: Josh craved drama. I get that. I've chased it my whole life. I noticed early on that people only believe a pain performance if you're seen to be *trying*: if the pain blooms into something useful, instead of taking over your life. If the pain is the root of your identity, not its flowers and leaves.

I ask Adam how Josh might have performed his pain. His tone changes, to something kind and practiced. He knows that the interview has always led up to this. How badly my motives must show: I need him to say that he, too, might've sent Josh home. But Adam is a doctor who first believes. Why weren't we better friends in college? Sometimes, in stories, a minor character walks out of the past, delivers some vital thing, a scene or a word, and vanishes again. That person is so often a doctor.

"Josh made threats," I say. "That's supposed to mean it's not serious."

"That's the clown shoes in a minefield," Adam says. "Sometimes, you follow the signs and you're still wrong. In medicine, zero failure isn't attainable. So, we try to believe everyone."

"It's like the Pascal's wager of medicine," I say.

"Every doctor you'll ever talk to," he says, "from this moment till forever, has a story of someone they missed. During my residency, someone convinced me and the psych that they were fine. 'Doc, I just got really heated. I didn't mean it.' They went home and killed themselves."

I feel certain now that Josh's trouble was this: he performed his pain badly. Though his mental illness was real, his enactment of it fell short. I wish I had shown him what little I'd learned. I might have shared the weird and wonderful hinges I found, between corporate negotiation tactics and asylum storytelling, the deliberate but often true theaters we perform on dates, and in doctor's offices, and in front of documentary cameras, and how the ancient Greek dramatists created compelling arcs. I wish I'd said, "Look, if you want to manipulate, fine. Let me just show you how other people get away with it."

But it's not that simple. Outside one's own body, pain manifests as something abstract and ugly; those rare connections when it becomes briefly tangible to someone else, merging with their past, like a beam refracted from another universe, happen by chance. For those with power to help, Josh just never stumbled into that congenial beam of light.

I tell Adam about the ravine films. As I speak, I imagine a ghostly old woman, ambling down a frozen road. Somewhere offscreen a quick, sharp voice instructs, "Wipe your eyes; now turn this way please." The grandmother progresses from body to body, lost in her search for tangible things—a familiar hand, a yellow scarf, a mole—then, ripped from her quiet prayers by the unseen voice, she looks up, nods. The cameraman reminds her to thrash the sky.

Afterward, Adam tells me about an ancestor who ran into the woods to escape the Nazis. A soldier caught her, but let her go, because she looked like his daughter. She was saved not by strength or wit or quickness (he had all the power and she had nothing to offer) but because he was transported into some parallel narrative that he preferred for himself; some other part of him overpowered his ideology. She lived because she stumbled into the role of his terrified daughter and, briefly, maybe just for seconds, she was convincing in it.

———

In fall 2019, we moved to Paris so I could take up a fellowship. A season of great joy followed. We bought salmon and scallops at the Sunday market, clicked over cobblestones in our good shoes, ate in bistros with daring chefs. We joined a writing group, found a babysitter, and shared early drafts with strangers. The pandemic came, and lockdowns. We paced our city apartment for two months, chewing our nails raw, then hunkered down in a village with friends.

The commune sprouted organic rules, and in daytime we succumbed to routines: diligent writing, quick lunches, long walks, vegetarian meals capped by mugs of chicory. Jennifer and Manu sang songs. Laleh shared nuggets of sublime writing she'd found in paperbacks next door. The vegetarian food became more varied and sophisticated. Charlie's chestnut Bourguignon, Aleks's chunky borscht, Laleh's mushroom frittatas, corn breads, and bowls of roasted root vegetables. I made Iranian eggplant-whey and creamy balsamic mushrooms, and for a while became obsessed with making a perfect lemon meringue pie. I made six that season.

In school, Elena learned to pronounce the names of all her classmates: all those French n's. It seemed that always mid-Benjamin, her nose became suddenly blocked. Her spongy young brain immersed deeply in a new language, sometimes she absorbed someone's deviated septum.

Our Sunday market walks grew chilly. The cheese mongers and pickle makers and oyster fishermen learned our names, one by one. Charlie found me the saltiest, mushroomiest hard cheeses. Amid all that fungus, he'd open the fridge door and retch at the tiniest whiff of flesh, a piece of Elena's cold cuts, or a single sardine in Tupperware. "This doesn't smell like a vegetarian fridge! What creature is decomposing here?"

When the group talked literature, I felt like a fraud, repeating syllables, like Lindsay the faker of tongues or that manifest-destiny-shale CEO. Our friends had read so broadly, from obscure to canonical; Laleh moved easily between *Magic Mountain* and *Invisible Cities*, Hadrian's memoirs and Cioran's syllogisms, Baudelaire and de Beauvoir. I had to look up the word *syllogism*; afterward, the other Dina shook her head in shame and disgust.

Sam joked, "Do you know what Dina's favorite movie is? *Under the Tuscan Sun.*"

Not my favorite, but what's wrong with it? This bad movie I so stupidly love is ninety minutes of visual joy: yellow umbrellas over Tuscan valleys, beautiful mouths eating glistening pasta, olives, gelato, young lovers' crushing first glimpse, nuns gossiping with a local seductress, old bachelors and feisty grandmothers, surprise intimacies that mimic life. It's about how the love of strangers finds you in your worst moments, like a pain-seeking missile. It's about immigrants finding a new table, divorcees rebuilding, neighbors who badly want you to be okay.

"I don't get why you make so many excuses for *this* bad movie," says Sam.

I guess there's something in it that I believe. For all its flaws, I don't want to dismiss that.

"It's fine to love it!" said Sam. "It meant a lot to you during your divorce, I get it."

No. That it moved me while I was suffering and cynical is why it works, not why liking it is acceptable. I reject the notion that I've been tricked or enthralled by something false, by guile.

"But there's no strangeness, no deviation or choice. It's predetermined," says Sam. He's right. I don't want choice or surprises when I'm wounded. I want comfort. I want to dream.

The dreamer has no choices. It is easier to believe in formula and fate, a future controlled by those with extraordinary ability (divine, ancestral, or corporate), than to believe in randomness, hypocrisy, and negligence. Good and bad events are foretold, inevitable. In a world like that, it's possible to relax and forget about choices. "It's like BDSM," an actor friend says. "Both religion and bad artists who romanticize dying in a *chambre de bonne*, they want to submit. Having power is scary."

"The lure of melodrama," said Sam. "Not remotely dramatic or moving. No anticipation, just . . . tedious."

Sometimes that's what you want: no choices, no tension.

That night as Sam spoke, Josh was conjuring his ancestors, imagining them in their last days, or in happier days. Through books and meditations, he traveled back to Israel, to Eastern Europe, to the ravines where an entire branch of his family, parents and children, were murdered. He kept returning to his great-grandfather's faith, to his ancestors' lands, to their holy books. He was mired in melodrama, certain that his troubles and turmoil were imprinted in his body and unchangeable, a toxin released by the Shoah into his ancestor's flesh and passed down to him. *Yes*, his family told him. *It is true. There are family traumas, but . . . but . . . it's a bad choice for a life story, when it takes away all your power.*

Sam told a story about visiting his mother's church as a teenager. The pastor, sensing an unbeliever, kept glancing over and asking if anyone was ready to accept Jesus. "Bad stories are like that, always asking you to believe something obvious, repeat a trope like it's a revelation." He sipped his soup and, briefly, he vanished, his gaze in the middle distance as if he were reliving an earlier, better scene.

———

In the village, Sam started to go quiet again. Sometimes he took long walks, and if Josh called, he didn't tell me. Then, one evening in that listless November, I closed my laptop and dashed to the shower. I had been reading the Rogers Commission Report on the *Challenger* disaster, why the NASA managers hadn't believed the engineers. Charlie was plating cheese down in the kitchen. Laleh and Aleks were cooking dinner. As I came down the stairs, Charlie pulled out a bottle of champagne. "Tonight's one month of commune living," he said. November 24, 2020. "Let's drink to that!"

"I need a shower." I rushed past Elena watching cartoons at the kitchen table.

"I got you some really mushroomy Cantal," Charlie sang after me.

Laleh and Aleks, the dinner shift, were humming shoulder to shoulder at the stove, browning onions and wilting kale. In the bathroom, I stripped off my exercise clothes and turned the water to hot. The bathroom is old, and it's weirdly located inside the kitchen. I could hear my friends cooking dinner, laughing, through the door. Then, a beat of silence, broken up by Elena's cartoon. I leaned back into the stream and started lathering. I was covered in a thick layer of white foam when someone knocked.

"Be right out," I said, annoyed. Couldn't somebody else change Elena's cartoon or get her juice? Maybe they needed a towel? Another knock. "Just a minute," I said. "I'm all soapy."

"Dina, I need you to come out," said Laleh, her voice controlled but shaky. Was I using all the hot water? *Was Elena okay?*

"Is Elena okay?" I shouted, turning off the tap, wrapping my lathered body in a towel.

"Dina, please come out now," said Laleh, her voice small and frightened.

"Is Elena okay?" I shouted. I opened the door a crack and looked past Laleh's stricken face. Elena sat happily in front of her cartoon. I breathed out. "Where's Sam?" My heart plummeted. Sam wasn't anywhere in sight. Where had he gone? I clung to the rough towel, my fingertips remembering the scratch of his new beard. *My Sam is gone. Has he left me? Or—*

"Dina, come out now, okay?" said Laleh.

This refusal to tell me what was wrong was becoming strange. Behind her, Charlie and Aleks were stunned silent, busying their hands with dish rags and carrot peelers and cling film. Aleks turned off the stove, gently, without a word. I kept picturing Sam's skull, split open on a sidewalk. I imagined him sliced open, bleeding, his beautiful hair ripped away. As I opened the bathroom door wider, a clump of body wash fell off my body onto the tile at my feet. It would congeal there for the next three hours until, at last, from the kitchen table crowded with local relatives, Laleh spotted it and quietly wiped it away with a dishrag.

I scanned the kitchen over Laleh's shoulders. Her voice shook. "You should talk to Sam."

"Where is he?" I asked. "Where is Sam? Is he okay?" I could see her struggling; was it her place to tell me the news? "Please, just say what you know," I said.

I thought, *Sam is hurt. Sam has left me. She doesn't want to be the despised messenger.*

"You need to get dressed and go find him," she said, following me upstairs.

"Please tell me what happened," I begged. "The things I'm imagining, honestly—"

She took a breath, trying to decide. Then she said it, her voice cracking under the strain. "His brother killed himself."

I teetered on my ankles, stomach in freefall. A part of me knew before Laleh spoke. Or is that hindsight? When did it happen, I wanted to know? When did it *finish* happening? Because, let's face it, it started long before I arrived on the scene, and continued right before my eyes.

Laleh sat quietly on the living room couch, watching as I ran into the bedroom and threw on Flo's flowy jean skirt and stumbled into my underwear. I grabbed a T-shirt and fleece from a dirty pile, wetting both as I pulled them over my sopping hair. Obviously Laleh had gotten some detail terribly wrong, poor thing.

"It's not true," I yelled into the living room. "What they mean is he *tried*. Is he in the hospital? He'll be fine . . . it's called a *suicidal gesture*. Did he . . . how . . ."

I kept wanting to pull up a photo of Josh's birthday party in our apartment two years before: *See? There he is. There is his alive body, blowing out candles—So now you get it.*

"I don't know," said Laleh, miserably. "No, I think he actually killed himself."

He did it to himself. How? I kept turning over the mechanics of it.

The guilt arrived later. It didn't take long to remember that I had never believed him, and to ask myself why I had fought so staunchly against this reality we now so irreversibly inhabited. But right then, my first thought was: *Thank God it wasn't Sam or Elena or, oh God, Sheldon.* I wasn't ready for that loss. Sam wasn't ready for that loss. And even before I said my first prayer for Josh's soul, or my first private apology to his ghost, I thought: *Is Sam okay? What if he gets in a car? What if he's had a drink and gets in a car? I don't care if he doesn't love me, if Sam dies, I'll die, too.* It seems obscene, this melodrama. All I thought about was *our* deaths. In Josh's wake, I was obsessed with the state of *us.*

I zipped up my fleece, my hair still dripping wet, and I ran into the cold and down the street to Sam's aunt and uncle's house. Halfway down a steep hill, my fingertips lost sensation, and briefly I shook off the madness. *Josh is fine. He is smart, charming, capable. Remember the empty piñata, raining loose marshmallows onto the children? A suicidal gesture, a theater.*

Being believed, getting what you want, requires performance; this I've learned from a life of social extremes. *Josh is just putting on a show* . . . but what if he only *thought* he was performing? I remembered other medical spectacles, when you think you're fooling everyone, but deep down, you're trying on the only outcome that isn't excruciating to imagine. Sometimes, in desperate moments, we are exactly the thing we're pretending to be. Then the cold slapped my wet face and my naked ankles stung and my hair began to harden against my temples, and I thought, *Poor lost Josh. He tried so hard to convince us.*

Repeating

7.

On his final weekend, Josh went to the hospital with Flo. He spent half a day begging skeptical nurses for help, but they had heard the same story too many times. Long desensitized to young men like Josh, they sent him away. By then, Flo had already seen her son dismissed in this way dozens of times. She took him home.

I don't want to get in the way of Josh's inquest; I don't dare sniff around British nursing degrees or suicide protocols as I did with American ones. Ilan will do that work. And mine isn't that kind of investigation. But I do know that these two nations, my two homes in adulthood, believe, fear, and hope similarly. Their institutions are built on the same principles of potential and need, under a layer of aspirational nonchalance. And I know, too, that the story of Josh's death began years ago. So I've started thinking about true beginnings.

What about the caseworker who first listened to KV's story? Who was the cynic who tainted his record with farce? Kafka's authoritarians are often unseen, their wishes enacted by bureaucrats. They establish their case long before a victim appears. Then the bureaucrat need only point and say, "I see a criminal!"

But we don't live inside an allegory. KV's real-life trial began years before his asylum case, before he was a refugee, when he was a happy jeweler's son, sculpting necklaces in his father's workshop. I imagine it like this:

Somewhere in London, a young woman graduates with a two-year degree. She casts about for jobs. It's rough out there, competing with university and masters graduates. She sees an ad for a Home Office caseworker. She can be part of something good. If she's precocious, she reads up on the Refugee Convention, studies the harrowing photos of overpacked dinghies on a black Aegean night. Maybe she thinks, *I'll save some of these wretched people.*

At the Home Office, she meets a senior caseworker tasked with showing her the ropes. The older woman greets her. "Welcome to the toughest job of your life." She pauses, then adds, "Get ready to be lied to. A lot."

In training, the young graduate is told that her job is to root out inconsistency. Then a ritual begins, a drumbeat of danger and despair that over weeks and months wears her down. The ritual changes her. How can so many people come out of the same country with the exact same injuries? How can so many people have crossed the same bridge, met the same smuggler, worn out their shoes on the same treacherous mountain? It seems impossible that she should meet twenty men a day, all dark, with the same face, the same stature, branded with the same scar patterns, running from the same villain.

"They look exactly the same," she tells her supervisor. "They're taking the same meds. Telling the same story. Why are the scars so alike?"

If she had spoken to a survivor thirty years past her pain, or a lawyer, or a charity worker, these men and women might have told her: *Because something big is happening inside their small country—a tiny patch of the earth is spewing out refugees now. Yes, they are all young, brown men with many shared traits, and they look the same to you because you are white. They are fleeing a common villain, and that villain does have a single brand, a torture device, that he favors. As for why they tell their story the same way, it is language, culture, the fact that they all learned English storytelling from the same five helpers along the way.*

Instead, the senior caseworker shrugs. "They all buy their tall tales and fake papers from the same lot. God knows, probably they get themselves branded by the same thug."

The young caseworker goes back into her office. She stares at the bottomless pile of nightmares on her desk. Something clenches inside her heart. Later today, she will hear three new Sri Lankan cases, all identical to KV's—his captors back home have wounded so many brothers. None is special to this English woman; by now, the rituals have worn down her senses. The droning stories, one after another. She is tired. A single rote response has crystallized. *What dramatics. Maybe he did it to himself.*

Then KV enters her interview room carrying photos of his mutilated back that looks like every other mutilated Sri Lankan back, and medical reports that read like all the others, from the same NGO doctors. The caseworker sighs: another Tamil Tiger, limping and scarred.

———

The basis for KV's rejection, "Wounding, Self-Inflicted by Proxy (SIBP)," baffled the doctors and country experts who had worked on his case, and his story soon spread through the asylum support community. How could the Home Office suggest that KV did this to himself? Who had ever heard of self-infliction at this level of wounding? And in a country like Sri Lanka where there was, at that time, rampant documented torture? And who was this phantom "proxy"?

It seems to me that torture shouldn't be difficult to prove. The scars are so distinctive and many survivors are covered with them. Often authorities in a particular country repeat a technique: iron rods in Sri Lanka, toenail removal in Iran. But in the report *Proving Torture*, Freedom from Torture claims that asylum seekers find it "almost impossible" to prove their stories, and medico-legal reports have become more arduous, detailed, and costly. Today's torture survivors are subjected to unprecedented rigors and suspicions. Disbelief is the baseline: you are lying until you prove you aren't. Survivors are accused of inventing details, passing off unrelated injuries, even inflicting the scars on themselves. Meanwhile, expert medical and psychological reports are ignored, and little attempt is made to train officers on the effect of trauma on memory, or on international guidelines like the Istanbul Protocol, which acknowledges that doctors cannot know with certainty the cause of any physical mark.

But "Wounding SIBP" stems from the idea that all things are possible. If only one plausible cause (torture) explains a pattern of scars, and the Home Office doesn't choose to believe that cause, they can create a second possibility and, in rejecting the first, assume the second by default. How did KV manage to brand himself so cleanly on an unreachable part of his body? No one lingered on that question for long. "Maybe he had help," they said, and moved on.

"There were just so many," said my anonymous HOPO about the Sri Lankan cases, "and they all presented themselves with two things: antidepressants and scars on the body." Sometimes the scars weren't severe enough to move the officers. "There were the round holes, the cigarette burns, and lashes to the back." The photos of another brown back covered in the same scars just didn't seem like much, and their antidepressants were low dosage, and the expert medical reports seemed copied-and-pasted. "Sometimes I didn't even engage with the report," said the HOPO. Desensitized, she dismissed it like a television rerun. "This is generic stuff."

The medical reports (written by doctors in support of each case) were unhelpful, she said. These doctors "could never rule out that it was A or B. They were never conclusive. So how do we know? These experts would be paid so much money for repeating the same stuff. They literally copy and paste it. Coming from the Home Office side, I see that report and say, *They're lying. There's nothing in that report specific to this case* . . ." She paused, took a breath. "How do *I* know? All we can say is these are the options, and it could have been self-infliction."

When KV heard the reason for his rejection, his stomach folded, his knees buckled. He was smacked by the nausea of those ninety minutes in the back of the truck out of the detention camp. How was this within the realm of human logic or compassion? How was this possible in a "civilized" country? Did these officers feel no shame writing such lines to a torture survivor?

"Your removal," the letter said, "would not be a breach of our obligations under . . . the ECHR" (European Convention on Human Rights).

Sometimes I'm asked about quick fixes to the asylum process. While there are hundreds of real policies dealing with the right to work, housing, education, as well as cultural and training overhauls for our asylum gatekeepers, I think on my first morning in charge, the first thing I'd do is rewrite the haughty, tone-deaf rejection letter.

After the Home Office rejected KV based on suspicion of self-infliction, he went to court. In May 2011, KV's case was heard by a tribunal of judges who dismissed his appeal, but allowed for it to be retried by an Upper Tribunal. They said that this tribunal could also decide if SIBP could become a "general guidance" for the Home Office—a dangerous, frightening precedent.

Strangely, amid the disbelief, the court found KV's accounts consistent with reports about Sri Lankan state forces. But the court doubted parts of KV's story: what could possibly explain his father's surprising immunity from arrest and detention? How was KV's escape possible? Why were the Tamil Tigers asking for melted gold? Still, the court considered an analysis of his scars to be central to the case, and accepted that if the scars could be proven to be from a torture that is established as typical in Sri Lanka, then the rest of his story likely happened too. In the meantime KV had options: to live while waiting, or to suffer while waiting.

In Kafka's *The Trial,* Josef K is woken from his sleep and told he will soon face a trial. Though he's allowed to live in his home and to work, Josef K is consumed by his eventual fate. He follows a labyrinth to two men offering twisted insights into the court: a painter and a priest who have particular influence on the shadowy judges. The painter describes three kinds of acquittal that K can hope for. Sure, everyone wants *absolute* acquittal, but the other two can be just as good. In an *apparent* acquittal, the defendant is let go and the ordeal seems to stop, for a time. "Seen from outside it can sometimes seem that everything has been long since forgotten, the documents have been lost and the acquittal is complete . . . [but] the court forgets nothing." One day, after years or maybe just an hour, some judge picks up a case, remembers it, and has the man rearrested. Then the whole thing starts again, a ritual that might last a lifetime. Also possible is a *deferment,* which "consists of keeping proceedings permanently in their earliest stages." The defendant must be always on alert, always in touch with the court, making sure everyone is happy. This too is about repetition: "You must never let the trial out of your sight," Josef K is told. At the same time, to the outside, it must seem like something is happening. There have to be investigations and injunctions and questionings. "The trial's been artificially constrained inside a tiny circle, and it has to be continuously spun around within it."

KV spent much of 2012 and 2013 having his body examined by doctors, retelling the story of that awful day with the soldering iron and the petrol. He described the way he passed out and fell forward. He described what position he was in just before he fell forward: the army men were holding his neck and arms down, pulling his face toward the floor, to expose his back for branding. He described waking up to the realization that his back was now a repository of pain, one massive wound. He described and described, and he collapsed into sorrow—he hadn't accounted for such grief here in Europe. After everything, that the greatest obstacle wouldn't be surviving the glowing rod, or escaping the camp, or trudging past borders to a safe country whose rhetoric of humanitarianism and virtue echoed across the globe and into the classrooms and workshops and villages of his youth. The greatest challenge would be rescuing his story from fading into fiction—or rather, being tossed there, into a Neverland made for stories like his.

KV's lawyer, Arun, assured him that gathering proof was essential for the Home Office; that bureaucracies never accept uncorroborated memories as evidence. He joked that many frustrated Sri Lankan survivors throw their hands up in front of their lawyers; it's normal. "Was I meant to stop as I was escaping," Arun joked, "stick my head out from under the crates, and get a signature from the guy who branded me?" KV chuckled. He'd wondered that himself more than once. "So, you see, that's why there are doctors to see if scars match a story. Don't worry. They're seasoned and they're kind and fair. And it's all very clinical, they're rarely shocked."

Dr. Joy Odili and Dr. Enrique Zapata-Bravo had years of medico-legal reporting and deep knowledge of the 1999 Istanbul Protocol— the strict standards by which medical experts judge the likelihood that wounds and scars are caused by torture. The doctors were instructed by KV's solicitors to assess *all* the various ways the scars could have been made. Were they made by disease? By accident? Surgery? By KV's own hand? An accomplice torturer? And so on.

In October 2013, Dr. Zapata-Bravo, an expert in internal medicine and psychiatry, formally examined KV. Like Dr. Odili, he rejected every theory except torture. Dr. Zapata-Bravo wrote that there was no chance that KV could have branded himself, and a hypothetical torturer, friend or foe, could never have done it so cleanly if KV were awake. The body's "intense pain stimulus" would result in a "powerful withdrawal of the exposed body part in a fraction of a second," and even a small shift would have blurred the marks. That is, unless KV fainted and went into a temporary coma, which could only happen under the hand of a hostile torturer, exactly as KV claimed, since a coma would cause a "friendly" torturer to stop. Or unless—the doctor added in a rhetorical aside that, in my readings, always includes an imagined chuckle—KV were put under anesthesia. This would restrict his collaborators to medical professionals, which was unlikely (read: ludicrous). KV's scars, concluded the doctor, were consistent with his account of torture. After examining KV's entire body, Dr. Zapata-Bravo went on to say that the event with the rod was "a major disruption in the life of this middle class educated young man." When petrol was poured on his wounds, the doctor writes, KV was put under "extreme anxiety and horror, because he was sure that he was going to be killed by fire." But since KV's psychological state wasn't within the scope of his instruction, the doctor stopped there.

Everyone who read Dr. Zapata-Bravo's report, from the solicitors to Freedom from Torture to the Helen Bamber Foundation, found it deeply convincing, sympathetic yet professional: a report by an unbiased doctor who had scrutinized a story and believed. But—and the genesis of this idea stuns me—the Home Office zeroed in on the doctor's clearly hyperbolic point about anesthesia. From his twenty-page report, their primary takeaway: that anesthesia *was* a possibility. Their hypothesis now defied all reason: that KV had himself put under anesthesia—by a villainous doctor, the theory casually allows—and permanently scarred so he might gain asylum to the U.K.

I suppose one might believe it, if the U.K. were a paradise. What was it that Virginia Woolf wrote about theories? They're dangerous things, the germ of a theory being "almost always the wish to prove what the theorist wishes to believe."

———

One tranquil English morning, Josh hanged himself off a low railing. How does one die like that? I don't dare ask. I imagine he was found on his knees, leaning forward away from the rail, the rope taut. I can't say for how long he'd seriously planned this step, but he completed it sometime that November morning, in his Essex flat, a few steps from his parents' house. I didn't know these details that first evening, when I threw on my clothes and ran down that Provencal hill to his uncle and aunt (Jo and Annie)'s house, my wet hair freezing to my cheek. I imagined him in a hospital bed, drinking a box of juice, nursing a hesitant wrist wound (a gesture, theater) wrapped under three fingers of unstained bandage.

By the time I arrived at Jo and Annie's house, my breath was ice scratching up my chest. I burst through the door without knocking, and only when I saw Annie's horror did I look down and realize I was wearing Flo's long jean skirt, sneakers with the backs crushed under my heels, Sheldon's half-wet Brooklyn sweatshirt, and a mop of frozen hair. Later Annie told me she thought I'd been raped. *This is the wrong reaction*, I kept telling myself. *Calm the fuck down.*

"Where is Sam?" I asked. She didn't know. "We have to call Anna or somebody."

I took a breath. In French, my already scattered thoughts became nonsensical. I explained that one of our guests was telling me that Josh had killed himself, and please let's call the family now. We called Sam's sister, Anna. She was strangely calm. Sometimes her breath would quicken into quiet sobs. She kept saying, "Well, he did it. He ended it." I handed the phone to Annie, so she could get details. As I waited, I chided myself: *You have no right to make a spectacle. His mother gets to be hysterical. His sister. Not you.*

It's strange now, thinking back to that night, that I started to fret about my own behavior. I'm usually very unpolished, very open—what you see is what you get. Sam says I have no filter. But I was suddenly aware that perhaps I wasn't entitled to certain dramas. Because I didn't love Josh. I didn't love him and everyone knew it. Even now, my frenzy was mostly about Sam.

I had been texting Sam all night. Finally, he replied, "I'm in the garden."

I told Annie I was going back. She offered to drive me the thirty seconds up the hill.

Over the next hour, people trickled into the kitchen. The commune writers, Sam's local family. We set up the iPad for family in London. Eventually, Sam would need to eat, so Laleh and Aleks kept the food warm. I dropped into a chair and picked up a glass of wine. Laleh spotted the dollop of body wash at the bathroom threshold and wiped it up with a dishrag.

I went upstairs to look for Sam. I found him sitting on the balcony where he had arranged his writing desk and papers, large sections of his novel taped to walls as they had been years before at MacDowell. "Your manifestos," I had joked then because his cabin was covered in rows of printouts, taped together like scrolls. *Most of all*, I now reminded myself, *Sam is hurting. And this isn't about me, or us.* I hugged him and whispered, "I'm so sorry."

His voice broke against my ear. "I can't believe it," he said. "I just can't believe it."

There was a long, eerie silence. "Do you want a glass of something?" I said.

"I can't drink," he said. "I want to talk to my family again. I want to call David."

I left him alone. Downstairs, I chewed my nails. I poured a glass of wine to take up to him. "He doesn't want wine," said Laleh. "We tried earlier."

I took it up anyway. "No, thank you, love," said Sam.

I set the glass down. "Are you hungry?" He shook his head.

I thought, I have to say something now, or this will always be between us. The thing we do now, the way we acknowledge my history with Josh, will affect everything from here on out.

"I'm sorry," I said, "that I never believed him. I know you're not thinking about that now, but you will later, and I'm sorry. I was wrong." But I didn't think I had been mistaken. If I'm honest, I believed that Josh's suicidal gesture (another of his dramas) had gone terribly wrong.

Sam's chin started to tremble, and he pulled me into his arms. He told me it wasn't my fault, that nobody believed Josh, and that was part of the tragedy. It was the kindest thing he'd say about it, in the aftermath. In weeks after, he would remember my every cruel remark. I closed my eyes and promised myself that from then on, I'd behave the right way, I'd say the right things, I'd perform everything Sam needed me to, to reckon with what I had and hadn't believed. But I wouldn't fake it, or change history, or pretend I felt what I didn't feel. That unforgiving voice inside would be too disgusted. And anyway, my opinion never mattered. I was a drop in the avalanche of things Josh had going on. But now he loomed large in my life, a human reminder of all that might go wrong in moments of great change.

Sam and I went downstairs. He ate a plate of vegetables, and details trickled down to us.

Josh's body was not discovered for a while. Sometime in the afternoon (I'm unsure of the hour), Ilan's best friend, Dirk, came upon him slumped by that railing. Given Josh's lockdown isolation and Sheldon's recent cancer struggle, Dirk, who lived a few doors down, had taken on the job of looking in on Josh, so Sheldon and Flo could self-isolate. A kind bespectacled man with a family of daughters and a quiet way of slipping in and out of rooms, I imagine he walked into Josh's living room expecting not to be noticed. More than once, at past gatherings, I had looked up to see Dirk raising a glass or clearing a plate, having missed his arrival entirely. I imagine that when he saw Josh and understood, he gasped softly, then got to work. I imagine he didn't make a lot of noise. For many nights, the scene played in my mind: this delicate, peaceful man with huge glasses, laboring and struggling under Josh's heavy corpse, trying to lower it from the railing, then lay it flat, to spare others that horrifying permanent image—the next person to cross the threshold might be Josh's mother, or a police officer who didn't love Josh enough to be the first to touch him.

Within an hour, Sam was researching flights to London. I was determined to go with him. "There are lots of people here to watch Elena," I said. "I'm going with you."

Nobody contradicted me at first. They just smiled and nodded. But as the hours passed, and far-flung relatives gathered on Zoom, it became clear I couldn't go. Thanksgiving was a day away, and Elena's birthday soon after that. Then we'd all be back with the family at Christmas. It wasn't fair to saddle our friends with Elena's routines. It would weigh on Sam to have her alone, without a parent. Plus, the five of them needed to mourn in private, without partners or friends or neighbors or children—to be together as they hadn't been since before Josh was born.

That night, Manu offered to read the Mourner's Kaddish in Hebrew, and family from around the globe logged on to hear it. It was a marvel; within hours, in that small kitchen, we were forty or fifty. Just before we began, Laleh, Jennifer, and I searched Flo's cellar for dinner napkins that might double as kippahs. Manu examined them, rejecting the ones with yellow polka dots. We didn't want to make a spectacle, we just wanted to cover our heads.

Early the next morning Sam flew to London, and the commune turned its attention to helping me survive parent duties. "I want to go ahead with Thanksgiving," I said at dinner the following night. Jennifer and I had planned a big traditional American meal and now everyone seemed relieved. We texted Sam's aunt and cousin, to invite them to join us.

The commune's serenity now seemed a blessing, and our friends were constantly helpful. They slipped in and out of the house, taking Elena, leaving shopping in the fridge and pantry. They wrote quietly in daytime and knocked on the door for walks. Charlie invited me to exercise. Laleh baked loaves of corn bread and pound cakes. Jennifer helped me think through my words for the shiva. Manu distracted me with an idea for a short film. Aleks found new riddles. And for days, there were whispers. "The commune doesn't feel like the commune anymore," someone said on a long market walk. "Now it's this limping and truncated version of itself." Suddenly, a clock had started on our time together. We had been such fools to believe we could remove ourselves from the messy business of life—not just in lockdowns, but in goodbyes, aftermaths.

———

Jennifer and I delighted in our American Thanksgiving, though it mystified Annie and Ludivine, Sam's French aunt and cousin. Wearing Flo's skirts and shawls, we built a fire, made a variety of stuffing (Annie: "*Qu'est-ce que c'est . . . oh là là*"). We skipped the turkey because French shops don't carry turkey. Manu made a fruity duck *magret*. I made a key lime pie and creamy balsamic mushrooms. Laleh took care of Elena. She did the elephant dance around the table, and told excellent stories. "Agaathaaaaa," she'd call across the square.

Now, in my memories, Laleh's voice calling Elena's secret nickname conjures that strange, unearthly season, the autumn when we briefly escaped a pandemic and death found us anyway. It brings back the yellowing leaves, lavish meals, the stories told with both hands, the music of my daughter's laughter, the safety of friends at work nearby, the sense of a village finally manifesting. That night, we ate too much and welcomed winter. Jennifer and Manu sang "A Lady of a Certain Age" and I tried not to weep.

The meal was a release of two days' tensions: Sam's departure, the Thanksgiving shopping and preparation, and my first huge failure in the wake of Josh's death: to maintain Elena's routine while Sam was gone. That first morning, since we had been up past two, I let her sleep in and took her to school at eleven. I tried to explain in French that Sam's brother had died, Sam had left, and we were barely coping. The teacher glared. At day's end, she sent a stern note with Annie that even a village school is school; next time Elena wouldn't be allowed in.

Each morning after that, I woke with Elena at precisely 8:00 a.m. as Sam had done. I coaxed my daughter's warm body out from under her covers, I brushed her teeth, dressed her and gave her whole-grain toast and milk, while I made a pack lunch and a pot of coffee. We walked to the local school, my steaming mug in hand. By 9:01 (when I would normally still be in bed) I was alone in the square, where I rocked on a swing in my sandals and long skirt, finishing my coffee.

I came to enjoy the strict morning routine, the crisp watery smell of the village in the morning, Laleh and Charlie out on the balcony, Manu and Jennifer strolling to *la source* for spring water. By the third day, when it became clear that nobody from the commune was going to abandon me to this, that they had decided (silently or when I wasn't around) that they would stage some kind of rescue, or at least make themselves into a kind of safety net, the dark fog that had settled over me for all of lockdown began to lift. I felt guilty. Sam was in Essex burying his baby brother. I wasn't allowed to be thriving. And yet, I breathed easier, plugging ahead with Elena's routine, joining more group walks, reading more, cooking more inventive dishes.

Between grim errands, Sam and his remaining siblings went on runs in the Essex woods. It seemed each time I called, they had either just returned from one or were about to set off. Carrying a load of Elena's laundry to the garden lines, I pushed back ugly thoughts. *Sam doesn't have to do his mourning the way I say so*, I reminded myself. *He can go on runs. Just relax.*

Sam spaced out the most difficult chores, steeling himself for each one, taking big breaths as if he were entering a fumigated room. He cleaned out Josh's apartment, surprising himself by burning sage. He had never been superstitious, and he wasn't even sure he burned the right kind. Now Josh's room smelled like roast vegetables. Cleaning out Josh's desk, Sam pocketed the books he was reading. He rifled through his papers and found poems Josh had written, meticulous sketches, a beautiful mosaic of Josh's fractured mind. Over hours, he devoured them all. Then, a noise outside roused him. The mailman had left a package at the threshold. He tore it open—it was industrial strength duct tape. Sam shuddered, tossed it aside, and burned more sage.

Unsatisfied with the answers in Josh's papers, Sam made a

halfhearted attempt to open his iPad. He wondered if he'd have access to Josh's finger, if he might use it to open his devices so they could sort through his bills, and email his friends. After a while, sharing Josh's creative space (all that childish joy, all that potential) became too painful, and Sam began sorting his clothes. He packed a few items to keep. After that, he was always wearing something of Josh's—a shirt, a jacket, a wristband. Now and then for several months, I'd cringe at Sam walking around in unfamiliar things. I considered ordering him the same T-shirts and mixing them in, so I'd never know if my partner was walking around like an unhinged ghoul in his dead brother's laundry.

Cleaning the flat was the job of many days. Sam locked up. Days later, he returned. Another package had arrived. Oven bags. "How many ways did he consider?" Sam muttered to me on the phone.

The next day, Sam visited Josh's body. Before he entered the cold room, his mother asked him to take a photo, and he did, zooming in on the eyes kept shut with Vaseline, the waxy skin, the suit buttoned to his neck. He couldn't bring himself to open the iPad. Every day was like sifting through the grisly flotsam trailing a shipwreck. And so, Sam went on long runs, and joked with his remaining brother, and dragged his sister mile after mile until she was stronger.

Meanwhile, in the bosom of the commune, I focused on Elena. Plagued by a constant dread, I gulped the air randomly. Every few hours, I lost myself in survival fantasies and was startled back to reality. Why should I have apocalyptic thoughts? When Sam asked me to moderate the upcoming shiva, I felt like I was about to attempt some kind of celestial fraud.

In the months that followed, each time Sam said something out of the blue, unlinked to the chain of our ongoing conversation, I knew that he had been with Josh. "Have you heard of George Berkeley, the eighteenth-century philosopher?" he asked once. "His theory of immaterialism? Basically, that *to be* is to be perceived. I thought it might interest you." I tried to follow the thought to its root, but got nowhere. I kept thinking, one day Sam will write about this and answer these mysteries. Nevertheless, I counted the fibers. What had led Sam to immaterialism?

If I close my eyes, will this nightmare end?

Did it even happen, if I refuse to see it?

Was Josh altered, damaged, by other people's perceptions of him?

Maybe, since we continue to perceive him, Josh lives on in some real way?

A few weeks later, we watched Disney's *Coco* with Elena and Ludivine. When a dead soul finally disappeared from the afterlife, having been forgotten by everyone on earth, Sam wept. After that, Sam made a habit of tearing up at children's movies, or bad movies—broad-stroked, graceless films that would never have moved him in ordinary times. It seemed he was returning to childhood, where everything is new and astonishing. It reminded me of the day Elena, at three, wept for an hour after *Moana*. "I don't know why I cry. I love it and it's over forever." Her first emotional response to art. One night, shortly after Josh died, I left *The Godfather Part III* on in the living room as I cleaned. We hadn't planned to watch it; it was just on as we tidied and folded. Near the end, in the famously bad Sofia Coppola death scene, I chuckled and turned to Sam. He was transfixed, tears streaming, believing every melodramatic beat. Maybe, I thought, this will be the bad movie he loves secretly, inexplicably. In many years, maybe he'll even speak out for it, always with a lot of compassion for its flaws, but no shame.

———

Once the Home Office typed the words "self-inflicted" into his files, it took KV years to pry that vile narrative from the imaginations of the officers and Home Office workers. They used it to explain away many other victims' scars, and wrote it down as carelessly as the accidentally un-redacted "*Loser*" in an applicant's file.

In September 2013, a few days before his examination with Dr. Zapata-Bravo, KV updated his appeal statement. Mired in despair and unable to focus, he managed to write it just in time for court.

Though they're both legal documents, this amendment reads so differently to me than his first statement. Before, KV wrote as someone expecting to be believed. He summarized where the story called for it, gave pertinent facts, left out his own emotions and didn't appeal to theirs. Now his voice is broken. The appeal begins with an apology for being late, then dips in and out of visceral details of his torture and escape. Though he beseeches the court, behind the numbered paragraphs is the palpable understanding that there is no human heart to move, no flesh-and-blood listener on the other side. KV recites memories almost for himself, in tender snatches from across decades that cling like dandelion spores, like poetry, to the imagination:

> . . . We had everything that we needed . . .
>> . . . my father had a valued Morris Oxford and we later also bought a van . . .
> . . . helped in my father's jewelry shop and in his workshop . . .
. . . . and we all loved each [other] immensely . . .

. . . I had used a white flag and surrendered to the authorities. They had no justification . . .
> . . . I am a human being . . .
> . . . I did not inflict scars on myself nor did I ask someone to do this to me . . .

. . . I am not so strong-willed nor am I that careless about my life
> . . . nor would I ever harm my life in that way . . .
>> . . . I will have to live with the scars for the rest of my life.

In 2014, KV's scars became the center of another appeal argument. KV had always said that his captors burned his arms, he lost consciousness from the pain, then they burned his back. In Dr. Zapata-Bravo's 2013 medico-legal report, the doctor points out "that the scars on the back were long, narrow and parallel and that in particular their edges were precise." A perfect branding. This could only happen if KV was unconscious, as he claimed. Even if he had been forcibly held down, the doctor said, his body would have twitched and writhed. He would have flinched in pain and the movement would have blurred the edges of the scar. On his arms, though, the scar edges *were* blurred, shaky, and varied in shapes and sizes. It was an imperfect branding, because he was conscious and struggling.

In 2014, the Upper Tribunal rejected KV's second court appeal. One point of contention was how far Dr. Zapata-Bravo was allowed to venture in believing KV. The court took issue with the doctor's use of the "highly consistent" designation (from the Istanbul Protocol) which he applied to "KV's account." One judge said that the doctor "rather trespassed beyond his remit as an expert medical witness" in applying that classification to KV's story, rather than the trauma—by commenting on *how* the iron rods came to be applied, rather than simply on the fact that iron rods caused the scarring.

Next, the court of appeal questioned Dr. Zapata-Bravo about how long a person could remain unconscious while hot irons were applied to his back. The doctor was hesitant to answer. He didn't know, but other experts had established that poor health could affect the length of time, and KV had indeed been in poor health. Off the cuff, he offered ten minutes. Based on that hesitant guess, the court found it "an unlikely hypothesis" that KV would have remained unconscious through ten minutes of hot branding, and dismissed the rest of his claim.

Then the tribunal took its greatest leap of logic: it dismissed KV's appeal using an exercise of omission, an argument like: *If we can't meet the burden of proof on any of these options, then we default to a final option, one we don't have to prove or scrutinize.* It concluded that "the scars represent wounding which was Self-Inflicted by Proxy ("wounding SIBP"), in other words which was inflicted by another person at KV's own invitation in an attempt on his part to manufacture evidence in support of a false asylum claim."

One lone judge balked—were his colleagues listening to the same story? In his dissent, Judge Elias upheld the doctor's right to comment on the consistency of the story with the scars. Elias's bafflement at the very notion of SIBP and his support for hearing out expert medical judgment would later be quoted liberally in KV's U.K. Supreme Court case.

It seemed that self-inflection, a tired officer's whim, was becoming normalized with each telling. That it would even become an acronym shocked the experts, "as if it were a well-known practice with historic roots," Crawshaw marvels. But higher courts were saying "Why not?" To undo this mess, KV needed the highest court in the land.

———

At that first Kaddish, I was nervous about seeing Josh's parents. How would his mother's agony manifest? I kept imagining myself in her shoes. I would be like my father's cousin in Iran who, on the day of her husband's funeral, threw herself on the floor. She thrashed her bed, other mourners' chests. She screamed and rejected all sympathy. She wailed and ripped out her hair by fistfuls, demanding that God return him to her. She was barely thirty with a baby boy. She had loved her husband and he had died suddenly, without reason. For years, the loss consumed her.

How would Flo perform her pain? Soon into the call, I realized I wasn't the only one wondering. Family in France, England, U.S., everyone seemed to be watching her, listening to her. She was gracious and serene, accepting condolences from her Essex living room, nodding at memories, occasionally even consoling friends and neighbors. But there was one thing I quickly realized Flo was refusing to do: no matter how much friends and relatives subtly pushed and prodded, Flo refused to perform her grief for other people.

Who knows if she wept in front of Sheldon, or her other children. But she wasn't about to put it on display for people who hadn't been there, during all those years of suffering with Josh, dragging Josh to doctors, wondering if he was in this country or that, sleeping in his bed or on a street. She had nothing to prove, and didn't owe them theater. Where were they days ago at the urgent care? Where were they when he was sectioned? Fixing my stare on Sam's mother throughout that first call, I sensed a new kind of respect for her taking root. She was so firm, so decided: she wasn't about to make "grieving mother" her new identity. *Well done, Flo.*

And how would one even begin to prove the depths of one's pain to any of these people—whether compassionate or judgmental—who had been hit so much more superficially than Flo had? Even Sam and his siblings couldn't match what Flo must have felt. Whatever stores of empathy we claim, humans can't feel one another's pain. What they feel when they witness suffering is, first and always, relief at having been spared.

So the guests tried to draw it out of her. They went on and on. They displayed their own grief, their regret, their sympathy. Flo nodded. "You mustn't feel guilty . . . You mustn't feel bad . . . He is in heaven." I watched the changes on her face. She was serene.

A few years ago, I lost an uncle to suicide. He married my aunt when they were barely twenty; he was one of the most charismatic and clever men I had met. That he was English in an Iranian family made him fascinating and exotic. Over decades he deteriorated, then he made his exit. Since I was closer to that death, and to its survivors (his wife and sons), I know that there is a measure of relief at such times. Now the family can rebuild. In a day, months and years are freed up for work, for exploration, for stories, for love. Their lives are no longer about mental health care. The family has come to understand, years before, that this *could* be the way their ailing beloved might go. They are prepared. They've lived this eventuality many times over. It has been repeated, enacted; this is only a manifestation of a living truth that has long existed. And it is, mercifully, its final enactment. They can stop reliving it now.

And yet, in the aftermath, there are expectations. The relief remains a secret, the one sensation that no insider performs. It exists entirely in a private, even subconscious realm.

. . . and suddenly Flo said it. She *said it*, to the people on Zoom. She didn't care what they thought. They weren't her son, or her mother, or her God, and this wasn't their story. "This has been my life for years. I am relieved. He is released." *Flo*, I thought, *you are my hero.*

A few nights later, with the family gathered, Flo and Sheldon danced, a sweet slow song with a light beat. Sam recorded them, as they held each other, as Sheldon raised his arm and Flo slowly turned, her eyes closed, a prayerful smile on her lips. The far-flung family watched, comforted. This couple had spent decades in silent misery, in anticipation of this worst outcome, this nightmare. Every night they awaited the monster, were jolted awake by every sound. And now it had come, and it had plundered their family. And it was over; it would never again return for them. Amid the rituals they would now perform, the nightly Kaddishes and the shiva, their rejection of the hysterical mourner's script seemed profound. This wasn't about the rest of us, or what we believed. We were just spectators. They were the chief mourners. Flo, who had carried Josh in her body, would enact her grief however she liked.

In the kitchen of the village house, a photo of a young Flo and Sheldon leans on a mantle above a basket of loose onions. That winter, as we cooked and washed dishes and mopped the floor, we kept glancing up at it. It was taken when they were in their twenties, at a time when they were first in love, long before their children were born. It seems to have been taken in some nothing moment, not the day of their engagement or a family gathering. They're just squandering the day, staring naively in the middle distance beyond the camera lens, playful, vibrant, expecting only the good.

8.

After we accepted Jesus (on that London trip when I was six), my mother and I tried to embody our new faith and make it tangible. She had marched with revolutionaries in 1979. Now back in Isfahan, my mother scurried to underground churches, worked on a secret radio station, and telephoned fellow converts. I, too, acted out my Christianity, wearing a cross, praying to Jesus in the schoolyard.

In London, my mother and grandmother had explained to me that what made our Christian faith special was the lack of ritual. That's why we were Protestants, not Catholics. We didn't want our old Muslim conventions dressed up in a new way. We wanted a living faith, a relationship with God. "We don't repeat numbing rituals," they said. "We read the Bible in Farsi and talk to Jesus in Farsi, and think for ourselves and question ideas."

The rule about praying deliberately in our own language didn't apply to glossolalic chants, which were divine gifts of ecstatic relief and proof of God's presence among us. As for rituals, we did keep two: communion and baptism. But these were symbolic acts that Jesus had done. It wasn't our place to group them with meaningless, mindless ceremonies that priests had introduced later to the church. I think what defined "ritual" to my mother and her fellow underground church-goers wasn't performance, but rote repetition: inviting Jesus wasn't a ritual, but a rite of passage, like a wedding or funeral. You did it once. Neither was baptism a ritual: you got one, and only when old enough to consent. As for holy communion, it was symbolic; the grape juice would remain grape juice in our bodies. These two sacraments were infrequent, designed to remind us, now and then, of God's love and sacrifice and the cleansing of our sins through faith. But even to rebels and apostates, symbols mattered in small doses.

Is faith worth anything without some kind of enactment? Some sac-rifice, or semblance of stakes? Seventeenth-century philosopher Blaise Pascal (famously practical about such things) said, "Kneel down, move your lips in prayer, and you will believe." Repeating the rituals of a faith will cement it, and make it true. We remake *ourselves* through repetition, perform the parts of our identity into existence. Three centuries later, Michel Foucault applied similar logic to the "historical specificity" of the body: society creates the kind of bodies it needs through exertions of structural power and discipline. This reshaping is achieved by repe-tition, ritual, and punishment. Capitalism creates fit, strong bodies that can work. Prisons create docile bodies that obey. The West creates a particular femininity, and so forth. Along the same lines, says Pascal, the aspiring believer can create in herself a believing mind, by moving her lips and praying.

My first week in an underground church, I watched my mother enact her Christianity, her arms raised in prayer, as she'd never done before. In a day, praying wasn't bowing over a rug, forehead to prayer stone; now it was standing, dancing, arms to the sky. How had it changed? Why didn't it seem silly to anyone else? Or would point-ing out the silliness expose something? What were the stakes of calling out a performance as inept as that of, say, Lindsay the gum-smacking glossolalist? Would the whole system crumble down if one person were seen to be faking? Or is the risk more akin to turning Lindsay into an ecstatic, saint-like, misunderstood Mariette? Regardless, my mother repeated the new prayers, and soon they became normal, even to me. After a while, no one noticed the gestures, only the sacred and deeply personal intention—to reach God. Pascal's advice had worked.

Research has shown that repeated acts, from musical training to meditation, tangibly alter the brain, curbing depression and numbing pain. Rituals (even superstitious ones) have been shown to lower anxiety, help us recover from grief, and improve performance in sports. Part of Pascal's meaning is simply that, over time, repeated enactment makes a state of mind real.

In *The Universal Exception*, Slovenian philosopher Slavoj Žižek offers three more enticing possibilities for interpreting Pascal's words. Habits cement belief in a way that "is more complex than it may appear." The kneeling might create a "self-referential causality: Kneel and you will believe *that you knelt down because you believed!*" Memory is a liar. Why not make use of that? Why not kneel for the sake of a later recollection? Or maybe the gesture displaces the belief: "Kneel and you will thereby *make someone else believe.*" Or what if the invitation is to dispel one's own belief by performing it? If the belief is too close, too overwhelming, one can externalize it in ritual performance and be rid of it as something physical existing outside oneself, a tapeworm wrapped around a healer's stick. "Do you find your belief too oppressing in its raw immediacy? Then kneel, act as if you believe, *and you will get rid of your belief . . . !*"

Even as a toddler, my daughter triple-checked things. "Are you lying? Are you lying about never lying?" Now, she often asks me to repeat things, to chant them, in order to make them true. ("Say tomorrow is my birthday." "Say there's no more school forever.") At the same time, her belief in the rules of her childhood stories is resolute and unchanging: long sleeps can be broken by handsome princes, monsters can be made good if you love them enough. She stages these stories to calm herself, long after they've stopped entertaining her. They are an enactment of an unchanging, knowable world, preserved through repetition, like a ritual.

Early on in my childish Christian faith, I stumbled on another bothersome paradox. The puzzle at the heart of Protestantism is that you can't achieve salvation through good works, or through ritual performance. You can do nothing, in fact, to earn entry to heaven. You are a Christian the moment you ask Jesus into your heart, and only he knows if you're sincere in that. But (here comes the rub), if you *were* a true Christian, you would *want* to do certain things: to attend church to be nearer to him and your spiritual siblings, to pray, to do God's good work among the poor and the unbelieving. If you don't want to, then is your faith true?

Many Christians attend church to prove it to others, and to themselves, and that repetition replaces the truth of their faith. This is what my mother noticed on arriving in Oklahoma. "They go to church to show they believe." Forget Jesus's warning against praying like hypocrites who display their faith at the street corner or in the synagogue. As humans, there are codes we've collectively created that supersede even Christ's teachings: belief, we've decided, is truer when it's exhibited.

———

Five days after my C-section, I paced the bathroom in our London flat, careful not to move a muscle around my wound, as I wept over the most taxing bowel movement of my life. The nurses in the maternity ward had warned the new mothers about this. The pain medications combine with weakened muscles, hormones, and several days of communal bathroom timidity and postpartum muscle insecurity to guarantee a day-three (or four) reckoning. The longer you avoid it, the worst it gets. And I was on day five.

Sam and I had prepared, though. He had stewed a pot of prunes and poured all the juice and pulp into my porridge. He sat there and watched until I finished every mushy bite. My mother took Elena into the guest bedroom, inconveniently on the other side of the thin bathroom wall. And I was given an hour to myself, just to accomplish this one thing. I could hear them, though, in other parts of the apartment, anticipating, worrying. Listening. I cried some more, put on Freddie Mercury, and crawled around on my hands and knees. This was my punishment for cheating the universe out of a "normal" birth, I thought. I kept feeling a phantom popped stitch.

Half an hour in, I reached across the sink to change the motivation music on my phone. Sam had sent a text. *You can do it, love!* And then: *Your mom is in there praying. Can you hear?*

I pressed my ear to the wall; or rather I slumped against it from my perch atop the toilet. She was pacing on the other side, just inches away, praying in rapid whispers. What was she saying? Was that Farsi? *Oh, God, if she starts on the damn tongues of angels . . . What if she does it in front of my baby?* Briefly I considered fetching newborn Elena—I'd rather have her see a violent shit than a delusional religious rapture. *What if the speaking in tongues blocks me more, and I have to call an ambulance?*

Still, my mother's voice distracted me from my pain. After a while, it helped. In my childhood, my mother's prayers had always worked, and now that familiar whisper carried through the bedroom wall, a ritual of prayer that I knew and had counted on during other pains, other illnesses, and grief. Once, those same whispers had had power to alter physical realities, to calm burns and bruises. It had never been God—I don't believe that. The relief was just muscle memory. Now, though I was wounded and out of balance, my body remembered: women had done this before. Many women—for millennia, including my mother—had got through that first postpartum shit. It was a joke between them, with midwives warning young mothers of it every day in that London maternity ward. What's more, I had witnessed so many other varieties of suffering dwindle and vanish, when communities prayed. I remembered now that collective strength exists. Now I looked silly to myself, suffering over a temporary physical pain.

I shut my eyes, squeezing the last tears out. *Jesus, please.* I traveled back to all those church sanctuary healings, the revivals of my youth. Was I praying to a literal Jesus? Probably not. I just wanted to be saying the same words as my mother, to relive the last time we did that.

I couldn't hold the memory long. Those revivals, the prayers, will forever fill me with shame and rage. My mother's voice may soothe me for a second, but then it's always infuriating. Because the next words might be gibberish, and then the charlatans and scammers echo in my head: *Let the bodies hit the floor. Slain in the spirit! Name and claim your fortune.* How rough and sluggish the truth against such lofty promises. "When truth appears at least as true as falsehood," wrote Simone Weil, "it is a triumph of sanctity or of genius. Thus Saint Francis made his audience cry just like a cheap theatrical preacher would have done."

Faith healers understand that rituals have power, not over the body, but over the mind that processes the body's experiences. And so they begin the grift, not in that massive sanctuary, but in the living rooms and churches of those who attend their revivals. In certain evangelical circles, they are celebrities. And everyone who finds themselves at a healing service is already a devotee, already worshipful, emotionally wrecked, probably ailing, and desperate to believe, to continue believing. By the time the evangelist lays his spray-tanned hands on a vulnerable forehead, the believer is ready (and has long been ready) to seize any hint of a miracle, and the healer needs only to provide psychological relief for the rapturous hour or two that the petitioner sits under the same roof, praying. Those hours spent in a sanctuary or revival tent, in the anesthetic brume of community, all around friends joined in uproarious prayer, in worshipful mania. The pain, you can be sure, won't return until tomorrow, when the faith healer is long gone and doubt comes knocking again.

In Philip Larkin's poem "Faith Healing" a procession of reverent women, "rimless glasses, silver hair," approach a preacher, whose "deep

American voice" demands "*now, dear child, what's wrong?*" "Mustachioed
in flowered frocks they shake." Each may dwell for twenty seconds in
his warmth: twenty seconds to state her pain, to enact faith and receive
healing, to cement the memory. Each stares dumbly at the preacher,
"an immense slackening ache," clinging to the idea that they are singular, called by a loving father, about to receive some of the lifetime's love
they were denied. The preacher prays: "Directing God about this eye,
that knee. Their heads are clasped abruptly; then, exiled."

What causes so many people to fall down by the lightest touch? Or
a suggestive word? It's important to acknowledge first that lots of people are faking—consciously. It's been a long night. They're expected to
fall. They're ready to go home, so they partake in the climax. But what
about the rest?

In many firsthand accounts, a worshipper went in skeptical, determined not to fake it, but open-minded. That open mind is all the faith
healer needs, especially with skeptics who are nonetheless still part of a
faith community. They've had repeated exposure, and intuit the spectacle as divine ritual, deriving its power from the participation of insiders. These new recruits understand how much the ritual means to
everyone, that a wave of bodies requires full participation, that idle old
men, eyes watery and expectant, are watching. They know, too, that
not succumbing is a personal failing. If you feel nothing, your spirit is
weak, or closed, or faithless. In that revival room, they are surrounded
by regulars who were first "slain in the spirit" as children, back when
community pressure was enough to make one honestly buckle—people
who grew up believing in that formative event, that sweet day they
were overcome by the spirit. For the visiting skeptic, add to this environment hours of suggestion that God is in the room, that they *will*
fall down, that they *want* to fall down, that a miracle, triggered by a
particular song or word, will unleash God's power. That word, "Shout"
or "Fire," comes unexpectedly, a roar breaking a long, meditative bout
of silence or a soothing melody. The crowd has been hushed in prayer,

lulling, swaying, for many minutes. Then, without warning, the trigger word. They fall. This is hypnosis.

Over years, and again during the revival service, the trigger words are transformed by the leader into speech acts: *I promise you, these words, in this context, have power.* They alter reality by their utterance. And don't we, as communities and society, confer upon every speech act its power? "I declare you husband and wife" can only transform two people into a married couple because we (along with our institutions) agree that, in a given context, it does.

My grandmother arrived in London from Tehran in her thirties, just before the revolution and my birth. Having escaped a marriage forced on her in childhood, she refined her accent, edited her wardrobe, and embodied her church's standards. She disowned her old self. Though she lived on a fixed income, she spent money on snake-oil promises of love and prosperity. She saw the future respect and material rewards of believing as a worthwhile sign that she was made of tougher, more faithful stuff than most.

The televangelists are so brazen: they claim that God has promised them absurd riches like jets (to "burn up for the Lord!") because they boldly ask for these things; they claim them, unashamed of desires sown by God, who is apparently an American capitalist. ("If Jesus were around today, he wouldn't be riding a donkey.")

In order to achieve the same astronomical fortune, ordinary folks should prove their faith and "plant a seed" in their future. The sums are often specific, chosen by the Lord for his own reasons ($273 is one televangelist's favorite). Knowing their viewers' financial circumstances, the grifters promise that it will return to those who, for a short time, have faith enough to part with painful sums. In this way, they've gathered millions from pensions and savings of the lonely and the hopeful. As in a pyramid scheme, people pay, hoping someone down the line will return it, regardless of their own lack of platform. The televangelists, in turn, openly admit that this "turnaround seed" will be spent on extravagances they've claimed from the Lord; if a donor ever complains of never receiving the promised manyfold returns, then they weren't faithful, or they were hiding sin.

For my grandmother, believing against all reason is something to be proud of, because it shows the depths of her trust. This is the logic that evangelical churches use when they gather children in a circle and bid them to speak in tongues. "If you believe enough, you can do it! If you can't, it's only because you doubted." It is eerily like the "I believe" chants that bring Tinkerbell back to life. When I first arrived in America, I found that many of the girls in my school were trained to believe in the power of their wishes; they strutted about the schoolyard, confident that what they wished for would come true. They wrote their wishes in lists, said them aloud, argued about them, and acted them out. They didn't talk much about work or sacrifice, as my Iranian classmates had done. By third grade in my Islamic Republic school, all the bright children knew how many hours of study it would take to pass the Konkour, and how many years to become a surgeon. We knew that buying one thing meant giving up another. We knew that the only people who'd tend to our dreams were us, and we felt lucky to have the chance to try for ourselves. Who taught American and British children that they matter so much?

As a child, I, too, listened to fantastical stories in a village at my grandparents' feet. I didn't read Western storybooks until I was ten, and when I did, I found them bizarre. Why are American children told, in dire times, to close their eyes and wish harder? That chanting "I believe" will stay a fairy's death? Don't they know fairies are mostly tricksters? Demons in disguise? Don't they know that everybody lies and that there are many kinds of lies, each with its own name? Don't they know that death comes for us all? That too much believing makes you the fool? The universe is so vast, so old. Who taught them that the pain of small children matters to the universe? Children die all the time, in excruciating ways. Don't *their* wishes matter?

For some, every speech act, even the ultimate plea for rescue, is drained of its protective power. *I am a refugee*. Even a minor functionary can defuse that with *I don't believe you*.

Soon I learned that the fairy tales were only the beginning of a long and alarming education for these lucky kids. This collective fairy tale conditioning—the doctrine of exceptionalism of the elect, a chosen few who get to speak their desires and expect fulfillment—prepares for an unexamined adulthood in which the believer never questions why so many of her wishes have been fulfilled till now (never considering the accident of birth, the privilege of race, class, and nationality, even the kindness of neighbors, or the strength of a community). It also means she never has to face such questions in the future, since she is trained to proudly and boldly believe against data, history, science, and reason. After all, faith, according to every storybook tale, is worth so much more. And those who *truly* believe are so few, and ever rewarded.

This Wonderland Doctrine is a first addictive taste of communal pain relief. Founded on otherworldly promises and group pretense, it is cemented by sanctioned rituals and speech acts, and upheld with tight control of the common knowledge. Some people leave it behind, of course, and join this flawed but tangible world. But for those who find too much suffering, sacrifice, and inequality in the real world, there are two options: revolt, or prolong the magic. Maybe that's why my grandmother dove so eagerly into evangelical Christianity—she had lost her youth to a child marriage. And here was a magical Western adolescence for her thirties, a continuation of something that, had it not been cut short, should have still ended long ago.

———

"Words have power," my mother says—you can make true things happen by saying them with faith and force, by demanding them. She doesn't mean that God is waiting around to make believers rich. Her understanding is more complex, part of a far more ancient mystery, akin to the Jewish Kabbalist teaching that words create our reality. God is in the words. God *is* the word. *In the beginning was the word.* We can make some things true by saying them. Sometimes we have that explicit power ("I bet fifty dollars"); sometimes our words influence or indoctrinate ("You will fall"). "Don't ever say *I can't*," my mother warned, because then it becomes true. *Death and life are in the power of the tongue*, the Bible says—and so do fairy tales.

Chant some words and people become frogs; princesses fall asleep. Sometimes when she's angry, Elena aims her fist at me and says *wshhhhhh*. She's making me disappear. Fairy tales teach the mighty "no" of the inner beast, the one that stops evil if you're brave enough to utter it. That "no" fails once or twice, before the protagonist finds the strength to make it stick.

Anticipation is fertile soil for the sturdiest convictions. If a storybook boy or girl says "no" once and is laughed out of the scene, you can bet that "no" will be her means of triumph at the end. If a bird flies into a prison window and says a rhyme once, then twice, you can be sure that the third repetition, the one that makes it a ritual, will mean freedom or death. First acts decide outcomes. They trigger a ritual, and tell our subconscious what to anticipate. Act one of a faith healing happens in an evangelical living room, where a transfixed child watches Benny Hinn drop fifty adults with a word and thinks, *I'd like to see that for real.* That boy, when he finally attends a revival, will make the spectacle real for the next generation glued to screens. Caught up in the moment, he performs his belief. The event grows into a substantial memory, then becomes mythic, a sacred pilgrimage or *hajj*. Does his act cement the belief, as Pascal said? Or is it submission to something larger (community, or God's unknowable ways)? Regardless, it is a relief and a closure simply to do what others expect, even if it feels false.

Maybe that's why no one ever calls out fakers and naïfs pretending to speak in tongues. Everyone in a room can know something, but it wields no power until someone says it aloud. In 1969, American philosopher David Lewis introduced the theory of "common knowledge." Two people can both know something, but they might not know that the other one knows it. And they can both know that the other one knows it, but they might not know that the other one knows that they know it, ad infinitum. Only when the thing is spoken aloud do they know fully, infinitely, of the commonality of the knowledge. This is why two people in a small room might remain silent after an obvious fart. Making it common knowledge is different from both people knowing.

A fascinating logic puzzle illustrates common knowledge. I admit, I've lost a few hours trying to make it feel intuitive. It never does, but once you glimpse it, it explains so much:

One hundred blue-eyed people are kept on an island by a powerful despot. They are told that they have blue or brown eyes. Each night, islanders get a chance to leave if they correctly guess the color of their own eyes. If they get it wrong, they're shot. If they communicate with each other, they're shot. There are no reflective surfaces. Each blue-eyed islander sees 99 other blue-eyed islanders, but has no way of knowing the color of her own eyes. You, as an outsider, are allowed to visit the island and to make one statement to the crowd. But if you offer any hint of new information, you will be shot. What do you say?

The answer is this: *I see one blue-eyed person.*

The despot laughs. They all already know this. But you have just introduced it as common knowledge. Imagine if only two islanders were listening. If only one had been blue-eyed, she would look at the other person's brown eyes and leave that night ("The blue-eyed person must be me!"). But on the first night, nobody leaves. The next morning, both blue-eyed people realize they too must have blue eyes, since the other didn't leave. And so, they both leave on the second night.

This next turn in the logic is hard to accept:

With 100 blue-eyed islanders, they all leave on the hundredth night.

If a single one of them was brown-eyed, that person would realize that they're not blue-eyed when the other 99 left on the 99th night.

This riddle's logic is counterintuitive and difficult to unpack. I don't suggest you go down the rabbit hole, as I did—it will never be satisfying. But it does answer one question for me: why does nobody at an evangelical revival ever stand up and say, "I see one person faking"?

Even in game theory, a logical, mathematical realm free from superstition, saying things aloud (or writing them down) makes them truer than they were before.

When I was eleven or twelve, newly arrived in Oklahoma, my father, the unapologetic bon vivant and lifelong atheist, got a visa to visit us from Iran. He spent most of the visit trying to find Iranians with a good pipe. He devoured banana splits and barreled down waterslides in tangerine shorts. And, in a brilliant comic third act, he allowed himself to be dragged to church, where he performed a highly convincing Protestant conversion, eyes squeezed shut, opening them only to wink at me as he parroted the words. The man even endured a real church baptism. I wanted to scream, "Can't you people see that he's faking?" That this was, at best, a Pascal's wager (a "just in case") for him? More likely, it was pure farce.

Maybe they knew. Anyone could see he was acting, trying not to spoil the mood, like a skeptic standing before Benny Hinn, a crowd of expectant believers behind him. He considered it cultural politeness, a foreign guest following the rules: *when in Rome*. Yet it was vital for us to be able to say, "He is saved." Baptism is a holy sacrament, one of only two accepted by Protestants. It doesn't stop being sacred with a hammy act—the whole thing is spectacle. The outsider doesn't make a mockery of a sacred ritual until the instant someone says aloud, *That man faked it*, and makes it common knowledge. Sometimes just staying silent is enough, makes the underlying wish true enough, to carry on in faith.

———

For thirty nights after Josh's death, Sam's family gathered on Zoom to read the Mourner's Kaddish. We repeated the prayer in Hebrew, French, English. I even looked for it in Farsi. The ritual began late on the night of Josh's death, in the kitchen alongside Sam's French family and our commune. Manu suggested it, and the idea blazed across phone lines to Sam's scattered family in England and America, who gathered within the hour with their kippahs to send Josh's soul up to God.

On that first night, Manu read in Hebrew, half singing, like a cantor. I breathed out, and decided to say a private word to Josh, something more honest than the unabashed, unqualified apology I had offered to Sam an hour or two before. I looked at my feet and I said, maybe to no one, maybe just to myself, *I'm sorry I didn't believe you. If I could do it over, I'd be kinder. And if I could do it over, I'd believe a little bit more. Not everything, Josh. But more.*

Then I added, like a traitor, *You weren't trying to kill yourself, though, right?*

Why did that seem like a betrayal to his family? When, a few days later, I suggested to my literary agent and friend that he might have bungled a cry for help. *What if he didn't mean to?* I texted. She texted back promptly: *never say that to Sam.*

Was it so ugly to think that maybe a lost, broken Josh had meant to shock us and *stumbled* into a suicide? It would absolve him of a greater sin, if there is such a thing as sin. His uncle, a devout Jew, had gone on and on about how Josh had no choice, how he was forgiven and heaven-bound. So why was it so awful to think that he wasn't making that choice? And wasn't everyone thinking it? The possibility was already in the air.

I think what my friend was saying was this: don't make this ugly theory, the fact that you're thinking it, common knowledge that has to be dealt with. She was right; it seemed a cowardly thing to lay at poor Josh's door, this last ultimate goof-up. To many, his final act seemed brave. I admit, it cast my own uncomfortable memories under a layer of forgiving sepia. *He peaced out. He walked away.*

It was decided there would be a post-funeral Zoom shiva, and that I'd be the organizer. I'd run the technical aspects, organizing the speaking queue and recording the ceremony. I spent the day a nervous wreck, and most of the event drinking and shivering as the commune members refilled my glass and tried not to overburden the rickety Wi-Fi. Sam joined from his parents' garden in England, along with the British side of his family and their neighbors. The Provence faction spent the evening quietly consuming small comforts. Charlie drove to another town, breaking lockdown curfew to get us Indian food. Laleh tried to make us tea, but the noise of the electric kettle startled me and she stopped. Jennifer and Manu sat statue-still, and quietly rotated Elena's bedtime routine with Aleks and Laleh. For hours, we held our breath and watched Sam's face on the iPad screen, reading his smallest gestures, listening to his words. For his turn, Sam read a collection of sentences from Josh's diaries that he had rearranged and edited into a poem. It was mesmerizing and strange: a suffering man's frantic explosions of creativity made into art by the talented brother whose shadow he had struggled for so long to escape.

For me, the shiva happened as two distinct halves: before and after I got through my own words. The ritual expulsion. I had considered my words for a long time, much longer than I ever think about readings. In my literary life, I never prepare for events—after many years, nobody cares if I mess up a little, and the memory of the event is better cemented if I have a nice dinner instead. Today was different. I wanted to be subtle, to have gravitas, and to become invisible. I wanted the family to know that in no way did I want to make this about myself. I wanted them to understand that I wasn't faking. And this part is strange: I wanted them to understand somehow, through my performance, that I knew (and I knew that they knew) that I didn't love Josh, and that I wasn't pretending to love him now. Yet, I still mourned him;

they could believe that mourning because I was admitting this: that to me, he was the embodiment of my greatest fears.

For that, I needed to read the words dispassionately, serenely, as in a courtroom. Any tears would be melodrama. *Please God*, I prayed, *grant me the strength not to fake it, or to be overcome by my own shit.* I told his family that Josh was a mystery to me (*someone thrown out of this world*). He was unintelligible, like Cassandra, or a glossolalist. My mythologies are all about trying, and Josh had stopped doing that. I guess I bought into the dogma that some youthful flame in the belly is enough, is everything. I joined the cult of passionate intensity, of potential and need.

But, in all of Josh's misfires, I watched Sam run to his rescue; I watched Sam love his little brother like I've never seen anyone love before. I didn't believe Josh, but I believed what I saw enacted, day after day, by his family: their devotion, their agony—when Josh arrived at the door, cheerful, unbroken, how they sat around him, how they drank up his words. How they missed their little brother, and dreaded the hour he'd slip away again. Even the most perplexing and unknowable people show themselves, sometimes, through others' grief. My dose of the real Josh *was* something tangible and true: I sensed him the way you sense a gust of wind. You can't see it, but you know it's there because suddenly, all the leaves move in one direction.

I cried throughout. How? I was astonished in exactly the same way that skeptical newcomers to a revival are astonished as they collect themselves from under Benny Hinn's feet. For months after, they wonder on blogs and in chatrooms, *Was I tired? Hypnotized? Carried away? Did I fake it?*

Some things can't be said aloud because they are too ugly, or uncomfortable, or messy. But here's the unspoken thing I kept wishing I could have made visible to Josh.

We're all fakers.

Nobody speaks the tongues, Josh. That's the big secret, the collective grift of every tribe in our species: nobody is completely okay. There's no platonic leaf, and nobody knows what they're doing. What's that old saying? "No one makes it out of this life alive." Squeeze your eyes shut, and you'll see, sooner or later, that everyone is waiting for you to just try. Utter the words, the usual metaphors, the syllable patterns and intonations. Listen to others in the circle. Now say it like them, with their sparkling certainty. Kneel down, move your lips, and you will believe (and persuade others), not in some vague redemption, but in the specific possibility of you.

But Josh was gone, and I had a ritual to complete. For the rest of the ceremony, and for many weeks after, I felt obscene, like a child with a streak of mucus on her cheek.

THE UNBELIEVER

9.

Mimi was born in Myanmar without a birth certificate. Growing up, she never knew her exact birthday, though the local mothers had guesses. As a girl, she learned all that the Karen people—an ethnic minority whose struggle for independence started in 1949—suffered at the hands of the Burmese government.

But eventually, like many other young Karens, she spoke up. I'm not sure if Mimi became a full-fledged activist—her lawyer didn't go into those details—but then I spent a day or two with this story, trying to figure out what "being an activist" means when you're entrenched in the persecuted group. For someone like me, past my troubles as a refugee with a place in Western society, activism is a clean-cut, respectable thing. But what of those who have to scream out on their own behalf because the media has disappeared? I learned in negotiation class that advocating anything that benefits you makes you less credible, so you should include a request that doesn't benefit you. What a strange luxury. For those stuck in the jaws of the beast, struggling to survive looks more like agitation, complaining.

Today many thousands of Karens live as refugees around the world, stuck in Thai border refugee camps, internally displaced in Myanmar, or in other neighboring countries. In 2011, over 73,000 were resettled in Western countries, most in the United States. Mimi followed that wave.

As a teen, she fled persecution in Myanmar to Thailand, where she lived in a refugee camp with many other Karens. Life in the camp was brutal and restrictive, and Mimi slipped away to work in Chiang Mai, Thailand. But soon the Burmese government caught up with her and arranged to have her deported back to Burma. Facing certain persecution back home, Mimi considered her options. In Burma she'd forever be a second-class citizen, harassed and disenfranchised. But there were places in the world where other Karens had found welcome, nations that had signed the Refugee Convention, pledging to help those without home or country.

Mimi is clever and resourceful. She is forthcoming and honest in her dealings. But in that desperate moment, about to be deported into danger with no passport, birth certificate, or other proof of identity or nationality, knowing that her only safe route was westward, Mimi began searching for any way to avoid being sent back to Myanmar. She paid a Thai woman, Dao, for her birth certificate. She then used Dao's birth certificate to obtain a Thai passport. With that passport (issued in Dao's name), Mimi got a U.S. visa. In America, she was sure to find a Karen community. At every point along the way, on Burmese roads and in Thai camps, at the passport agency and in the embassy where, in her best skirt, she waited in lines and received her (or Dao's) student visa, Mimi thought, *When I'm safe, I'll tell them. I won't have to live with this lie.*

"So you understand," the lawyer said, then paused. "A legitimate U.S. visa was now attached to a fraudulent underlying passport, in the wrong name." I winced. Bureaucratic nightmare ahead.

Mimi passed the checkpoints and boarded a plane. The minute she landed in New York, Mimi asked for immigration authorities. Alone in the tiny room, she gave herself up. "This is a fake passport," Mimi told the officers. "This is not who I am." She told them her story. "I used this document to reach safety because I have no access to proof of who I am. I've never been granted my Burmese citizenship because I'm a Karen. I never had a birth certificate. But I'd like to claim asylum, as myself."

With that, Mimi waited. She had pressed the button, triggered the long saga for which she'd prepared for weeks, maybe months. Other refugees had warned her, quoting a line from a famous book: *once it's begun, you can never let the trial out of your sight.* She took a breath.

—————

In every life, some words are more noteworthy than others. Some are more than mere words. They don't say something, they *do* something. "I take thee," "I bequeath," "I christen this girl," "I bet a grand," "I relinquish my right to counsel." Such utterances alter reality. In his 1962 book *How to Do Things with Words,* J. L. Austin argued that we use words not just to inform (to describe existing truth) but to act (to change that truth). These speech acts, or "performatives," as Austin called them, either trigger a response or, just by being spoken, alter the state of things—for example, commanding, betting, promising, taking an oath. Such words are actions in themselves, made true simply by being said.

My first conscious speech act was when I sat with my grandmother in London, fresh off a flight from Iran, and said the words "I accept Jesus." Another speech act was the day I allowed an Islamic Republic school teacher to put a bullhorn in my hand, so I could lead the "death to" chants. *Death to America. Death to Israel.* The first speech act made me a Christian, the second a baby Judas.

Linguists distinguish between illocutionary speech acts (the ones that alter reality instantly by their utterance) and perlocutionary ones (the ones that cause something else to happen). Illocutionary enactments are ceremonial, ritualizing an outcome: the utterance completes the act. "I take thee," for example, or "You're fired" are illocutionary speech acts. In Islam, you can divorce someone by thrice saying, "I divorce you." The divorce becomes real in that moment, and enterable as fact into the public record. On the other hand, a perlocutionary speech act might be something like a leader calling citizens to arms, or a person shouting "fire" in a crowded theater, famously not covered by the First Amendment precisely because it's not speech, but an *act*. When uttered, it unleashes a chain of events, like a fairy tale spell.

Naturally, since performatives are more action than statement, one can't judge them as untrue. Speech acts can only be happily or unhappily enacted. They can be misfires (e.g., the wedding officiant isn't licensed), or abuses (e.g., one party is a bigamist). Maybe the love wasn't ever there, and that too is either an abuse or an unhappy outcome of a marriage vow. Whatever the case, "I take thee" isn't a truth or lie so much as a success or failure.

Why is the phrase "China virus" a part of our public discourse, appearing in think pieces, news reports? Why is it a part of the pandemic narrative? Even before his second presidential run was over, Trump began performing his most frightening speech acts, declaring widespread voter fraud, an accusation he later tried to legitimize with frivolous court cases. Watching it unfold, it was clear he wasn't counting on judicial wins. Aside from the obvious theater, he was trying to alter the public record. The election was officially questioned in court—a true but dishonest history. Meanwhile, we waited for the one patriotic speech act that would never come. *I concede.*

On November 4, 2020, Trump tweeted, "We have claimed, for Electoral Vote purposes, the Commonwealth of Pennsylvania (which won't allow legal observers) the State of Georgia, and the State of North Carolina, each one of which has a BIG Trump lead. Additionally, we hereby claim the State of Michigan if, in fact . . . there was a large number of secretly dumped ballots as has been widely reported!"

Twitter went wild. People started "hereby claiming" things from money to a full head of hair to Liam Hemsworth. They meant, *You don't have the power to do that just by saying "hereby."* As an illocutionary speech act, the claim had no force. But Trump never meant "We claim

Michigan" as an illocutionary act, like "You're fired." The performative was calculated for its consequence, its perlocutionary effect, like
"China virus." He wanted the damage, and had no delusions about the
official impact of "hereby." He had expensive lawyers, after all, and
an instinct for performatives of both kinds. Perlocutionary speech acts
are performed upon others, for the response. Similarly, when a president calls migrants "thugs" or "criminals," he enters those words into
history, an accusation that their children and grandchildren will have
to answer for decades, privately, in the subconscious of their neighbors
and classmates and coworkers. Simple visual metaphors become red
herrings in the public memory. Once refugees are a swarm, Mexicans
are rapists, women are banshees, it is trying, Sisyphean work to untangle the image from the reality—the red herring remains lodged at the
story's center. For a red herring to be forgotten, a single compelling and
inevitable truth has to emerge and overpower the trick.

Why does public memory matter? As recently as the 1960s, textbooks in the American South taught children that southern slaves were
better off than northern factory workers, that the Civil War was entirely about states' rights. Even in recent years, textbook publishers have
used terms like "workers," "indentured servants," or "immigrants" as
synonyms for America's Black slaves. The public memory continues to
make heroes of Confederate generals, and people turn out to protest
their erasure from public landmarks.

After WWII, many Germans claimed not to have known what the
Nazis were doing. Maybe this was true, for some. But "an extreme case
of the distortion of the memory of a committed guilty act is found in
its suppression," writes Primo Levi in *The Drowned and the Saved*. "Here,
too, the borderline between good and bad faith can be vague; behind
the 'I don't know' and 'I do not remember' that one hears in court-
rooms there is sometimes the precise intent to lie, but at other times
it is a fossilized lie, rigidified in a formula." The fossilized lie is public
memory, the last battleground. Historians might say that Trump didn't

understand truth, that it didn't exist for him. Maybe so. But for an opportunist and a grifter, truth is a feeble match for a good performative. Trump may not have understood the truth, but he understood something more powerful: how to alter it.

———

Speech acts at their most extreme appear in children's stories as magical spells, enchantments, and the kind of *I love you*'s that end century-long sleeps. A staple of children's storytelling is the all-powerful "No!" as in Gandalf the Grey's "You shall not pass." In an episode of *Stranger Things*, a doomed but kindhearted Sean Astin (the ideal actor to sell the power of "no") tells our boy hero that all he has to do is stand up to the monster and command it to go. All he had to do was *perform* the bigness and bravery of his heart; disastrous advice.

Wishing doesn't have any force; it is an exhalation, a release, of one's existing power.

When carried over to real life, fairy tale speech acts (the kind backed by spirit, wit, or determination, rather than by financial or institutional power) can be moving, but often they're just misfires. Sometimes a "no" will put a powerful opponent in his place, but not if there's money on the line. Sometimes a "please" will earn you goodwill, but not if your foe has something valuable at stake. Fairy tale speech acts work if the powerful want them to work. And yet we begin our storytelling lives learning that our heartfelt speech acts will land where we lob them. What cruel and dangerous miseducation.

The claim for asylum is a speech act. The utterance changes the petitioner into an asylum seeker, and it attaches the grounds to their case. A major struggle for asylum seekers is having attached the wrong reason to their case in that confused moment of first utterance, having been ashamed to say "I'm gay" or "I was raped." That first speech act declares a particular identity and establishes fear of danger on account of *that* identity. It is that fear, not previous harm, that makes a Refugee

Convention refugee. That first speech act commits the petitioner to one kernel of the self (a story, an identity) and triggers a chain of bureaucratic responses to it. It also establishes a series of smaller facts: your name and country of origin, age, family ties. In other words, it brings you into existence in the host country's records: you are now "in the system."

Mimi's claim, though, created some problems for the asylum officers. Three speech acts, each requiring action: she claimed asylum ("I am a refugee"), denied the identity on her papers, forcing it into official question ("This is not who I am"), and confessed to a crime ("I've entered the country on a false passport"). It bound together a grimy tangled hairball of falsehoods that now needed to be scraped off the public's books, so that Mimi could live as herself.

And here was another problem: forensic testing on the visa (an American document easily tested by U.S. authorities) confirmed decisively that it was legitimate, an irrelevant finding that Mimi had already explained, which felt nonetheless instinctively meaningful to the officers. How could the passport possibly be fraudulent if American immigration authorities had believed it credible enough to grant a visa? Accepting that would mean accepting that an American officer had been duped. The passport, by way of the visa, had been accepted and legitimized.

The officers now had two options: untangle the hairball, or refuse to acknowledge it. They chose the easy line, and converted it to belief: the public record is always right. "They refused to hear her asylum case," Mimi's lawyer said. "They insisted that the U.S. visa was legitimate and that she was lying about her fake credentials. That she was legitimately in the United States on a student visa." Never mind that many refugees enter into safe countries on tourist or student visas at first (this was my family's route when we entered Dubai; we went in on a tourist visa, then we claimed asylum)—so, the legitimacy of the visa didn't by itself invalidate Mimi's asylum claim. What the authorities chose to disbelieve was her entire backstory and identity behind it. To the American government, the passport was real now. Mimi was no refugee, but simply a visitor on a visa. Mimi, the Karen refugee, was now Dao, a Thai student.

Ana Reyes, the American asylum lawyer, told me about a case in which government lawyers had found a newspaper article in which a client's age was misreported. Reyes and her team had to find corroboration outweighing the newspaper's credibility; the wrong age might have entered the public record via human error, but it could only be excised with a mountain of evidence and a reputable lawyer known for extreme vetting. If the discrepancy had happened to an unrepresented client, the case would have been thrown out for credibility issues. Had the reporter himself been reachable, his word alone might not have been enough. Similarly, each time a translator mistranslates a detail of someone's life, trying to correct it is like trying to change history. The mistake is treated as sacred fact, and no proof of the translation error seems to suffice. Meanwhile, errors can slip in covertly, through repetition. News media pick up stories from each other, without fact-checking, and a faulty detail can be repeated in twenty journals before it's caught. The repetition doesn't make that detail any more solidly factual. And yet, it has now become more compelling, entrenched more deeply in the public record.

———

Just after midnight on August 31, 1994 in East Baltimore, Anthony Wooden was shot in the head with a .44-caliber bullet. Witnesses described two men running into the night, and some remembered speaking to the men before the shooting. No one could identify them. But the very next day, police stumbled upon a lead: Diane Bailey, who lived two blocks from the scene, had cooperated with police before. After a previous shooting, she had exchanged testimony for rent—a practice that, apparently, doesn't get a witness laughed out of a modern American court. This time, as they had done before, the police offered to move Bailey and to pay her rent if she would testify against their chief suspects: brothers Kenneth "JR" McPherson and Eric Simmons.

Though Bailey was paid, and claimed to have seen the crime from a third-floor window 150 feet away, her testimony slipped into the public record with the same legitimizing language of an impartial witness. In fact, she became a cornerstone for the prosecution's case. Their other key witness, a thirteen-year-old boy, was threatened with homicide charges until he named JR and Eric. This, too, is common enough to bypass the collective conscience of the police. Aside from those two shaky witnesses, the police had no evidence tying either brother to the crimes.

Before trial, the boy tried to recant, but it was too late. Like Mimi's fake passport, his testimony was part of the record. During trial, he tried *again* to recant. It made no difference.

JR and Eric spent twenty-five years in prison for conspiracy to commit murder. In 2019, a joint investigation by the Mid-Atlantic Innocence Project, the University of Baltimore Innocence Project Clinic (UBIPC), and the Conviction Integrity Unit at the Baltimore City state attorney's office reinvestigated the case, confirming both alibis and dismantling the state's shoddy case. When they were exonerated in May 2019, JR and Eric were forty-five and forty-eight, respectively. I saw their photo on Facebook, happily walking in front of my college friend, Mid-Atlantic Innocence Project attorney Frances Kim Walters, who represented JR (Eric was represented by UBIPC). *Twenty-five years.* I looked at that photo for a long time. They seemed so hopeful, after all that.

In those twenty-five years, their lawyers grew up. My friend Frances transformed from a girl with a tennis racket and a pile of textbooks wrapped in brown paper to the kind of legal professional who can free the wrongfully convicted—a person who can challenge and rewrite the public record. In 1994, when the brothers were convicted and shut away, Frances and I were fifteen, in high schools across the country. By the time we were dressing up as Charlie's Angels and bickering over Econ scores and butterfly clips in her Princeton dorm, JR and Eric had already lost half a decade.

It's a mercy that they didn't know then that they had two decades left to wait, that Frances was now drinking Diet Snapple and looking for her first job. That their other lawyers, too, were still young and unsure, with so much to learn and do before they'd even know the names JR and Eric. Frances still had two degrees to go, a few internships, that first job, then another. She had to become interested in the law, to take the LSAT, to apply to law school, to move, attend hundreds of classes, to marry, have children, get eight dozen haircuts and drink seven thousand cups of coffee, to watch the news day after day, wondering, *Where is the justice in this world?*, to stay up nights with her babies in her lap, fuming over racial and wealth inequality, to lose many of our classmates to cynical money jobs, to hear their language lose its charming contours, then stiffen and cement into an evasive code, always ahead of the law, to decide to take her talents to the Innocence Project, to come across JR and Eric's names in a file. To see the words *paid witness* and *tried to recant* and *twenty-five years*.

It can take decades to unwrite a story that was crafted in hours. And yet, that story can be written with words bought for rent money by a dogged, badly incentivized police force, with details wrenched from the mouth of a frightened child who is granted no further right to correct it. Truth or lies, innocent or guilty, never talk to police, lawyers tell us, because all you're doing is establishing a focal point for some future absurdity. Innocent or not, the chances that speaking to police will help you are precisely zero; once something enters the record, it's impossible to pry it out, and once there is any kind of narrative, the system turns from hunting near and far for truth, to proving or disproving that narrative, however silly it might be. Sometimes that starting point isn't what you said, but an oversimplified piece of what you said. And if you're a young Black man questioned by police, your aim is to make no impression, give no information, invite no second visit—to vanish from memory.

"We see that police form a theory of the crime based on the first identification and quickly start bucketing information," Frances told me. "Anything that fits is believed; anything that doesn't fit is a lie . . . Tunnel vision can happen when you truly believe someone is guilty or when you are under pressure to make an arrest." Of 2,505 exonerations in the U.S. (as compiled by the National Registry of Exonerations) up to the date of our talk, 1,500 involved perjured or false testimony or bad confessions (e.g., the Reid Technique). Frances thinks the world has grown skeptical, "believing that all humans are inherently self-serving. Admissions of guilt are readily believed, while pleas of innocence are dismissed out of hand."

"So, people are pushed to say things," I asked, "then blocked from recanting because every lie has to be self-serving? What about human error, or frailty, or coercion, or remorse?"

Frances chuckled. Then she sent me a pile of documents about Lamar Johnson, a man who spent thirteen years in prison for a murder he didn't commit.

———

Fourteen-year-old Ashia sits in a stuffy interrogation room, staring at photos of men. She knows some of them. An officer reads her some words, then stands there, arms crossed, waiting. She wants to leave now. *If we pick one,* a voice whispers, *we can leave. We should've just kept our mouth shut.* The man was so blurry; he ran so fast. *Just pick one. Pick the closest.*

On March 26, 2004, in broad daylight, with thirty people nearby, a dark-skinned young man in a skully hat fired three shots into Carlos Sawyer's body, leaving him to die in a gutter. The shooting happened at a bustling intersection of Baltimore, near shops, restaurants, churches, community and health centers, a street where lifelong residents regularly pass neighbors that they recognize by name, nickname, face, or recent local gossip (relationships, babies). Many heard the shots, and some even talked to Sawyer and the shooter, before and after Sawyer died. Police spoke first to a reverend who worked at a youth center nearby.

She hadn't seen much. They left her with their details and posted a flyer asking witnesses to contact the police. Before long, the flyer was scribbled over with FUCK THE POLICE. Rumors of the shooter's nickname were already flying around the neighborhood. Within a day of asking around, the police came upon an informant who told them that the gunman was "BooBoo who dates CeeCee." Police then showed the informant mug shots of local men with past arrests. He identified Lamar Johnson as BooBoo.

It wouldn't have taken long for police to figure out that Lamar Johnson had never been known by that nickname. Because of past drug charges (for which he was never convicted), Lamar appeared in a Maryland Lotus Notes database. That database also includes a nickname search, which shows that Lamar was called "Mar" on the street. The police also knew of several *other* men known as BooBoo, yet there is no indication that they investigated any of them.

As early as the arrest and indictment, the victim's family was insisting that Lamar Johnson was not the shooter. "We don't want to let Carlos's murder create two tragedies." But by then the police's collective jaws had sunk into Lamar's haunches, and nothing short of the real killer's confession would loosen that grip. The police never presented any physical evidence tying Lamar to the crime. No motive, absolutely none, was ever presented—the jury was simply left with the image of a violent neighborhood, where thugs kill each other for no reason.

The day after the murder, around the time the informant told them the killer was "BooBoo who dates CeeCee," the police received a call on behalf of two girls, cousins who claimed to have heard several shots while on their way to buy socks. When Ashley (seventeen) and Ashia (fourteen) were brought in on March 27, they were terrified, nervous, out of place. They had never been in a police station before and, if what happened to the church flyer was any indication, getting involved in murder cases wasn't the wisest move in their neighborhood. Nevertheless, Ashley's sister had called the police and here they were. The girls told detectives that after hearing several shots, they saw a dark-skinned shooter, between seventeen and twenty years old, running away.

A few days later, on March 31, the girls were brought in again to look at a lineup of mug shots. The detective read each girl the protocol: that the photographs "may or may not contain the picture of the person who committed the crime." On this second visit, too, Ashia and Ashley were nervous, half listening to the officer's practiced drone (everyone knows what a lineup is from movies, right?). Having been called in for this important task, the girls believed they were *required* to choose one of the six men in the photo array. And if the man wasn't there? To help the detectives, they believed they had to choose the face that looked most like the shooter's. They were shown mug shots of six young Black men arranged in two rows.

Frances tells me that such "six-packs" are no longer best practice; officers now show photos one by one. But even when using six-packs, only one suspect should be placed in each lineup—the others ought to be fillers from the database. We don't know how Lamar's mug shot ended up as part of that initial lineup of suspects from which the informant picked out the man he thought was BooBoo. Did police ever create a six-pack with several local boys they suspected? Surely at that point, before the informant identified Lamar as "BooBoo," they had no reason to suspect Lamar at all. So his photo must have been a filler for another suspect, or one of several men in a game of whack-a-mole. Did they compile an array of all the young men seen earlier at that corner? If so, they introduced a huge logical error into the investigation—as in the 2006 Duke lacrosse case, wherein the photo array had no fillers, only Duke lacrosse players, "a multiple-choice test with no wrong answers."

Whatever caused the police to put Lamar's photo in the first lineup, after being picked out by the informant, Lamar became the police's top suspect, and the only person of interest shown to Ashia and Ashley. In the younger Ashia's mug shot array, Lamar's photo was in the top center position. In Ashley's, it was in the bottom left. This time, unlike in the lineup shown to the informant, the five non-suspects sat against a light background, further back from the camera, their faces smaller. Lamar's photo seemed almost blown up: his face menacingly close and noticeably larger, his shirt and background much darker than the others. Most appalling, the contours of his headshot looked larger (especially in Ashia's array, where it was centered); his photo took up slightly more space than the others, but his darker background and larger face amplified this effect. The photo screamed "pick me."

And both girls did. Ashia struggled with the memory, since the man ran away so quickly and she wasn't wearing her glasses. Ashley recognized Lamar's face from the neighborhood; she had seen this guy around, though she had never seen the shooter before. Feeling pressured to choose, this darkest-skinned, darkest-dressed of the six men looked most like the shooter.

I decided to try a little test. I called Elena into the room and showed her the headshot. I had covered the witness signatures with a text box, so she saw what Ashley and Ashia saw. I said, "Elena, pick a man."

In both lineups, without thinking, she chose Lamar. When I asked why she picked him, she shrugged. "I choosed the man. Come play!"

In their testimonies, the girls seem nervous and wholly uninterested. They were just walking and heard something. Like children, they were ready to move on with their day. At the station, it's easy to imagine that, feeling intimidated, they wished they had just kept their mouths shut, bought the socks they were shopping for, and gone home for cookies and juice.

Lamar Johnson was arrested on April 1 and taken to the homicide office. Thinking he was only in for questioning, he didn't remain silent—whatever rote words the police read to him had, like dead metaphors, lost their meaning. He kept thinking *I don't want to be a witness in this.* So, instead of saying nothing, he claimed to have been nowhere near the shooting.

At trial, the girls tried to recant. Ashley was shown the sentence she wrote on the back of the photo array: that Lamar was (not *looked like*) the shooter. She said: "No, because at the time I was writing I was nervous." The prosecutor ignored this. Later, Ashley said that she had seen Lamar around the neighborhood, and had known him for about five years; the shooter, on the other hand, was someone she had never seen. "When I went down there, I felt as though that I had to point someone out," Ashley testified. "But nobody forced you to do that," said the prosecutor. "That's my question, Ashley. Did anybody force you to do that?"

Throughout the trial transcript, the police and prosecution speak to the girls in this same *let me just tell you what you're saying* style. They dismiss repeated attempts to clarify that the girls felt coerced, which is what matters: not the intent but the outcome of pressure, the desperation to choose a suspect and leave. Each time the girls tried to express this fear at trial, the prosecutor pressed that nobody forced them to do anything, that the officers were well-meaning. He held fast to the implication that their speech act on March 31 was somehow more credible than their every subsequent caveat and clarification.

An honest listener would give the same weight to both statements. A dishonest listener grabs the part that helps their case, and ignores all else. But prosecutors aren't honest listeners. Their job is to win the case handed to them by police—a case built by selectively compiling only the pieces of evidence that support a detective's first hunch.

An officer's hunch is the seed of the story that enters the public record. Those first recorded clues, even if they're red herrings collected in slapdash ways (like the Duke lacrosse photo arrays with no fillers, or a nurse hastily scribbling "very dramatic" in a triage note), nurture that hunch. Nothing can uproot it from the prosecutor's mind. Once Ashley and Ashia's signatures were beneath Lamar's photo, no recantation mattered—the story had already sprouted.

When Ashia took the stand in Lamar Johnson's trial, the prosecutor asked her to read from her police statement, to refresh her memory when she forgot details about the day of the murder. He said things like, "Referring to the second page, your first answer, do you recall . . ."

Once, reading from her police statement, Ashia said, "Boo had a gun."

Defense objected. At this moment in the transcript, I held my breath. *Is anyone going to mention that she called him Boo in a statement given within days of the shooting, before she had seen Lamar's photo?* But defense's objection was to a different absurdity. "He's basically asking her to read her statement rather than testifying."

It surprises me that the police statement is shown to her at all. Isn't it better to ask again and see if her two stories match? Doesn't society insist that, for refugees and those who need help, a discrepant memory is a sign of deception? When the court sustained the objection, the prosecutor instructed Ashia, "Don't read the statement. If you can remember based upon looking at the statement, then you can testify after you look at the statement."

So much for an unimpeachable public record. So, Ashia did as she was asked.

During defense's cross-examination, Ashia grabbed the chance to say that she wasn't certain, that she saw the event from across the street without her glasses, that she meant to say that Lamar *looked like* the dark-skinned shooter. "He was like telling me how the person look and he was like, does he look like him and I said yes. That is what I said." When asked if she chose the darkest of the six men, she said yes, that the others were medium-skinned. From far away, without her glasses, with people running this way and that, a blur of color was all Ashia saw.

———

Minutes before Carlos Sawyer was shot, a man named Watkins was sitting on a stoop across a bar, arguing with Lavar, better known as

BooBoo. Watkins met BooBoo in 2000, but they weren't close. They each had a child by the same woman. Now, BooBoo dated Watkins's niece, CeeCee. That afternoon, BooBoo was fuming at Watkins's refusal to lend him his rental car, when Carlos Sawyer approached Watkins to buy two bags of weed. When Watkins went to get the weed, BooBoo snapped and Carlos laughed. BooBoo's anger turned to Carlos, and the two men faced off. Carlos pulled a knife. BooBoo left. Thinking it was over, Carlos headed to a friend's garage to retrieve a dirt bike he had stored there. Ten minutes later, Watkins heard shots, ran to the noise, and saw his friend Carlos dying in the gutter.

Remembering the argument with BooBoo, Watkins rushed from the body to CeeCee's house. BooBoo was there. "He was in motion," Watkins said at trial, where he specified that Lavar, not Lamar Johnson, was BooBoo. "He was like sweating, wiping his face . . . He was like sweating real hard. He was walking towards me and he had his shirt and he was wiping his face . . . [his face] was like when you go into seeing somebody that's hurt, somebody that's in your family that—like for instance, if I'm going to a funeral of a family member or a friend of mine and how I would be hurt. It was one of them type of facial expressions."

When he was arrested, Lamar Johnson knew none of this. He knew only that he was accused of murdering Carlos, and strangely, also rumored to be involved with Watkins's niece, CeeCee. Sometime later, in a detention center, Lamar ran into Watkins. He said he was arrested for the Sawyer murder, adding, "They saying that I messed with your niece."

Now Watkins understood what had happened. The police believed Lamar to be BooBoo, CeeCee's boyfriend, whom they understood to be Carlos's shooter. It was a simple case of mistaken identity that the police refused to see clarified by neighbors who had lived in the same community for years. I wonder if in another community, group knowledge would be more easily relayed, understood, and accepted. The conversation between the men reveals that they had long ago accepted the impossibility of communicating simple facts to police, even facts verified by the police's own database.

"That's when I had said to him was [sic] you got to go ahead and believe . . . you know what, you got to go ahead and believe it to your lawyer and trust him—I'm sorry, trust it to God, because I was locked up before for a murder that I did not do and I know how he felt."

Did these pained words move the exhausted jurors and officers of a Baltimore city court? These errant men, who stops to believe them? In and out of prisons, being falsely accused of murder is for them an everyday experience. Their stories vanish, even when they're so nakedly honest, so consistent with the system's known flaws. Watkins's testimony didn't take root in the jury's hearts or minds. Maybe it was the way he spoke, or the fact that he was a convict. Lamar and Watkins aren't the sort of men who know the path to a judge's sympathy, the codes that make judges wring their hands and say, "But I can't ruin a promising young life."

I told Sam this story on a forest walk. He asked, "If you had information about a crime and it was a little messy, would you go to the police? What would you do?"

"Are you kidding me?" I said. I'd give it to my lawyer and wait around to be summoned.

With all its singular detail, the texture of everyday life, Watkins's story rings true: BooBoo wiping the sweat on his shirt, the recurrence of CeeCee in both men's lives, the dirt bikes, the argument over the rental car. Watkins was no friend of Lamar, and he had no reason to testify, especially with BooBoo so close to his niece. The day after the killing, Sawyer's wife told the police that her husband Carlos had been heard laughing at his shooter, and that the shooter said, just before he fired, "Who are you laughing at now, motherfucker?" She said this to police *before* she knew about Watkins, whose story about Lavar matches. And, at this point, both the informant and Ashia (in that slip-up) had called the shooter by Lavar's nickname.

Why was all this reasonable doubt not easily seen?

Unable to decide, the jury were rushed to judgment under threat of an extra day. Meanwhile, Lamar's lawyer gave an abysmal performance—asking the wrong questions, in the wrong way, failing to rephrase after sustained objections. Sometimes the court had to remind her of basics, like what constitutes "leading," or that you can't introduce wild factoids (like a $2,000 reward nobody had heard of) without a basis. Though, finding basis was also her job: if a reward did motivate the girls to call the police, and the lawyer didn't go out and find evidence of its existence to use in cross-examinations, that is even bigger attorney negligence.

Once, when the court reminded her that one of her objections should actually be her rebuttal, Lamar's defense replied, "Huh?"

Again and again, the defense lawyer fumbled, mangling questions and putting unprepared witnesses on the stand. One had to be chased down under threat of arrest, because the defense hadn't bothered to follow up on a summons. Scrambling to save the case, the lawyer put Lamar on the stand—the same day, without any preparation or even a strategy. She asked whether Lamar knew Carlos (no), whether he had killed Carlos (no), what he was doing near the scene (talking to a girl), and why he told detectives he wasn't there (he was afraid; murder witnesses get killed). For those obvious answers, so easily presented in closing arguments, she exposed Lamar to cross-examination—a foolish trade.

Under cross-examination, Lamar broke down. "You just want a conviction on me. You don't care if I really done this. All you want is somebody to go down . . . You're not worrying about this. You still get paid, regardless if I go to jail for something that I didn't do."

Why do such outbursts of frustration make others think we're lying? I am most frustrated when I'm telling the truth to no avail. Elena, too, bursts into tears from that injustice.

In February 2006, Lamar Johnson was sentenced to life plus twenty years in prison.

Lamar appealed, citing (among other complaints) the suggestive photo array and his lawyer's performance. But the court held that, according to precedent, "a lineup to be fair need not consist of clones." Further, the photos were color mug shots from a database, and their sizes and colorings were predetermined, so there was nothing improper about the procedure—here the focus seemed to be on whether the police intentionally made Lamar's photo suggestive. "Once the motions court ruled that the procedures employed to secure the pretrial identification were not impermissibly suggestive, that court would have no obligation to inquire into the reliability, *vel non* [or not], of the identifications"—a sentence Kafka would love. It didn't matter that the photo *was* suggestive, only whether the police made it so.

Across the Western world, the law is full of such logical knots. An American lawyer reading this would yawn and say, "Well, that's only for admissibility. You can still argue it's bad evidence." Right—but only after jurors get to see it, and be influenced by it. I never understood in trials when judges say things like, *Jury will disregard that last mega-damaging thing.* Does the law expect us to believe, or merely to pretend, that we can stop being biased, suggestible, weak humans once we cross its threshold?

As for reasonable doubt, well, the appeal court's role is not to retry the case, Lamar was told. The rule for the appeal court was to look at the case in the light most favorable to the prosecution, and ask if *one* rational person could have found you guilty. If so, the judgment stands, even if the case is full of reasonable doubt. If you were badly tried once, that's it for you; your rights to justice and "innocent until proven guilty" are gone.

Over years of investigations, Carlos Sawyer's family held firm that Lamar was not the killer. Eventually, the case was picked up by the Mid-Atlantic Innocence Project and the state attorney's Conviction Integrity Unit. And Lamar's story lived on in the neighborhood. As years passed, it weighed heavily on those who had been there. One by one, three new witnesses came forward. Though they were strangers to each other, they all pointed to the same killer. Two had been at the scene during and just after the shooting. And in the weeks after the crime, when Lamar was in custody, a third witness heard the real killer confess to having shot Carlos.

Lamar spent thirteen years in prison before the Innocence Project proved the judgment wrong. After years of research and lobbying, once the Mid-Atlantic Innocence Project convinced the prosecutor's Conviction Integrity Unit, it took one day for their joint motion to be granted, and for Lamar's convictions to be vacated. *One day.*

"I finally got justice," Lamar says. In interviews, he sounds grateful, hopeful that his story will be shared justly. But what is justice when the world is composed of a collection of voices, all clamoring and self-motivated? At the base of a great pyramid the vulnerable flock, their voices too small to reach past those who love them. An entire neighborhood might shout a story for years and never be heard. At the tip, a formidable few can declare that same story true in a day. The best anyone can do is plead to the next tier and hope the truth keeps traveling upward.

The Innocence Project warns that many vulnerable people are wrongfully convicted because of bad lawyers—some are overworked, exhausted, unprepared. Others are jaded, even drunk on the job. At a stressful moment, her case falling apart, Lamar's lawyer looks up at the witness. I imagine a tired breath, an icy palm to her temple. She says, "Ma'am, can you speak in the microwave?" Was *microwave* a slip of the tongue, or of a court reporter's finger? It's in the public record now, forever a part of our collective history.

During his long empty days removed from the world, with no purpose, work, or family, Lamar got his GED. In news footage of his 2017 release, a woman runs into his arms. In the background, ignoring the news cameras, Frances takes photos of their euphoric reunion. By now she knows that the events you don't document yourself can vanish.

On a muggy Florida morning in February 2013, I crawled out of a hotel bed to untangle myself from the mistakes of my twenties. I was a student at the Iowa Writers Workshop. Florida was the easiest place to get a divorce without a partner present. Sitting in a courtroom arena with the day's other uncontested divorces, with baggy eyes and a tight, wet bun, I watched the thirteen stories on the docket before mine. Near the end, an old man shuffled to the front. He hadn't seen his wife in more than a decade and wanted to set her free. The judge, flabbergasted that he'd not heard from her in so long, asked questions. Soon, it became clear that this woman was likely dead. But instead of telling the man that, the judge just granted the divorce. Rather, she said the old man could consider himself free and unmarried or some such. Her words were taken down. Maybe a clerk attached the real story in a memo.

What if that old man went back to his neighborhood and declared himself divorced? What if his wife's mother, her wounds reopened, demanded that he acknowledge her daughter's death? What if the court reporter took down "*You are free*," the judge's merciful speech act (which doesn't feel like an abuse or misfire, but technically was, since the man was a widow), as a divorce ruling? A community can insist and insist and never convince the law that such folksy stories, passed orally between neighbors, are truer than stamped papers and certified depositions.

In the end, Mimi, the Karen from Burma with the hairball of a triple speech act, had to resort to the power of her community to pry the false story out of dry cement. Mimi's lawyer began calling everyone who had ever known her. For over a year, she gathered letters and petitioned the FBI. She kept explaining that the ruling party in Burma doesn't recognize ethnically Karen people as Burmese, and therefore her client couldn't get a birth certificate. Yes, said the FBI, but Mimi had to establish that she *was* Karen, and that she was the specific person she claimed to be. Mimi's lawyer called ministers, school teachers, playmates, women who had watched her when she was five. She gathered sworn declarations, and found a Karen interpreter in New York to speak to Mimi for hours and declare that she had a native vocabulary and accent.

After a year, the FBI granted Mimi a proceeding.

And what about that other identity, the one she had purchased? Mimi could have chosen the easy route. She could have enrolled in school on her student visa, found a job, a way to stay outside of the asylum system. For skilled people with American jobs, the path is truly not that hard. You don't have to be remarkable; just on somebody's payroll. She could have lived a full life. But that life, Dao's identity, would be a massive lie.

"I've rarely met someone with greater integrity," Mimi's lawyer said. "There was no way she could live this lie. She said, *I'm not going to do it the easy way.*"

Every refugee knows: your judge is your destiny. Reading Mimi's stack of letters, the many neighbors vouching for her, her desperation for a card with her own true name, and the easy out always within her reach, Mimi's judge was moved. "From then on," said her lawyer, "the judge wasn't willing to give an inch to the government lawyer to push questioning. You know, it's often the judges that save people from the government's asylum lawyers."

More than a decade after arriving, Mimi works for a Burmese NGO. She's an activist. With American papers, her motives for activism are no longer suspect to American natives. She still doesn't know when she was born. "How can you not know your own birthday?" people ask. She shrugs. It's no longer a credibility issue, just a strange detail from a long, eventful life.

10.

"You're not a real believer!" my mother muttered through tears in a crowded Amsterdam restaurant. It was an accusation, and a damning one in our family. My mother had suffered for her beliefs, fled her home, started a new life. It was 2009, and it had taken until I was nearly thirty for her to face my lifelong doubt. Saying it out loud was something like reaching across the table and pulling a wig off my head. People stared. I turned a shade redder. I shouted that she had no window into my heart and mind. Out of the corner of my eye, I saw a youngish man listening hard, definitely with me on this. Did he have a mother praying for his soul? Forgetting our food, we argued for a long time. I said the wrong words. It was all so new, my unbelief. What I wished to articulate was that I felt no higher power protecting the vulnerable or preserving justice, and that I was finally becoming aware that believing in Him was mere distraction, sucking oxygen from all the urgent human stories waiting for a response.

Whom should I believe, after such massive failures of judgment? Is there a method of believing such that, even if I'm proven wrong, I can be sure that I did my best, that I haven't been immoral? *Give me the way to do my very best.*

At two, any time Elena found me sad, she'd sit with me, arranging her skirt around her knees, mimicking some grandmotherly gesture, and say, "Was it a crocodile?" Sometimes I'd nod. Sometimes I'd say no, and she'd ask if it was a crab or a lobster. At some point I'd have to pick one; she'd grow alarmed as she searched for increasingly worse creatures to suggest. Then, once it was settled, she'd press a hot cheek against mine and, as if to end my suffering, she'd say, "I believe you, Mummy."

I struggle with the shame of pretending. Often, I wish it were as easy as in childhood, to bow my head, to kneel, to move my lips in prayer for someone else's sake, to give them their rituals, as I did when I accepted Christ for my grandmother, or my father did when, on a visit to America, he casually let himself be baptized.

When Elena was five, I wondered, what does my daughter believe now? So, I asked her. "Elena, are you *inside* your body, or *are* you your body?"

She furrowed her brows. "I *am* my body." Then she paused and added in her mixed-up French-English, "And we all, *tout le monde*, live inside a huge *baleine*."

"A whale?" I said. "We all live in the whale?"

"Yes, and it's a magic *baleine multicolore* and we can ask it for things."

In a godless household, Elena has created a god. Maybe she started creating her sea-creature god the day she saw her mother brought to her knees by that crab, or that crocodile. She craves an existential myth she can refine, then spend her life protecting.

Psychologists like Daniel Kahneman have long argued that the mind seeks homeostasis, just as the body's systems try to maintain a relatively stable state. Despite changing outer conditions, the body tries to stay within a given range of temperature, heart rate, blood sugar, and other variables. The mind, too, wants to keep things in balance. It wants its core beliefs to remain true, for its idea of the self to go unchallenged. So it will create shortcuts, a way of making sense of a fast current of observations, with the singular purpose of preserving what it already knows.

I like stories of trying, of skills sharpening into weapons, of purposeful people finding agency, saying *no*. Are those my sacred myths? And when will they harden into dogma, blinding me to the burns and lesions that just don't happen in the world I know? Have I, like my mother, escaped from one religious fever dream into another? Am I capable of seeing truth that doesn't fit my doctrine? Should I write to the unfortunates who have trusted me with their stories and tell them that I have the dirtiest lens? Should I tell them that I'm a cynic, an unbeliever?

How do you know if you have a bad heart, when you've only had the one?

My strange struggle with faith has taken me from blind belief, to an impassioned rejection of my mother's faith, to Simone Weil. "You found Saint Simone," my friend, a Christian ethics professor at Emory University, writes to me. "Or, she's found you."

Weil, a Christian mystic, writes that false things give the impression of truth and that true things seem false. That the ability to *receive* truth requires work. When I failed to speak in tongues, I thought I hadn't done the work of receiving God, that I was missing a muscle or a gene. Later, I believed it all a scam. Was that survival instinct? In order to survive, writes Weil, we use falsehoods like armor "secreted by what is unfit in order to ward off the danger." Without this armor, the unfit thing would meet a natural, Darwinian end, so it toils to ward off truths that might destroy it. "There is as it were a phagocytosis in the soul: everything which is threatened by time secretes falsehood in order not to die, and in proportion to the danger it is in of dying."

The pride survives many humiliations, Weil writes, thanks to this armor of lies. If we allowed ourselves to truly see our worst selves, we might crumble. My pride, too, secretes lies, delusions that I'm desperate to see as plainly as I see my mother's armor or my grandmother's.

Maybe I should just let it die, whatever it was in me that failed.

Weil compares the not-yet-understood and the incomprehensible to dust on a window and the view beyond. Reason makes the glass transparent. But we don't see the glass (reason), only the dust or the view—we wipe the dust off the glass in order to see the view. "The uncomprehended hides the incomprehensible and should on this account be eliminated."

I yearn to do the math this time. For weeks, I put away my notes. I let KV's story grow stale. I read Western philosophies about belief. They're dense, calming. I should've studied them closely back in college, when I was busy calculating net present values and looking up market bubbles. I dig around for clues in the dark, newly aware of so much that had once been invisible, like a mushroom hunt at the turn of a season, new shapes and hues to search out. We don't see the things we're not looking for. For months after a forest scavenging, you may spot every lone gray mushroom, but you miss the hundreds of lost marbles in the village square, splashes of color slowly losing their gloss, until you go looking for your daughter's lost marble.

———

In 1877, philosopher William Clifford posed a moral dilemma: a shipowner prepares to send a passenger ship across the Atlantic. He knows it's old, weathered, ramshackle after many voyages. Nevertheless, he sells tickets, telling himself all the while that she's arrived safely at every previous destination. And shouldn't he trust in God, who will protect all the poor immigrants onboard? And anyway, why is he having ungenerous thoughts about honest builders and contractors? In this way, the shipowner convinces himself that his ship is safe and seaworthy, forming a "sincere and comfortable conviction." He sells tickets, loads the ship, and waves goodbye to the passengers "with a light heart," sincerely wishing them well. When the ship sinks and tells "no tales," he collects the insurance money.

This shipowner, Clifford says, is guilty of killing his passengers since he "had no right to believe on such evidence as was before him" and he "acquired his belief not by honestly earning it in patient investigation, but by stifling his doubts." Clifford's principle says that "*It is wrong always, everywhere, and for anyone to believe anything on insufficient evidence.*" That includes the maintenance of a belief over time: it is *always* wrong to glibly ignore or dismiss evidence relevant to a belief you already hold, even if you had good reason to form that belief at one time, or to sidestep new evidence that goes against it, or to privilege faulty data that supports it. We're duty-bound to override the instinctive answers we want to believe. Not having malicious intent is no excuse for persisting in ignorance or harm.

But what if the ship had arrived safely? "Will that diminish the guilt of her owner?" Clifford asks. "Not one jot. When an action is once done, it is right or wrong for ever; no accidental failure of its good or evil fruits can possibly alter that."

That story used to make me think of faith in God; now I think of climate change.

But what about Josh's death? Using Clifford's logic, the information (Josh's plan) was handed to me by the source, and I didn't believe. I'm guilty. And I'd be guilty if he had lived. Though if he had lived, wouldn't it mean that his threats weren't credible? The shipowner knows his ship is shoddy, but I couldn't see inside Josh. I believed Josh was seaworthy, but I didn't send him to sea. I wasn't the shipowner, I was the person whispering "don't worry" in the ship owner's ear.

American philosopher William James, also an evidentialist, added a few caveats to Clifford's principle. He made room for "live" hypotheses, as long as they were "forced" and "momentous." If an idea is live "among the mind's possibilities," that means one is still reasonably grappling with it (e.g., the existence of God, which might be a lifelong question). But the liveness of an idea must depend, in part, on the community as well. Scientists are no longer grappling with evolution, for example. Would James see it as a "live" hypothesis?

WHO GETS BELIEVED?   241

James, who shaped and popularized the philosophical tradition of pragmatism, argued that truth is by nature workable and dependable. It can be acted upon and its results can be predicted and counted upon. "What concrete difference will [a belief] being true make in anyone's actual life?" he wrote. "What experiences will be different? What, in short, is the truth's cash value in experiential terms?" A truth is true so far as it is useful, enacted and realized through experience.

The truth's cash value. I always pause on this strange metaphor. James's frequent use of it was controversial among his contemporaries. He meant: let's not argue in the abstract; what practical difference does any truth have on individual lives, on physical sensations and experiences? Cash value *in experiential terms.* Some took it as evidence of James's capitalist frame of mind. Pragmatism *is* the most American of philosophies; developed in the 1870s, it has empowered industrialists, politicians, and every MBA applicant since the first business school opened its doors. But it keeps being misused. Modern-day confidence men chase profits and argue that they've done the moral thing, because they've created value (for someone). I think that James would suffer to see his ideas so mangled.

Maybe James's logic will be kinder to me than Clifford's: I believed Josh's threats had no practical impact because he was bluffing. Josh's seriousness was a live hypothesis for me, but simmering on a back burner, because I had no practical choice to make. I wasn't one of the experts or decision-makers.

Professionals sent Josh home. But had they studied enough, practiced enough? Did they know what they didn't know? How knowledgeable are the people who decide if we live or die?

There's a scene in the movie *Backdraft* in which Robert De Niro describes a fire as a living thing. "It breathes, it eats, it hates." He tells Billy Baldwin that the fire goes where it wants to go, that its embers tell a story, and that you have to learn to think like it in order to beat it.

"For the longest time," Frances (my lawyer friend) told me, "fire-fighters would designate certain fires a clear case of arson." They had a sort of folk wisdom that was passed down from firefighter to firefighter. Over time, people assumed that their experience contained the rigor of real science. On stands across the country, firefighters presented themselves as a definitive voice in fire science. No one's seen more fires than me, they'd say. "But unless you have a scientific way of making sense of all those fires you've seen, that's a fairly meaningless boast."

There used to be a mantra that "fires burn up." If a floor was burned or had holes where the fire had burned *down*, an accelerant must have been poured onto the floor. Confident on the stand, firefighters would say, "That's not how fire works. I'm sure something made that fire burn down." Another kernel of folk wisdom was that natural fires don't get hot enough to melt aluminum—for that, you need an accelerant. So melted aluminum, too, became a sign of arson.

During the 1990s, firefighters responded to a series of deadly California wildfires. In many of those houses, they found holes in the floor and melted aluminum. Gradually, some wondered, *Are we passing off guesses as knowledge?* Meanwhile, in 1990, a fire broke out in Jacksonville, Florida. It killed two women and four children. Known as the Lime Street Fire, the case was seminal in discrediting previously trusted fire science. Gerald Lewis, husband and brother to the two women, escaped with his three-year-old son. He stood outside, stunned as the house burned with his family trapped inside. He claimed that the fire had been an accident, that it began on the couch. But when firefighters discovered streaks, or "pour patterns," on the floor, Gerald was charged with arson and six first-degree murders.

Enter fire science skeptic John Lentini. Though he was part of the "fire tells a story" community, he was curious, and prone to doubting folk wisdom. He asked for permission to recreate the fire in the abandoned house next to Gerald's. The two houses had been built at the same time, by the same people, using the same materials and an identical floor plan. To stage an exact recreation of the original fire, Lentini obtained a replica of the couch, resurfaced the interior with the same sheetrock, and found matching furnishings, including wallpaper, curtains, and carpet. Then he set the couch on fire. Without an accelerant, the team expected flashover in twenty minutes, but the house was engulfed in just four. The detritus included floor streaks. It seemed pour patterns had nothing to do with pouring at all.

"I had come within twenty-four hours of giving testimony that could well have sent an innocent person to Florida's electric chair," said Lentini. "I was chastened by the experience. My professional life was never the same again."

And yet, there was no knowledge flashover. The shocking implications of the Lime Street experiment didn't spread. The old "fire scientists" kept testifying about how many fires they had seen. They kept peddling their outdated wisdoms and sending victims to prison. When Michael Ledford, the autistic man whose false confession was coerced through the Reid Technique, came to trial in the late 1990s, the National Fire Protection Agency had already created *NFPA 921: Guide for Fire and Explosion Investigations*. However, there was no accepted standard to abide by the guidance at trial. That change was only just beginning. In Dru (the dramatic man)'s trial, prosecutors said that a fire that seemed to have multiple starting points was a sure sign of arson, despite the new knowledge that after flashover, it's nearly impossible to pinpoint an origin. The fire has now engulfed the house; there is no story hiding in the ashes.

Remembering the Lime Street case, Lentini quotes the old adage, "Science advances one funeral at a time." Erroneous experts are never convinced of their mistakes—they're replaced. The Innocence Project has piles of wrongful convictions (like Michael and Dru), people who've lost decades because of debunked theories like fire science or shaken baby syndrome.

In 2004, Cameron Todd Willingham was executed for arson

murder based on junk science. Those who defend such convictions argue that the fire science was just one aspect of it, that there was a "preponderance of evidence" pointing toward guilt: maybe there was marital or financial trouble. They don't want to believe that they got it so wrong, and so they fight for the truth they once knew.

"Convincing a prosecutor to join us is a tall order," says Frances. "Even in DNA cases, prosecutors have fought to save their convictions." Who wants to reopen an old wound by believing in a second victim? "I can't imagine the cognitive dissonance." Yet the troubling truth remains: that conviction was achieved not with motive or a plethora of circumstantial evidence, but from those things plus a so-called expert's word—his intense, fiery certainty.

"Those stories," Sam says, "are part of the American dogma: Money knows best. Anything is possible. Anyone can do anything, *fast*. Expertise is a myth."

Maybe this is why Americans have such trouble believing real experts (those grumpy old doctors and scientists, nothing like the heroic fire guys or sweet young nurses), why they call learned knowledge elitist and prefer a more organic lived kind of knowledge. But not every field is learned by witness or instinct. Some things require long, rigorous hours in the company of the previous generation's experts. The most complex human discoveries are passed down deliberately with sacrifice, over years, to the few with intellectual power and curiosity, the worthy and dedicated. There's nothing organic about it. We pass it on, so we don't have to re-learn that collective knowledge.

Sam and I passed a small farm, waved. Earlier, we had been talking about Josh and about the great-great-grandfather who dug his own grave. Sam told me that in rural France, anti-tech, anti-vaccine, ecological agrarian politics is starting to coincide with a high incidence of Holocaust denial. Somehow, this anti-Semitism was becoming part of this belief cluster, along with hating Macron and buying used clothes. The more the denials were spoken aloud, the more acceptable they became to say aloud. The doubt had leaked, drop by drop, into the cluster's values.

"The smart ones are alarming," Sam said. "How do you talk to a person in 2021, who has an education and a sophisticated understanding of how to use the internet for research, and still believes all that nonsense?"

A discredited old report has recently resurfaced in Provence, fueling absurd doubts. The American-funded Leuchter Report (1988) was a so-called expert analysis that empowered a generation of Holocaust denial. It claimed to have found fewer compounds of hydrogen cyanide from Zyklon B in gas chamber walls than in the walls of the disinfection chambers. So, the report concluded, Zyklon B was used only in cleaning. Real experts quickly pointed out that the walls of the gas chambers were in ruins and exposed to the elements, while the disinfection chambers were intact, and that Zyklon B was used to kill people for thirty minutes per day, whereas it was left on the walls for twenty-four hours at a time in the disinfection rooms. The report is dismissed now in a statement by the Auschwitz memorial as an attempt, "concealed beneath an academic-looking smokescreen of graphs, analyses, and calculations, at misinforming readers who have no access to the scholarly literature—or who are looking for precisely the sort of conclusions that Leuchter offers."

"What's scary is that it sounds like expertise," said Sam. "That farmer who comes across it, he reads just that one report, and it's in scientific language, and it validates his dark fantasies." One day, if you greet that Provencal farmer, he might offer you an organic tomato, maybe warn you that smart gas meters are just surveillance. Then he might say, "Did you read that there's no residue in the gas chamber walls? To me that says everything." That farmer doesn't consider himself an anti-Semite. He's setting up a shibboleth: will you respond, "That's lazy, sloppy hogwash"? Wrong answer; you're an outsider. Or will you respond with something openly racist? Also wrong answer. Or will you nod, eat the tomato, and mutter, "Interesting"?

———

Not all opinions matter equally. I am not a suicide expert. But the fire scientists weren't fire experts, either. So how can an ordinary person judge? In whom do we place our trust when the circumstance eclipses our own education?

My quest takes me to Kant, who questioned the basic assumption that all belief even counts as belief. I read on, thinking maybe my *dis*belief didn't count either. In his *Critique of Pure Reason* and later in his *Lectures on Logic*, Immanuel Kant distinguishes between three types of "taking as true." He defines them like this:

Knowing is taking something as true, because any rational person with the same information would be logically required to take the thing as true. For example, stepping outside, you know it's not raining on this street at this hour. Any logical person would have to accept it.

Believing is taking something as true because, given the evidence, *you* are logically required to accept it, but you understand that other rational people may not be (most religious fervor falls into this category).

Having an opinion is taking something as true even though, given the evidence, no rational person is logically required to accept it as such, not even you.

Kant scholars have done a lot of debating about the difference between believing and opining. Kant argues that the logical requirement for one person is often proved by the fact that they have lived that way. A life of devout living proves that the existence of God *was* logically necessary for that person, given the evidence.

I might hold true that sugar is poison (I've seen the studies), but I just had a cookie. So clearly the idea that sugar is poison is just an opinion for me. It may be perfectly appropriate as an opinion, but it's clearly not sufficient to require acceptance, and so doesn't rise to the level of belief for me. If everyone who ate a spoonful of sugar dropped dead, we would all be logically required to accept that sugar is poison. It would be knowledge, certain and universal. But it isn't. It is my *opinion*, a person who just ate a cookie. I have a friend who hasn't eaten refined sugar for a decade. For her, "sugar is poison" is a belief, not opinion, and the only observable proof is that she has lived this way. It's circular, but how else would we establish an individual's logical mandate?

Kant gives the example of a doctor who, after examining a patient, holds the opinion that the patient has consumption. This becomes a belief, as soon as the doctor treats the patient for consumption. The diagnosis has moved from opinion to belief simply because the doctor treated it. If the treatment quickly works, I suppose, that diagnosis would become knowledge that the patient has consumption.

At what point does the belief of many experts become knowledge? If an expert is logically compelled to take a thing as true (she *believes*) and if, after decades, a thousand more experts believe, too, then at some point don't we all just . . . *know*?

Maybe an expert's role is to move the rest of us up and down Kant's ladder of acceptance. If enough experts move from opinion to belief, then the gap between individual belief and collective knowledge closes. To compare the belief of an ordinary person to that of thousands of experts is a false equivalence. To ask experts to make room for the beliefs of ordinary people is irrational. Simone Weil wrote in her meditations *Gravity and Grace*: "We have not to choose between opinions. We have to welcome them all, but arrange them vertically, placing them on suitable levels." In judging the mysteries of the universe—God and creation and the afterlife—the intelligence must be "keener, more discerning, more precise, more exact and more exacting than for any other."

Today, working American politicians push expertise and public belief onto the same plane without a moment's thought, demanding that schools teach evolution and creation side by side as competing theories, or equating the opinions of businesspeople and corporate lobbies to those of climate scientists so that they can claim that the matter is unresolved or disputed, a Jamesian "live" hypothesis. I wonder what James, the evidentialist, would say to the current practice of keeping questions artificially alive and momentous through sheer myopia, stubbornness, and magical thinking. If you squint hard enough and ignore the world as it reveals itself to our brightest minds, any dead and buried question can appear shattering and be thrust into public debate, no matter how exhausting to those who understand.

Weil believed in a rigorous scientific practice; she was hard on modern scientists, wanting them to reflect beyond their narrow expertise to examine larger truths. Seeing today's body of knowledge, she might say that God has revealed a part of the mystery (the how) through the science of evolution, and we should humble ourselves enough to see it. "There is nothing nearer to true humility than the intelligence . . . for we know that even if we became an idiot the following instant and remained so for the rest of our life, the truth would continue unchanged."

Expertise, then, starts with observing a thing at a slant, and perceiving the vastness of what you don't see—the many angles hidden from view. Then, maybe, it's accepting that you will die without seeing the whole of the thing, and continuing on.

I came out of McKinsey with utter confidence in my every thought. I knew how to shut down debate, to make the other person think before refuting me, a standard that I didn't apply to myself. The key was to call the other person on every logical inconsistency—on straw men, on lack of data, outdated data, insufficient data, too large a margin of error, results within a margin of error, too many outliers, weird collection methodology, spurious correlations, and whatever else I could think of—while making my own claims with no such rigor, but with carefully worded caveats and asides: *My theory so far . . .* To some, a theory presented in a credible voice becomes fact. And that credible voice could be cultivated—it *had* to be.

At Harvard, I started giving presentations on career networking to the undergraduates. I was fiery and bold, telling my students just what to do. Before long, my audience grew, and when Career Services picked it up, I was speaking to full auditoriums. To be fair to me (which I always am), I did it for free, for fun. Still, one day I got a call from a business school section-mate. He asked, almost apologetically, "What makes you an expert in this?"

"Because I made the PowerPoint," I said.

He laughed; the conversation drifted elsewhere. I wonder if he remembers it. For me, it was a moment of reckoning with expertise: I can make people think I'm an expert by packaging common sense. Later, many of my classmates would publish popular books about how to manage your time, how to be your own boss, how to work less, how to have better sex. But none of that was expertise. It was bombast. We stumbled onto something useful and made a framework for it. Like young consultants. Or fire scientists.

From a young age, I craved expertise, credentials, all that soothing certainty. And yet, the years have offered only more questions. Am I doing my best? That drive for insider knowledge and sureness, in recent years, has changed. Now it's more like this: In *The Writing Life* Annie Dillard writes about a student who wants to be a writer, but is astonished when asked if he enjoys sentences. "If he had liked sentences," Dillard writes, "he could begin, like a joyful painter I knew. I asked him how he came to be a painter. He said, 'I liked the smell of the paint.'"

At forty-two, I'm not sure if I've achieved any kind of expertise. Certainly, I'm less confident about what I know than I was at thirty-two or twenty-two. There's never a single day when you become an expert, is there? Slowly, other people decide for you. But it happens privately, too, in thousands of mystifying questions that enrich or challenge what you know, and many unscheduled journeys into the weeds. There are eras in life marked by the disconnect between the two, the public and private stores of knowledge. I suppose my experience has included both: I've been granted trust and confidence in things I was only beginning to understand, but I've been mistrusted, too, long after having proven enough.

I can't make fiery speeches anymore. I prefer slow slogs. I'm afraid that one day, in a crucial moment, I won't know what I don't know. One day, I'll make a huge mistake. It's bound to happen, right? One day, standing in the opening pages of an obvious tragedy, I'll help it along.

I know now that expertise is gained quietly, alone in dark hours, digging into the dirt as the skills to present that knowledge erode. When so many professionals are satisfied projecting bulk onto a fun-house mirror (craving only the prescription pad, the office, the veneer of expertise), who's going to believe the quiet hermit who appears like a frightened kitten on television? We've relaxed into our shortcuts, and we're primed to be fooled.

But I want to seek out the knowledge keepers, the infectious disease experts, the legal scholars, the craftspeople—those who know—and I've finally figured out just where to look. The best withdraw deep into their craft; you'll find them staring in wonder and amusement at one spot (in bright pink shirts or boat shoes, with wonky glasses or food in their hair), slowly, obsessively picking at a single question, never turning toward the noise, for decades.

Goodbye McKinsey confidence training.

Rilke advises artists to seek and welcome solitude, to immerse yourself in it, to come alive. Go deeper into the recesses of your mind. Be porous to others' stories. A story is like a speck of dust in an oyster, a mentor once said. It's the hours spent turning it over that make it a pearl. In those hours turning over the details, the fires of youth die down.

One summer, years ago, Josh arrived to a garden dinner for Sam's birthday. Many of our friends were there. We sat in a circle on an untrimmed lawn. Josh was cheerful, talkative. But when he tried to tell stories, something was off: his words, his pacing. He was meandering, struggling to find his way through the story, pulling up blades of grass, always the almost-right word. He lacked the usual metaphors, and people strained to follow. Unaccustomed to social performance, he seemed a forgery of his healthier self.

Taking a break from the philosophers, I pick up an anthology Sam has left in the hallway. I flip through it, trying to cleanse my mind from all the academic writing. I stumble onto Walt Whitman's "Song of Myself." I arrive at a section that hits me in the chest, and I remember that garden party, a few summers before Josh died. Maybe this book was mislaid here, just so I would open to this page, to these lines that remind me of this family, Elena's family and Sam's, and Flo's grief, and people like Josh, their lifelong struggle at parties, to convince people like me.

> "A child said *What is the grass?* fetching it to me with full hands;
> How could I answer the child? I do not know what it is any
>   more than he.
>
>   . . .
>
> And now it seems to me the beautiful uncut hair of graves."

The uncut hair of graves. Children know by instinct: *This is grass. That is a leaf.* Any other name is a forgery, one thing posturing as another. Or maybe it's not a forgery. Maybe it's a new metaphor born into the world. Children are alert for lies, for inconsistency, but only briefly. *This was once a leaf, but now it's a crunch pile to stamp.* Then they switch on their imagination, a wondrous other universe that will one day fade from view. And even an incredulous child, when looking through a kaleidoscope, a tube filled with pieces of glass, falling and rearranging themselves at random, will now and then catch her breath as a new shape tumbles into place and whisper, "Look, Mummy, leaves!"

11.

A man from the country approaches the Law, where a doorkeeper waits. He asks to enter, since the Law is supposed to be free and accessible to all men. The doorkeeper says that he cannot enter the Law now, and warns him not to try, as he is powerful and even more powerful doorkeepers wait further inside, at inner doors, so that the man has no hope of passing them all. He might be allowed to enter later. The man can choose to wait, though there are no promises. The doorkeeper even offers him a stool. Years pass, and the man grows old. He learns every flea in the doorkeeper's collar. He sells all he has to bribe the doorkeeper, and the doorkeeper accepts only so the man doesn't think he hasn't tried everything, but the bribes make no difference. As age makes the man childish, he begs even the fleas in the doorkeeper's collar to help his case. Finally, one day, he asks an obvious question: Why in all this time has no one else sought entry into the Law? The doorkeeper answers, "No one else could ever be admitted here, since this gate was made only for you. I am now going to shut it."

"Before the Law," a fable in Kafka's *The Trial,* has the feel and logic of a familiar nightmare. There is no arguing with the doorkeeper. It's folly to find fault in the system, and folly to waste your life waiting at the door. Could the man simply have walked through the door, into the Law? In the end, he didn't battle with the doorkeeper. He stayed outside out of fear and respect for a self-proclaimed authority. He trembled before the rules. Should he have gone in and challenged the ultimate doorkeeper, instead of hunkering outside, intimidated and obedient?

In *The Trial*, a painter and a priest advise K. The priest asks the bigger moral questions: *Why are you submitting to this?* In life, refugees don't have the strength or the power to rise up and defy borders and gatekeepers. Most follow the wisdom of artists. The painter's advice is to live and find joy in the spaces opened up by the system. So, refugees find a kind functionary to keep the case churning ("deferment," the painter calls it), or they are arrested and released from detention, again and again ("apparent acquittal"). Their lives are squandered. Some are released from the cycle after decades, those who never stop appealing to higher authorities, who won't accept disbelief, but push past door-keeper after doorkeeper until they find the mightiest one. This takes a Herculean will. And it takes the willingness to have the door slammed shut, to be told "no" for the final time and be sent back to death. For some, that is preferable to endless waiting, crouching outside the door, like a dog.

The system wants to squander your life, your sanity, Kafka says. Know your power.

Does "entering the Law" mean rushing past the many layers of il-logic and mediocrity, doing what is necessary and untrue, to reach the human core, the rational inmost judge?

The priest tells K that he is deluding himself. "The court doesn't want anything from you," says the priest. "It accepts you when you come and it lets you go when you leave." Stop struggling, he seems to say. "You don't need to accept everything as true. You only have to accept it as necessary." However dishonest, we must find a way to seize control within the logic of the nightmare. "Depressing view," K responds, "the lie made into the rule of the world."

———

Near our tiny village, down a small road, an actress has a house. The house has a special history, and over the years I've come to like its new owner, because she lifted herself out of extreme poverty with guts and drive. We don't have much in common, though. Despite her achievements, all the actress wants, her metric for female worth, is an upper-class husband. It's a panic I understand: once displaced, now she craves security, proximity to those whose safety society underwrites. She doesn't want to stumble far from clean spaces, even if they're populated by those who do nothing, give nothing. She wants to belong there, even if they judge her for her upbringing. Sometimes I imagine her marrying some dull Englishman with a title and no cash, handing over the keys to her properties, bragging about his much smaller achievements, slowly abandoning her career, bringing him pots of tea. I want to scream, *But you're finally free!*

"Why do you care?" said Sam.

"I don't," I said. "You see someone about to step in dogshit, you want to grab their arm."

After our commune disbanded, the actress arrived with a young man from the English upper class, a handsome blond Londoner who claimed to work in finance. It took about three questions to realize this was no Harvard MBA type, or even a Noah. He spent four hours a day managing money for "a small fund," the kind that doesn't cast about for talented money managers, but hires from among its own drowsy sons. And he didn't care to create a likeness. For him, the job was just a gauzy cover-up for being born rich. Like a skimpy garment, its purpose wasn't to hide what's underneath, but to display it more tantalizingly while following the social convention of not arriving naked.

Instinct kept telling me to be ugly. To show up in pajamas and leave out the compost.

Throughout their stay, the actress hinted about marriage. He evaded. Having always been the most desired person in the room, she was oblivious to the rules most women know: don't ask for everything you want, don't be thirsty, loving more, needing more. Watching her without a script was tragic; all the years of performing love on screen, she couldn't fathom that she might not be the leading lady. Still, I admired her brazen attitude; to her, rejection was unthinkable. He casually remarked that his grandparents wouldn't love that he was dating an actress.

Alone with Sam, I fumed. "At least she does *something!*"

Sometimes the aristo was kind, nurturing. He cooked dinners. He sent over a drone with a single chocolate egg. How do you dislike someone who does that? And yet, a voice kept reminding me that he was part of a terrible class system, built on colonialism, imperialism, racism, and theft—a system I want dismantled, its spoils returned. At a barbecue, he cast out a shibboleth to Sam. He did it so subtly, it might've been subconscious. He had spent much of his childhood in India (he cringed each time I said "colonialism") but had never dated a South Asian woman. He said, casually, keeping his eyes on the grill, "I've never had yellow fever."

Sam and I looked at each other, stunned. Later I asked Sam, "Was that a dog whistle or some kind of racist tic? I honestly can't tell."

The next night, the four of us spoke about English quirks. He pretended not to have heard of RP, or "Received Pronunciation," the upper-class accent. The actress was confused. "But I see it all the time on scripts!" We started talking about university. Sam mentioned that in his first year at Oxford, he intensified his Essex accent. He wanted to signal that he got there on his own steam. The trouble was loads of rich kids were doing the same. The aristocrat spoke of certain forbidden words, the ones that signal a middle-class try-hard ("tea" instead of "dinner," "serviette" instead of "napkin").

The actress said, "But I heard you say *time for tea* . . . that night . . ."

He laughed. "You weren't meant to understand that, darling; it was an inside joke."

At whose expense, I wonder. The aristo explained that the middle classes always try to sound French. "What if they're part French?" I asked, thinking of Elena. "Would my bilingual daughter be allowed to say 'serviette'?"

He chuckled and said kindly, "If she's speaking French."

Damn it, I liked this man. He'd make a charming farmer or doctor or mechanic, had all usefulness not been bred out of him.

That night I found Nancy Mitford's biting mid-century writings about English upper-class words: how the U (aristocracy) differentiate themselves from the non-U (middle class), while seeming not to care. They pretend that their nonchalance has made them sound like the working classes. Counter-signaling is the notion that if one has something in abundance, one doesn't care about signaling it, and behaves like those with none of it. The billionaire in jeans and sandals, the goddess without makeup. Their counter signals differentiate them from the middle, the only border that matters. The language of the U is simple, unadorned, effortless. The message is that the upper class don't have to care what words they use; they are always correct by virtue of innate sensibility.

I hit the roof. I slammed my laptop shut and stormed into Sam's workspace.

"Is this totally mediocre person secretly thinking that I'm a non-U?"

"Of course," Sam said, laughing. "You have a non-U personality."

"Explain," I said. "Explain *now*, because this snobbery . . . I have *three* master's degrees!"

"Right there," said Sam. "U's are subtle. You're like a blowfish. Someone touches you and poof . . . out comes the three master's degrees."

His precision stung. But then I was confused; if abundance is counter-signaled, then why do I keep talking about these credentials that I definitely have? Maybe I'm not confident that they truly belong to me, or that I deserve them. Maybe I've conflated them with entry into a tribe, one to which the aristo effortlessly belongs.

"But I *earned* those," I said, stung.

"You hang your degrees on your wall!" he said. "I'm not saying it's bad, but if you're asking about those people and their rules, it's non-U to display that stuff."

"Like wearing the Chanel Cs," I muttered, arms crossed.

"What?" he said.

"Maybe you're not supposed to display social class because it's stolen and unearned and they know it," I said. "But I earned my degrees. Plus, they're in my *office*, not over the living room couch. If you ask me, hiding them under the bed seems way more self-conscious."

"It's more work to frame them and hang them," he said.

"They *come in a frame!*" (They don't. I paid a hundred bucks for each.)

"You're right." Sam smiled kindly. "But you care so much. Everything's a fire."

I admit, I don't like to be on the outside of things. I'll be arguing with doorkeepers until I die. And I mourn for the forbidden words, so easily discarded. What a waste. The first time I heard an English person refer to dinner as "tea," I was charmed. I imagined a light meal of sandwiches. I heard the clink of the glass, the fizz of sugar dissolving in hot liquid. How grotesque to dismiss someone based on a wrong word uttered while offering hospitality. And why? Because it signals trying, caring—the best things a stranger can do.

Though insider language evolves over generations, one upper-class signal hasn't changed, because strivers can't mimic it: coldness to those burdened by need, a trait they consider an evolutionary failure of the lower classes.

A few days later, after a few bottles of wine, the aristo showed us a video his prep school friends were passing around of an old brown man who, for five pounds, would get naked and wave his genitals at the camera. In one video, rich English boys laughed cruelly, slapping the man on the back, like a friend. *Look how well we get along with this man from the gutter.* In text chains they repeated his price; how cheaply a fellow human will sell his dignity. Maybe this is amusing, when you have so much; maybe it's a triumph to walk away with the film, having offered only five pounds. Sam and I stared; the aristo was oblivious to this ugliness. Catching Sam's eye, I knew he was imagining the old man steeped in quiet dignity just before he took a breath and stripped for the camera. What was the calculus of that five pounds? The actress looked adoringly at her ordinary man, leaking value with every longing look and bated breath.

Back at the house, Sam seemed distracted.

"I get it now," I said. "Cruelty is the currency of his tribe." All his life, this aristo's indifference was rewarded, the way effort is for others.

Sam kept looking at his phone.

"Are you listening?" I asked.

"Sorry," he said. He didn't want to talk about the Englishman anymore. Recently Sam had started doing editing work; lots of business school applications. "You know," he said, "I'm editing another McKinsey person? Listen to this: her sister tried to kill herself. So she's telling business schools she wants to cultivate more effective leadership."

"Fucking hell," I said. A rogue laugh escaped my lips.

Sam smirked, and recited in his best business-wanker voice: "Leveraging my current vulnerability, I'm ideally suited to manage . . ." He paused. "She actually says *showcasing my vulnerability* . . . That's the verb she chose for it. Showcase."

"She learned English in the corporate world," I said. "You can't blame her."

Sam took a breath. I feel exposed when Sam reads stomach-turning McKinsey-to-Harvard essays, the kind from my past. I remind myself that I never wrote one like that, that my bosses warned me that I sounded young and unsure. Maybe I was leveraging my vulnerability, too.

"You know every one of them tries for a discount?" said Sam.

"Please tell me you tell them to fuck right off," I said. "You never give discounts to these people. They *want* you to say no. It means you're worth it."

That night I couldn't sleep. I had been so in the weeds, thinking so much about the tension between potential and need, I had missed disease deep in the roots. Now it seemed the lie at the core of the world, the greater structure of it, was becoming visible. To be seen and believed, what do you do with your vulnerability?

The powerful upper classes hide it: subtlety is the long-term absence of every need.

The bourgeoisie curate it as a part of their fire and potential (*try, burn, roar*).

The vulnerable have no options: they dramatize it. Naked at the fringes, they have only their need, displayed like entertainment for the top, judged on its authenticity by the middle.

In the end, there is an order to things. Everyone must verify their identity to the doorkeeper at the gate.

This caste system manifests in every realm, even art. Western writing students are told that good stories are like a still river. The water roils below the surface, but at the top, all is calm. You earn respect, we are told, by writing quiet stories, by burying intensity and keeping your cool so the reader can feel something entirely on their own. It is a Western aesthetic, born out of European class hierarchies. Iranians don't function this way. For us, love is drama. Pain is drama. Lovers don't leave subtle notes; they rip their shirts. It's disconcerting and alluring.

What kept me awake that night, though, wasn't the McKinsey kid showcasing vulnerability or the poor old man stripping for five quid. I kept returning to that third tier: *Why do we still let them do it?* Why do we bicker about meritocracies and gatekeeping and who deserves which passport, and still allow the children of colonialists to carry insider-ness around with them from country to country?

––––––

Just before he died, Josh was reading Kafka's parables and I was reading Kafka's *The Trial*. I didn't know this until Sam went to clean out the apartment and found the book on his desk. Over the weeks, in a strange mourning ritual, Sam had begun layering on Josh's clothes. First sweaters, then winter coats—despite constant poverty, Josh had excellent coats, from massive sheep-scented shearlings passed down from Provencal uncles to waxy Barbour hunting jackets. That afternoon, Sam slipped the Kafka into the pocket of Josh's big raincoat and walked away. A part of me itched to thumb through it. What had Josh found inside those pages?

"I almost read the doorkeeper's fable at the shiva," said Sam. "Because Josh was the man standing at the door of the world, asking to be let in. Never realizing the door was his fate."

For over a year, I've been thinking about KV. I keep asking, *What should he have done?* Should he have gone home and courted death? Taken power into his own hands, as Josh did?

Kafka's allegories of our twisted bureaucracies seem concerned with something beyond. Kafka seems to say that we have some power: to reject authority, to look away, to refuse to play a part or even to twist into the knife. In accepting the knife, we wake up from the nightmare. Is that it?

Sam is hunched over Josh's manic emails. I'm sitting in front of a dying hearth, wearing an old puffer coat I found in a closet. Briefly I wonder if it belonged to someone who has passed, then I find another crusted half vitamin in the pocket that can only have belonged to Flo, and the idea seems silly. Clothing changes hands all the time; it can only belong to the living, to those who can feel the cold. I wonder if KV still has that bloody shirt.

In December 2018—after two tribunals of judges (in 2011 and 2014) both upheld the Home Office's rejection—the U.K. Supreme Court heard KV's case, allowing intervention from the Helen Bamber Foundation, Freedom from Torture, and Medical Justice. It was a hot-button case, full of dramatic theories. Did the doctor overstep? Would a normal person have themselves tortured for asylum? As all this was being debated, the court noticed a troubling inconsistency: it seemed that the court of appeal had misread a key part of the doctor's report. They seemed to think that *all* the scars had precise edges, even the ones on his arms. So clearly, the tribunal said, he was unconscious the *entire* time (from anesthesia), rather than passing out from pain.

The Supreme Court was stunned: "*ha[s] the tribunal mislaid the pivotal point?*"

When its mistake was pointed out, the tribunal's response was flimsy, pompous, and grasping. If it mistook the scars on KV's arms as precise, the tribunal said, then the doctor must have been vague or confusing in his oral statements. Though the doctor's written statements were clear and entirely consistent with KV's story, the tribunal claimed that the doctor must have said something different elsewhere which had misled them (implication: the tribunal is infallible). And, since KV had failed to provide a transcript of every oral remark, the unprovability of the tribunal's claim was his own fault. The courts and the public must assume, the tribunal held, that the doctor contradicted himself somewhere: "Without a transcript, there was no basis for criticising the tribunal."

In its March 2019 ruling, the Supreme Court rejected this dangerous suggestion: that a court officer could explain his error by attributing it to an unrecorded oral testimony contradicting everything a witness has said on record. "The court of first instance should be expected to record the oral evidence on which it places reliance." In his medical reports and in transcripts of his oral testimonies, the doctor is always clear about the difference between the scars, and the Supreme Court accepted that the doctor had never wavered from that. It also disagreed with the lower court's assertion that the doctor had overstepped in his designation of the story as "highly consistent": the doctor was giving valuable evidence about how it's possible to lose consciousness, then remain unconscious as the rods were applied to the back.

But the most vital point in KV's lower court ruling was in the designation of "SIBP" as a routine guidance for the Home Office to use as they wish. The made-up acronym, some foolish caseworker's nonsensical phrase, had cemented into bureaucratic shorthand, an ordinary reason to reject. The lower court then waded deep into the waters they had just polluted, dismissing all of KV's evidence with the following rationale: the doctors had eliminated every explanation except two, torture or self-infliction. Since the torture claim didn't meet the Home Office's preferred level of scrutiny, they were left with only one option. No, they couldn't say that it was *definitely* self-infliction, but it didn't matter, since it was the only option left.

In other words, they treated it like a Jamesian "live hypothesis." It was alive among their minds' possibilities, the only one they couldn't discount, so they felt morally clear to believe it. As a parting shot, they made a stunning logical leap. Though they had chastised the doctor for going too far, believing the story (instead of only assessing scars), the lower court did exactly that, leaping from their disbelief of the scars to disbelief of the entire story, with defiant certainty: *"We find that after 2003 he . . . remained in Colombo and at no stage then or thereafter did he come to the adverse attention of the army or police before coming to the UK."*

The Supreme Court's response has a tone like Clifford's shipowner parable. Do you think you're morally in the clear now? *Not one jot.* A live hypothesis can't be live in one mind alone. It can't revive a dead question or defy experts. It must be live in the mind of a community.

To paraphrase the Supreme Court: if you claim that there are two real possibilities, then reject one of them, then you are necessarily claiming that the other possibility happened. You cannot shrug and say, "Well, it's the only one left, so let's take it." You have to put both possibilities through equal scrutiny before dismissing either one. Neither gets to be a default. In short, you can't create a catch-all bucket for when the only other real option is too unpalatable to accept. "That there was extensive torture by state forces in Sri Lanka in 2009 was well established," said the Supreme Court, "[including] burning with soldering irons and suspension of detainees by their thumbs." Self-infliction by asylum seekers "was almost non-existent."

In 2019, eight years after he arrived in the U.K., the court directed the tribunal to give KV a fresh claim against his refusal of asylum. "It is an extreme measure," the judges wrote, "for a person to decide to cause himself to suffer deep injury and severe and protracted pain." Plus, KV would have needed help from a doctor. Even if he had managed that, how do you explain the frantic scars on his arms? And why did he need so many? "One or two strategically placed scars would equally well have supported a claim of torture."

The Supreme Court closed by quoting the only lower court judge who had heard KV's story honestly. In his dissent, Judge Elias said, "[V]ery considerable weight should be given to the fact that injuries which are SIBP are likely to be extremely rare . . . This would in all probability have required the clandestine co-operation of a qualified doctor who would have had to be willing to act in breach of the most fundamental and ethical standards, and who had access to the relevant medical equipment." It was simply too absurd, thought Judge Elias. "That was his view," the Supreme Court ruled, with the finality of a society's last seat of judgment. "It should also, I suggest, be ours."

————

The cruelty and audacity of KV's rejection shook the humanitarian community. Activists and lawyers saw it as a chilling new low in disbelief culture, a warning that standards had shifted away from refuge toward barred gates. Did we as a society no longer understand that some truths are contained only in the memory, without papers or proof? Were we forgetting that the burden of proof on refugees is rightfully set below that of criminals? The Home Office was now openly teaching its gate-keepers bad-faith techniques, incentivizing and training them to trap survivors in surreal logic games. If they offered a place to anyone, it was because they had lost.

Will the Home Office continue to use self-infliction as a reason to reject asylum claims? I wouldn't bet against it, since it takes a long time for caseworker biases to change. What's more worrying is that asylum officers around the world are searching for such tricks, and that they're rewarded for them. They will find new ones—cleverer, more danger-ous ones.

Though the media barely looked at KV, the human rights activists couldn't stop talking about him. What a farce his trial had been. *Prove it didn't happen*, the Home Office and the lower courts seemed to say. But they knew. They knew by Kant's definition of knowing, because anyone who saw KV's back would be logically required to know. Scars on a back are evidence; they tell a story. We don't curate them. KV's trials reminded me of a line in French Napoleonic era writer Joseph Joubert's notebooks: "Nothing that is proved is obvious; for what is ob-vious shows itself and cannot be proved."

But the Home Office wasn't looking to prove anything. The people arguing the other side of KVs case understood, as any human would, that a U.K. passport isn't worth your body's health. Self-infliction was, and continues to be, entirely disingenuous: a catch-all invented pre-cisely to justify dismissing cases wherein torture is the only plausible story. "It's a box-ticking exercise," says Juliet Cohen, head of doctors at Freedom from Torture and an advocate for KV. "So they created a new box," a default fantasy box to increase the burden of proof on all other boxes to arbitrarily high levels.

When KV first told his story to veteran doctors and torture experts, they all believed him. His story isn't rare or improbable, and it has plenty of singular detail. The credibility issues arose from those inexplicable events that may not happen often, but could easily happen once: Sri Lankan authorities overlooked KV's father; someone helped KV escape. Life is baffling. Strange things often happen one time. Is it unimaginable that a story that ends in permanent disfigurement and displacement might contain some of those singular events?

Long after KV's final court case, I sat in a London legal office and talked to his lawyer, Arun, a careful but forthcoming man who, over many years, has grown close to KV. When KV joined us, I was struck by his ease. Physical detail spilled out of him, a tendency of trauma survivors who are remembering, rather than inventing. KV talked about his grandmother's busy mornings, about her food, the physical process of melting gold. As he spoke, his lawyer watched my face, as if to say, *You see? Everyone involved knew this man was honest.* That he was treated like a liar and a criminal was a matter of policy, not credibility.

"People don't have a certificate of torture," said FFT's Dr. Cohen, "so, doubts and biases creep in." To encounter others' pain is to doubt. As in criminal interrogations, asylum officers give in to confirmation bias. They use their imagination. If a theory occurs, they look to confirm it. We all look to verify what we think we know.

Sometimes, caseworkers make meaningless observations that seem clever. Scars on body parts opposite a dominant hand may strike the officer as self-inflicted, but if they occur in unreachable places, the same officer might suggest a proxy. In one case, Dr. Cohen tells me, a woman was deported to her country. She escaped again with new injuries and was accused of having given consent for those. "But fake injuries tend to be superficial, on parts of the body that are easy to access, not intimate parts, inflicted by a single method (all scratches or cuts). There is often a mismatch between what the person describes and what you observe as a doctor, and a mismatch between the psychological impact of the injury in torture versus with consent."

What causes PTSD, says Dr. Cohen, is the overwhelming fear of the unknown. Someone who has commissioned a torture will know exactly what is going to happen. And it isn't easy to fake PTSD before a trained doctor with years of expertise and thousands of cases spanning many ages, many cultures. Medical experts don't use a single scar or lesion as proof. They make a holistic diagnosis, following many exploratory questions and objective exams. "We know how to move them off script. Every person is different. Some people cry; others don't. You need experience to see the impact on a life. You can't look for a single behavior as a sign of deceit."

During a lull in our conversation, Arun told me a story about a client who was wanted by the government in Sri Lanka. He was riding his bike when police cars passed him, headed toward his home. Knowing precisely why they'd come, he kept his pedaling calm, then, as the cars vanished from sight, he turned and sped away in another direction. He never offered this story to the U.K. asylum authorities. It was too cinematic, too astonishing. "What court would believe a coincidence like that?" Instead the man said he was out when the police arrived and stayed away after news of the attempted arrest reached him. This more typical story might be believed.

I asked KV if he was in touch with his family. He told me that his father was paranoid, that he spoke of clicking sounds on his home phone. Once, he had called KV for three minutes on a borrowed phone, to warn his son that the authorities were hunting him. Later, I read about the call in KV's testimonies. How crucial three minutes can be in a year, a life.

Arun smiled kindly and offered me water. His entire career is dedicated to proving these unbelievable stories. A lawyer in Kafka's *The Trial* tells K that lawyers often fall into a depression, because the cases that win were always destined to win, and all the small triumphs that

give joy during a trial often amount to nothing. The court believes
what it wants to believe.

Was there ever a doctor willing to breach every ethic, sedate a patient and inflict torture scars for the price a tailor or a jeweler could
pay? We stumble into fear, and we build scaffolding around the truth.
We set up doorkeepers and we grow our burdens of proof beyond the
most hostile caseworker's imagination. Perhaps the most honest reaction to such contortions is the simple bafflement of the U.K. Supreme
Court: *It is an extreme measure.*

Having lost track of time, I rushed out of my meeting with KV.
He ran after me to say goodbye. He gave me his real name, his email
address. He was frantic with worry. Would another writer let his story
pass by? Why should he trust me when his story, as it unfolded, had
hardly had a moment's media attention? Stories disappear all the time.

At the end of Kafka's "In the Penal Colony," the Traveler refuses
to support the brutal machine and its guardian. He judges the Officer
inhuman. So the Officer, who has dedicated his life and all his thoughts
to the design and outcome of the apparatus, climbs in himself. Impris-
oned in his own logic, he submits to the Harrow, his life's work, inflicting its punishment on himself. The Traveler rushes back to his own
country. When two refugees try to board his ship to escape the penal
colony, he fights them off, denying them refuge.

Which man, Officer or Traveler, has lived honestly according to
the logic of his own convictions? Before submitting his body to the
machine, the Officer loads a text in the Inscriber. His sentence reads:
"Be Just."

———

That winter and spring, we reckoned with the wounds, our limping
family. Sam ran the hills and hiked through the forest. I whipped
meringue and read dark stories. Elena played with the other Iranian
girl in her school. We met local families, blended into the community.

Sometimes my father in Isfahan left voice memos about the pandemic. "Who would've guessed being a dentist would become so dangerous?" He described the "space suit" he wore to work, and how he couldn't smell his patients anymore through the layers of plastic. If he'd had a few drinks, he'd go on about Rumi, the Sufi mystics, and the mysteries of the universe.

"There was a time," Baba said late one night, "when I wanted to follow astronomy. It's a beautiful field, opens the eyes to another world. To think that after 400 million years, some light reached us from the Andromeda galaxy. And if there were people there living, maybe they communicated in UV lights. Imagining these things from here . . . you laugh. They're marvelous."

I dropped into a chair, awestruck, like watching my mother untangle a logic puzzle. *I come from weird, wonderful people; I can cobble myself together from them.* But I'm certain that only I and my father plan to be finished when we die. Despite his Oklahoma baptism ruse, my father falls somewhere between an atheist and a Sufi. He likes the spirituality of poets, seeking peace in never knowing for sure. I imagine Rumi's Islam is like Weil's Christianity; I want to tell him about her writings, but doubt he can find a Farsi copy of *Gravity and Grace.*

I told Baba once that I find relief in devoting my hours to the present, rather than to some promised afterlife that may never arrive. He agreed. Then he grumbled about growing old. I told him that I was feeling the years, too, and he said, "You're not old. I'm old because love is over for me." I smiled; what's life without the occasional dose of Iranian melodrama?

Old, I wanted to say, *is when you can't discount away the afterlife anymore.* In finance, you learn to discount future gains by their likelihood, then by a discount rate that obliterates distant outcomes. Present dollars and joys are worth more than future, improbable ones. In youth, then, it's irrational to prioritize afterlife happiness at the expense of current happiness (though believers keep reminding us of the "eternity" part of the equation). In *Pensées*, Pascal argued that against even the tiniest possibility of God and infinite gain, any finite loss is worthwhile. I answer Pascal's wager by saying that the cost isn't small for me. And even if it were, zero-probability plus my personal discount rate of nearly 100 percent on gains beyond my death shrinks paradise down to almost nothing. This seems dishonest: in my last year, I will feel differently.

But enough with the afterlife spreadsheets—I stopped believing in Jesus, is all. Or, rather, I stopped believing in the evangelical Jesus. That Jesus's agenda seems too closely correlated with that of the rich and the male. And motives factor in when I decide whom to believe.

But is "decide" the right word? Can believing be muscled? Is it a skill or a purely rational outcome of external truths? In the long term, faith and skepticism are part of our identities, embedded in the spirit, much the way Pascal, after a mystical vision of Jesus and God, wrote "Memorial" feverishly and sewed it into his lapel, carrying it around for the rest of his life. "Certitude. Certitude. Feeling. Joy. Peace." Pascal's "Memorial" is manic. "Complete submission to Jesus Christ and to my director." In the end, Pascal's belief had nothing to do with the math.

So. I still pray sometimes. It's useful, my friend Joubert whispers from across the centuries—though, he adds, it doesn't alter destiny.

And when I pray, I say "Jesus." And sometimes I fall asleep knowing that someone has heard me. Yet I don't *believe* that someone has, certainly not the historical Jesus.

I'm not a believer. Maybe I never was. My mother says that a true Christian can never fall away. Maybe in my adolescence I was just a math nerd, hedging.

Sometimes, in moments of doubt and near waking, I read "The Unbeliever" by Elizabeth Bishop. It describes a sleeper on top of a mast, his head suspended, his bedsheets the sails. He is dreaming. A cloud speaks to him. A gull speaks to him. Their perspective is rooted in the dream. They see the reflections in the sea, the marble air, and they believe it as the world. The unbeliever continues sleeping, perched precariously on the mast, his eyes closed, though perhaps not for long. "I must not fall. The spangled sea below wants me to fall. It is hard as diamonds; it wants to destroy us all." The dreamer is becoming lucid, aware of the dream, and maybe aware of the sea as the marble-hard floor of his room. He is the only voice who can exit the dream. The sea wants him to wake, to destroy the cloud, the bird, the sleeper—the part of himself who believes. Is it freedom or death, to stop believing?

I relish the dream; I need it to survive.

One morning at Flo and Sheldon's, a hymn from my childhood played on a podcast. I don't remember the name. Did I mutter a response? Flo squeezed out her teabag. She snapped the top onto her mug and said, "That's not the reaction of an atheist." Then she walked away.

Now, deeper into her sixties, my own mother has mellowed. She no longer calls me an unbeliever. She doesn't ask about my faith, and I don't ask about her inner life. Instead, when we talk, we talk about collapsing meringues, the dirt road to our old village in Iran, vaccines. In February 2020, she complimented my writing. I can see her itching to tell Elena about Jesus. Her mouth tightens when Elena declares that "we all of us live inside the *baleine multicolore*."

I understand that my mother needs to believe in my salvation. She doesn't want to imagine her child burning up for eternity. It's hard to rage at her for choosing the comfortable ending, the one that allows her to keep her sacred myth, to reject the unimaginable.

Over the years, I've heard many believers bear public witness to the deathbed salvations of loved ones. I wonder if, after I die, some comatose neighbor of my mother's will wake up claiming to have spotted me in heaven and swear that I secretly believed. Probably. There's always someone ready with such mercies. And, anyway, the group wisdom is that, like my dad, I'm logical and mercenary: after a lifetime of preoccupation with every kind of gatekeeping, I'm not about to get stuck behind the ultimate door. The likeliest outcome, the one to put money on: having done Pascal's math, I probably went to my grave reciting *all* the prayers.

————

A few days after the commune ended, we went for a walk in the mountains with Sam's cousin Ludivine. We visited a litter of newborn sheep. We drank soup and coffee from thermoses and stared into the wintry green expanse of the Luberon valley. On the way back, we visited the churchyard cemetery where Sam's grandparents are buried. Elena kept pointing to tombstones and asking, "Who died here?" as if the dead had each traveled to this spot and lay down under the stone to die. She asked in French, which made it all the more difficult for me to answer.

"Where is Josh?" she asked, scanning the graves. And when I told her he's in Essex, she said, pining for her grandparents' home, "He's there? But I thought he was dead!"

Sam was starting to stare out into the distance again. I kicked his foot gently and waited.

We stumbled onto a Muslim grave. It didn't have a stone, and I told Sam that below this earth, the man is probably wrapped in a white biodegradable shroud, a *kaffan*, so he can decompose more elegantly into the earth instead of becoming a puddle of goo in a marble coffin. I remembered my father's reaction to Iran's pandemic funerals: *even his soul can't get past that.* The last time we exchanged voice memos, he was still bothered by it. He explained that the body needs its space, even in death: "In Islam, you dig a grave. And you dig half of it a little bit deeper, to put the nose of the dead on the dirt. And you put two sticks under his arms, so that the dead can sit up in front of Nakir and Munkir, to answer the questions, and name the Imams."

Nakir and Munkir are terrifying angels that are said to appear to the dead, to ask the three vital questions of faith. Their answers decide if the dead are allowed into paradise. "But now," my father continued, "they're so worried about the virus escaping, they dig a giant swimming pool and put you in plastic and shove you in. If you're poor, no one bothers to bury you one by one. They push you into the swimming pool and seal it with cement so nothing can get out."

"I want to be buried in a shroud," I said to Sam, as we scanned the graves in the churchyard, "but stick a straw in my mouth, just in case."

"Just in case you're alive, you can starve to death?" said Sam.

"No, if I wake up, I'll dig myself out." I paused. "I'd like you to bury me really shallow."

Sam laughed, which was nice. A dozen old tombstones were leaning against the church wall. Sam explained that you buy a plot only for a hundred years. After that, they can bury someone else there.

"What?" I said. "How is that fair?"

"They move the older tombstones into the church," said Sam. "They're historical relics."

"But what about the bodies?" I said.

"They've decomposed," said Sam. He's been obsessed with the bodies of the dead lately. He showed me the photo of Josh's body, his eyelids held down with clumps of Vaseline, his cheeks rouged. I wanted to stare at it for longer than he'd let me.

"What about the bodies that are a puddle of goo in a marble coffin?" I asked.

"They're under the new ones," he said. "They get buried really deep."

We walked and squinted at the old tombstones, trying to read the dates. "So, they just get their stone moved inside and forgotten?" I asked.

"The old ones don't have anyone who visits them," said Ludivine. "Everyone's died."

"I change my mind," I said. "I'd like you to grind me up into a powder and hang me on a chain around your neck until you die, then I'd like Elena to wear that chain, then her children."

Sam laughed again (*Twice. Good*). "How about if we put some spikes on the necklace as a constant reminder? And a little microphone with your voice saying, 'Are you listening to me?'"

"Elena," I said, "promise you'll make me into a necklace when I'm dead."

"Okay, Mummy," said Elena, picking wild daisies for her great-grandmother's grave.

Near the end of forty years of notebooks, Joubert, the Napoleon-era writer, seems to realize that he'll never complete his great book, his uprooted epiphanies growing out of nothing, the stories lost inside his aging memory. He fixates on age: ". . . but in the end a year comes when you find that you are getting old." In his last few years, Joubert grows morbidly funny, like elderly villagers, and my dad. "Flowers in cemeteries," he writes. "They must be uprooted; this earth spoils them—and let the skeletons smile. Horrible amusements."

So, we let Elena carry on with the wild daisies.

On our way of the cemetery, in a somber moment, Elena started chanting "*Josh est déjà mort. Il est vraiment mort, oui? Hyper mort!*" I held my breath.

"Children are severe. Why?" asks Joubert. I wonder what his son had said that morning.

Sam chuckled at Elena's chant. "Her candor is weirdly cathartic . . . Josh is *really* dead."

"All the new thinking is about loss," writes Robert Hass in a poem. "In this it resembles all the old thinking." In a "first world of undivided light," there was some nameless harmony without words, there were physical things, and childlike wonder, amazement at the thing itself. At brambles and blackberries. Then came concepts, words, the idea that "a word is elegy to what it signifies." Turn a word over on your tongue. Does it contain the marvelous thing? It invites grief, because the blackberry or the bramble or the bread has leaked out of the word.

"*Hyper* dead," I said. It did feel good to be so literal. The word *dead* somehow felt close to the thing itself, to the bodies just below our feet. Closer than *blackberry* to the nearest blackberry. Elena ripped some daisies from the ground. *The uncut hair of graves.*

"He's dead," muttered Sam. *Forever.* He took Elena's hand and we left the cemetery.

———

One morning around that time, as I was dressing Elena, she looked at me with big, imploring eyes. "Mummy, how many days do I have?"

At first, I didn't get it. "Have for what?"

She searched my face for a precise answer. "How many days do I have till I have to die?"

It was a punch to the chest. I scanned my memory. Had we spoken too loudly or too often of Josh? Had we properly explained to her the death of Oscar, Flo's beloved dog, shortly after?

Elena kept waiting. Caught off guard, I could think only of the math.

"If you take good care, about 36,000," I said.

She stared with those eyes. "Is that a lot of days?"

So I began counting: "One, two, three . . ." I imagined all my daughter's future pains, her confusions. In coming years, she'd run to me weeping over a lost love or a crushing defeat, and maybe I'd pull her into my arms and count her remaining days into her ear: so many still left to live. I'd stop when the vastness of the number smoothed out the furrows in her brow, made her giggle and move on from her worries. That first morning, it happened at "forty-three."

Elena keeps asking versions of this question. "How many days have you had already?" But she's never asked me where we go, after we die. She is focused on this life, how many days, hours, do we have left to play, to swim, to read stories?

In her meditations, Weil writes: "When we listen to Bach or to a Gregorian melody, all the faculties of the soul become tense and silent in order to apprehend this thing of perfect beauty . . . should not faith be an adherence of this kind? The mysteries of faith are degraded if they are made into an object of affirmation and negation, when in reality they should be an object of contemplation . . . The object of our search should not be the supernatural, but the world."

In writing stories, I peer into dark corners and I find bright threads in unlikely places, the echo of one thing in another. I don't pray or speak in tongues. I reflect on all that I *can* know, ever briefly, with my earthly senses, and I unstitch the embroidery of the world. That's enough faith for now. Like Saint Simone, I fill the void with my imagination and logic.

"Of two men who have no experience of God," Weil writes, "he who denies him is perhaps nearer to him than the other." Weil believes that in such cases, God has *chosen* to go unseen: "When God has become as full of significance as the treasure is for the miser, we have to tell ourselves insistently that he does not exist . . . It is he who, through the operation of the dark night, withdraws himself in order not to be loved like the treasure is by the miser . . . If we love God while thinking he does not exist, he will manifest his existence."

Jacques Derrida, who called himself a "man of prayers and tears," agrees in his reflections on prayer that atheists are closer to the divine than theologians, that perhaps it takes an atheist to truly pray. In a 2002 talk at the joint meeting of American Academy of Religion and Society of Biblical Literature, he is asked, since he is an atheist, "To whom are you praying?"

Derrida responds with his own question: Why ask this publicly of a non-theologian?

Derrida says that his prayers (*if* he prays) are secret; private prayer interrupts something in the community. In the Book of Matthew, Jesus calls out the hypocrisy of public prayer. "When you pray, go into your room, close the door and pray to your Father, who is unseen."

A person who performs prayer isn't talking to God but to an

audience. Derrida says that, as a youth, his first rebellion had to do with public, common prayer. He articulated his prayers in his own words, always in intelligible language (no glossolalia for him), and he kept them private. Yet his prayers are also a ritual, "a mixture of a secret and sacred idiom and some common ritual in which the body accepts to make coded gestures." They contain childlike imagery, iconography of God as a severe, merciless, but ultimately just grandfather and also as a forgiving mother who believes in his innocence. At the same time, they contain an adult layer: the atheist, the unbeliever asking, who am I talking to? "Who do you expect to answer these prayers is part of what the prayer has to be in order to be authentic. If I knew, that would be the end of prayer. That would be like ordering a pizza." Derrida says that we must give up any expectation, any certainty of an answer, if our words are to be a prayer. Perhaps this is what creates a wider gulf between God and the theologian than God and the atheist: the theologian is too certain. His humility is leaking out.

Maybe God, then, removed himself from me, even in those girlhood days. Maybe he saw that other Dina, so certain, smirking through all that clenching prayer, all that fighting to be let in. That's a comfort. I'm not going to let that Dina go. Though she's cruel, she is also my imagination and my reason. Maybe she's my superego, or armor for my identity. Maybe she remakes the truth to help me survive. And even in that, she is my best thing.

God would agree, if he were sentient. I still imagine him with a kind, fatherly face, though I know that he is only a manifestation, other people's imprint on my heart. He is all the human goodness that I've known, the portion of love I've been granted, the love I've craved and let slip away, the small pleasures that landed briefly on my cheeks, then vanished, leaving their memory for me to chase. These sensations come together and take a God-like shape. Some people spend their lives feeling for contours, instead of standing back to see how (and from what) it's made.

"This is as inevitable as gravity," Weil writes in *Gravity and Grace*. "A beloved being who disappoints me. I have written to him. It is impossible that he should not reply by saying what I have said to myself in his name."

———

In this village, elderly relatives often need our help. In 2020, I've eaten more dinners with seventy-year-old Frenchmen than I have the entire rest of my life. I've baked more pies. I've watched the damage a single year can do.

One morning, a neighbor, a bored, meddling type, came pounding on our door. One of Sam's relatives, a woman in her eighties, had fallen for a love scam again. "There is no talking sense to her! She knows she can't convince us this time, so she lies!" Every decade this woman has slipped a new man into this community. Some have stayed. Some have run away with her cash and furniture. Now, though, she simply denies that this new lover exists: no, she isn't buying him ten pre-paid shopping cards a week. She isn't selling all her antique furniture to give him money. The cash borrowed from relatives doesn't disappear into his pockets. He doesn't exist. We're imagining things, making baseless accusations.

"Poor thing," the villagers say, "she's lost her grip on reality." They invite her to church.

"Imagine if only one person believed in Jesus," says Sam. "How the story would sound."

"Imagine if you cut a poo with a knife," says Elena, in a serious joining-in way.

Sam laughs. I mutter something about the finality of death. Elena says, "When I die, I'm going to say *I don't want to be next to Dina*." Later, blowing bubbles, she apologizes to each one for its demise. "Forgive me, my dear! I'm sorry, *chérie*," she whispers to each bubble.

Death has settled over our household. We're stuck in aftermaths. Sam is mired in the long, slow work of recovering from Josh's death.

At Sunday market we run into people from the Constellations performance therapy that Josh had tried to convince the family to join.
Sam talks to them for a long time. At home he is despondent. "I have a
hole in my heart," he says. "I'll always have a hole in my heart." Sam's
love for Josh is so consuming and parental. It's how I loved Sam at
MacDowell, and how I love Elena, with a big stupid love that scoops
me out and makes me feel like a ghost, but continues on, though its object just stands there and receives it, or bats it away, annoyed.

The weather is warming and Sam and I take a flask of soup to the
woods. We talk about our writing, how to choose good firewood, our
daughter's education. I ask about something practical, and he bats it
away. "I can't think about that now," he says. "I just lost my brother."

"But." I pause. It's been months. I blurt out, "But that can't be the
answer to everything."

He is angry now. We fight. For the first time since Josh's death, he
says the unspeakable to me. "You never believed him," he says. "And
you never believed *me*."

He storms off, leaving me in the woods. He doesn't go far, and I'm
safe here. I know this area and I have my phone. What is the story
brewing in Sam's imagination?

I sit on a dry patch overlooking the horizon. *This long dark winter will
be over.* I wrap Flo's coat tighter around me. I think about the eras in my
life passing like breaths, like lungs inflating and deflating. I think about
Sam's older brother, Ilan, holding the family together, making room for
everyone's rituals: human rights battles, Friday night prayers, Sunday
church service. He says he finds wisdom in these faiths, as practical
ethics and a good way of living. Twice I've pressed him to say more
about what he believes and why (*what should I believe*, I want to ask). "We
can talk about this later," Ilan says. He sounds tired.

Have I done my best? I want to believe that I've made good choices.
More than that, I want to believe that hard work cures all, that you can
claim the life you want. I crave stories of trying. Other stories trigger

my doubt. This is my ideology, a toothy creature composed of rapturous and bitter experience. I believe in discipline, but I want to be just. I want Elena to understand that believing can end suffering; it's a kind of love. I don't want her to repeat the mistakes of past generations, to turn and walk away from others' pain, or to crave submission, to kick responsibility up some imagined ladder where someone smarter, more powerful, supposedly lives. I want to touch earthly wounds without flinching. I want to ask *who did this to you?* And if offered a strange, unfathomable story, I want my imagination to triumph over my shortcuts so that I can silence the voices, move my lips, and say "I believe."

Later Sam searches the woods for me. I refuse to be found. *I didn't kill Josh*, I want to shout at him. *And I never wanted him to hurt, or to die. I wanted to scold him and force him to do more stuff.*

We don't talk for hours, and Sam gets progressively meaner.

The next day, the accusation escalates and picks up sharp debris. "You hated him, my beloved brother who died, you hated him."

The day after that, "You thought he was a liar and a thief. You said if he were in Iran—"

I try to remember what I said, the specific images, how much of it I said aloud, and how much of it was just inside my dark, pitiless head. *Even by that*, I want to shout, *I just meant some mustachioed uncle forcing him to do a bunch of squats.*

The weeks after Josh's death are long and excruciating, each day a complete drama that I will never write. As Sam recovers, Josh is absolved, sheathed in sainthood and rightness, and I'm becoming the villain. I find myself lashing out at an imaginary Josh, angry all over again.

All season, we stumble over each other and apologize. The wounds in his heart are scarring over, reshaping it, and he'll never be the first Sam that I knew.

Meanwhile, Flo paints. I read Rilke's *The Dark Interval*, letters to grieving friends. It strikes me as heroic how hard Rilke is working to console these broken people, to find meaning in their misery. He writes about a "tiny kernel of dark joy" deep inside the mourning. He writes about time, and how finished things are never lost. They belong to another era that is repeated forever. He writes about grief as one of life's beautiful intensities. What a waste to try to move past it instead of cherishing and using it, as we do other intensities. What great work is embedded in the life that remains. ("Is 36,000 a lot?" Elena asks.)

Over many months, we stop fighting. We read again, write again. We make friends in the countryside. We meet a joyful couple who invite the community for yoga and apéros. A Sanskrit meditation singer leads us in mantras we don't understand. A traveler offers me a book of French aphorisms. In my terrible French, I try to offer perspective and give up, tongue-tied.

The next day Sam tells me that in that moment with the Frenchman and his book, Sam was filled with an effervescent love for me. I was balancing such heavy things: French, kindness, and nuance. I realize just how long it's been since he's added that painful extra word. "I *do* love you," as if convincing himself. Somewhere along the road, that word vanished from our lives.

Sam goes to Josh's favorite mountain to collect a rock. He hauls it back for the stone setting ceremony. What stories will we carve out of this year, when we finally leave this village? The coming days are still shrouded in dark. But I've decided to override my fears for now.

Flo shows us her painting, a serene Josh soaring away alongside Oscar (Flo's dog, who seemed to have chased Josh through some open door). Flo's four grandchildren send gifts from the earth below. Elena releases a unicorn, her little face turned skyward. The wounded heart of the painting, though, the shattering corner, is Sheldon and Flo, all but forgotten in the wake, trying to lasso their youngest son's legs with a scarf, a rope, their arms raised up in desperation.

Josh craved entry elsewhere, into a purpose, friendships, love. We all crave welcome, each through our own unique door. By the time we're willing to harm ourselves, though, we're no longer trying for entry. Looking at Flo's heartbroken brushstrokes, her lost son flying away, I think: words so often fail mothers. God so often fails mothers.

Days later, an artist from a neighboring village brings her daughter to play with Elena. The girls run off to the living room to arrange their unicorns. We put out ripe cheese and pickled garlic from the market and talk about creativity, about platonic leaves and blades of glass, the uncut hair of graves. This year, Sam and I have both indulged in too many bad movies to judge stories anymore, but we talk a little about that too, and about language. We laugh about our own stalled efforts, the pages we've filled with bad prose. We talk about how sometimes, creativity is like a thistle, as mine has been this last year: its small beauties surviving a harsh landscape. And in other moments, as in times of grief, it is an orchid, a rare, exquisite bloom that withers outside congenial soil. We talk about how art springs out of brutality, and how precious few witness (or allow themselves to see) those errant virtuosic strokes of toil and inspiration—how every good work rescues its audience out of a sea of sophisticated cynics, critics, aristos. We talk about the cash value of a creative life, about negotiation, and loving bad actors. How little room the world leaves people to breathe out hard, to be needy, ugly, or just in someone's way now and then.

But now I'm lying. We talk about half of these things. The other half, I say to myself, alone inside my head, as I drink chilled rose wine and spread mushroomy cheese across my toast. I remember a mantra from somewhere: *Give me the chance to do my very best.*

After a silent beat, we refill our glasses. The woman settles into a story: growing up her mother was erratic and unreliable. A young wife in 1980s France, she tried to convince everyone that she was ill. When she failed, she took her own life. Now, decades later, her daughter tells us about a powerful new therapy where you perform generations of your family's pain. You act it out, releasing the pain into the void. You imagine the horrors your ancestors lived, and transport yourself into their bodies. Are they weeping in ravines? Branded by soldiers? Chased from their homes at night? Sam and I exchange a glance. He smiles faintly. "We've heard of this," he says.

There is a long silence. She stumbles on a thought, then starts again.

"Sometimes now, out of nowhere," she says, "I feel wrapped in so much love."

I catch a breath. Sam smiles, delighted after weeks. He reaches for my hand. Offstage, the children giggle and guffaw. They try on a word they've invented. I drink in my daughter's voice, *my favorite in all the baleine.* We pause to listen to their secret laughter.

AUTHOR'S NOTE

Excerpts from court transcripts, quotes from asylum interviews and decision letters, and unredacted asylum officer notes were printed with permission of each survivor's legal representation, lawyers at the Innocence Project and Freedom from Torture.

In these pages, I have recreated events, locales, and conversations from memory and interviews. I have changed the names of some individuals and places, as well as altered identifying characteristics and details such as physical properties, occupations, and places of residence. In general, if I have not provided a last name in the text, the first name is usually changed to protect the individual (unless they requested otherwise). Examples are Mimi, Meredith, and Dru. My family, for obvious reasons, is an exception to this rule. KV is publicly known as KV.

In recounting the stories of others, I have dramatized, putting as much as I could in-scene. I have only written about events that were carefully recounted to me by relevant individuals or their legal or medical counsel, were meticulously recorded in legal documents, or that I witnessed. Afterward, I researched the time and place, the context around each story, and brought the stories to life using sensory details that I found and imagined. Any mistakes are my own.

I have kept my language true to particular times and places, and tried not to sanitize thoughts or language after the fact. For events where I was present, my accounts are true according to my memory and perspective.

ACKNOWLEDGMENTS

Most heartfelt thanks to those who trusted me with their stories, especially KV and his lawyer Arun. Thank you to my friends Adam and Frances, who shared their expertise and personal stories with me. Thanks to the medical doctors, lawyers, and activists who spoke to me and sent files, as well as the Innocence Project and Freedom from Torture, particularly Steve Crawshaw, who first encouraged me to look into KV's astonishing story. Thanks to the Columbia Institute for Ideas and Imagination in Paris for supporting a year of this work, and to the American Library in Paris, where I was a fellow as I was editing it. Thanks to the Geschwister-Scholl-Preis for the confidence to carry on in this style of creative non-fiction ("the implicated witness narrative," I'm tempted to call it), and to the University of St Andrews for giving me a home after I was wrung out from the seclusion and hermitage that these pages required. Thanks also to Andy Hunter, Megha Majumdar, Andy Kifer, Jonathan Lee, Kate Harvey, Peter Haag, and Kathleen Anderson (and all my wonderful publishing family), who saw what the book could be and gave editorial and personal advice. Finally, thank you to my commune family, to the Leader family, and to Sam, who have enriched my life, challenged and deepened my thinking, and nourished my heart.

DINA NAYERI was born during the Iranian revolution and lived as a refugee for two years before being granted asylum in the United States. She is the author of *The Ungrateful Refugee*, winner of the Geschwister Scholl Preis and finalist for the Los Angeles Times Book Prize, the Kirkus Prize, and *Elle*'s Grand Prix des Lectrices. A 2019–2020 fellow at the Columbia Institute for Ideas and Imagination in Paris, and winner of the 2018 UNESCO City of Literature Paul Engle Prize, Nayeri has won a National Endowment for the Arts grant and an O. Henry Prize and has been anthologized in *The Best American Short Stories*, and she was a finalist for the 2017 Rome Prize, among other honors. Her work has been published in more than twenty countries and in *The New York Times*, *The Guardian*, *The Washington Post*, *The New Yorker*, *Granta*, and many other publications. She has a bachelor of arts degree from Princeton and master's degrees from Harvard Business School, the Harvard Graduate School of Education, and the Iowa Writers' Workshop, where she was a Teaching Writing Fellow.